CAREER OPPORTUNITIES IN THE AUTOMOTIVE INDUSTRY

G. Michael Kennedy

Checkmark Books®

An imprint of Facts On File, Inc.

Career Opportunities in the Automotive Industry

Copyright © 2005 by G. Michael Kennedy

Checkmark Books
An imprint of Facts On File, Inc.
132 West 31st Street
New York NY 10001

Library of Congress Cataloging-in-Publication Data
Kennedy, Michael (G. Michael)
  Career opportunities in the automotive industry / G. Michael Kennedy.
      p. cm.
  Includes bibliographical references and index.
  ISBN 0-8160-5246-8 (hc : alk. paper)—ISBN 0-8160-5247-6 (pb : alk. paper)
  1. Automobile industry and trade—Vocational guidance. I. Title.
  HD9710.A2K46 2005
  629.2′023′73—dc22   2004008438

Checkmark Books are available at special discounts when purchased in bulk quantities for businesses, associations, institutions, or sales promotions. Please call our Special Sales Department in New York at (212) 967-8800 or (800) 322-8755.

You can find Facts On File on the World Wide Web at http://www.factsonfile.com

Cover illustration by Art Parts/Ron and Joe, Inc.

Printed in the United States of America

VB Hermitage 10 9 8 7 6 5 4 3 2 1

This book is printed on acid-free paper.

CONTENTS

APPENDIXES

ACKNOWLEDGMENTS

I'd like to thank every person, corporation, association, agency, and library that provided information, assistance, or encouragement for this book. Specifically, this includes editor James Chambers, agent Gene Brissie, the Association for Manufacturing Technology, the Association of International Automobile Manufacturers, the Automatic Transmission Rebuilders Association, the Automotive Aftermarket Industry Association (AAIA), Automotive Engine Rebuilders Association, Automotive Industry Action Group, Automotive Industry Planning Council, Automotive Recyclers Association, Automotive Service Association, Automotive Training Managers Council, Automotive Warehouse Distributors Association, Automotive Youth Education System, Canadian Vehicle Manufacturers' Association, ERIC Clearinghouse on Adult, Career, and Vocational Education, Independent Automotive Damage Appraisers Association, Indy Racing League, Institute of Electrical and Electronics Engineers, Institute of Industrial Engineers, International Automotive Technicians' Network, International Franchise Association, International Motor Sports Association, National Automobile Dealers Association, National Automotive Technicians Education Foundation, National Hot Rod Association, National Institute for Automotive Service Excellence, National Institute for Metalworking Skills, National Limousine Association, National School Transportation Association, National Tooling and Metalworking Association, Precision Machine Products Association, Professional Truck Driving Institute of America, International Association of Business Communicators, Service Technicians Society, Society of Automotive Engineers, Society of Manufacturing Engineers, Sports Car Club of America, Taxi, Limousine, and Paratransit Association, MAACO, Midas Muffler, Truck Driver Institute of America, United Motorcoach Association, and the United States Auto Club.

HOW TO USE THIS BOOK

The job descriptions in this book are divided into six sections representing the different areas of the automotive field: design and production, repair and restoration, transportation, sales, racing, and "other automotive careers."

About Each Entry

As you reach each of the various sections of this book, keep in mind there are many ways you can be involved in an automotive career. Within each section of the book, you'll find information necessary to acquaint you with the important jobs in every area, from racing to design and fabrication.

There are two parts to each job classification. The first begins with job information in a chart form for easy identification; the second part outlines more detailed information in a narrative text. The key to the organization of each entry is as follows:

Job Title

The most commonly accepted job title goes here.

Career Profile

This section provides a snapshot of the relevant details for this job, including duties, alternate titles, salary range, employment and advancement prospects, best geographical location, and prerequisites (education or training, experience, special skills, and certification or licensure). This is followed by an in-depth discussion of each section.

Career Ladder

The career ladder illustrates a normal job progression, beginning with the entry-level job, followed by the current job title in the middle. The top rung of the career ladder lists those jobs or opportunities for which the central job is a stepping-stone. Not all positions listed in the career ladder are discussed separately in the book.

Position Description

This section provides a detailed description of all the duties connected with the job, offering a general overview of what the average person holding this position can expect on a day-to-day basis.

Salary Range

Salary ranges for the jobs in this book are as accurate as possible. Many are based on the most recent U.S. Occupa-

tional Outlook Handbook published by the U.S. Bureau of Labor Statistics. Salary ranges are also checked against actual classified ads for automotive jobs as listed in different sections of the United States. Readers should keep in mind that salaries for any particular job will depend on the size and location of the company, racetrack, or institution, as well as the person's own experience, education, training, and responsibilities.

Employment Prospects

A job carrying an "excellent," "good," or "fair" rating means that it should not be too difficult to find a job in this field. This section also discusses how many opportunities there may be, and why they may be increasing or decreasing. Industry trends are also discussed here. This information is based in part on the U.S. Occupational Outlook Handbook, as well as information obtained from individuals in the field.

Advancement Prospects

Once you've gotten your first job, this section will discuss how easy it will be to be promoted—and what positions might be available to you. Any special skills or talents that may be required will be noted here.

Education and Training

Jobs in sales, management, and design typically require a four-year college degree; jobs in repair, restoration, racing, and "other" generally require considerable experience and specialized vocational training. Transportation jobs typically require a high school diploma and may require special certification.

Special Requirements

Some jobs require special certification or licenses. In these cases, information about licensure or certification is included here. Even if certification is not required, it may vastly improve your chances of getting a good job in that field.

Experience, Skills, and Personality Traits

These tend to differ from job to job, but most jobs in automotive management require good communication and people skills and excellent computer literacy, experience, and willingness to work hard. Repair, production, and other highly skilled jobs in this field also require significant attention to detail, creativity, mechanical ability, and patience.

Unions and Associations

There are many professional trade organizations available for all types of automotive work. Joining an appropriate trade association offers a number of important benefits to the job hunter, including the chance to make vital contacts, attend workshops, and hear about jobs in classified sections of trade journals. Most associations have Internet Web sites that include at least one page of classified ads or "joblines" in which current jobs are listed. Most of these are free to anyone surfing the Internet.

Tips for Entry

This section provides at least three or four tips on breaking into the automotive field. You can use this section for ideas on how to get a particular automotive-related job, with details on helpful Web site addresses, magazines, or journals, and other inside tips.

Appendixes

Several appendixes are included to provide additional detailed information, including:

- names and contact information for professional associations
- information on automotive training programs
- racing schools
- automotive museums

INTRODUCTION

The automotive industry is big business in the United States—so big, in fact, that one out of every seven Americans is employed in the field in some capacity. *Career Opportunities in the Automotive Industry* explores this popular profession, providing clear, easily accessible information about a wide range of careers in the field. With comprehensive descriptions of more than 60 different jobs together with the information and resources readers would need to pursue them, the book is divided into six areas that represent the types of jobs in this industry.

The United States is the world's largest marketplace for motor vehicles due to the size and affluence of its population. According to the U.S. Department of Transportation, more than 210 million motor vehicles—131 million passenger cars and 79 million trucks—were registered in the United States in 1998. The number of light trucks has shown especially steady growth since the mid-1980s.

There are career opportunities right now for people who want to be auto technicians, auto electricians, body repairers, or spray painters. What many people don't know is that there are also many other career opportunities as well. For example, you can work in sales, administration, or training. The retail automotive sector can provide a vast range of career options. You can start out as a mechanic, move into sales or parts, maybe start your own business, or become a principal owner of a large dealership!

Finding a job in the automotive industry can involve a wide variety of career possibilities, beginning with auto design and factory production. The motor vehicle is an intricate series of systems, subsystems, and components, all assembled into a final product. Each manufactured part or component is integrated into the vehicle—none is developed to exist separately. To make things even more complicated, vehicles are constantly changing as new technology or reengineered components are incorporated, and as new and updated models are designed to keep abreast of the constantly changing tastes of buyers. Like their products, motor vehicle and equipment manufacturers are complex organizations that constantly evolve to improve their efficiency and maintain a continuing stream of commercially viable products in a highly competitive market.

Although motor vehicle and equipment manufacturing jobs are scattered throughout the nation, certain states offer the greatest numbers of jobs. Michigan, for example, accounts for nearly one-third of all automotive manufacturing jobs. Combined, Michigan, Ohio, and Indiana include about half of all the jobs in this industry. Other states that account for significant numbers of jobs are California, New York, Illinois, Missouri, North Carolina, Tennessee, and Kentucky.

However, the cars people drive are only a small part of the story in motor vehicle and equipment manufacturing. In 2000, about 6,500 establishments manufactured motor vehicles and equipment; these ranged from small parts plants with only a few workers to huge assembly plants that employ thousands.

Once a vehicle has been built and it leaves the factory, it becomes part of the retail automotive sector. Jobs in this field focus on the sale of everything from cars and motorcycles, to heavy vehicles like trucks and boats—and even racing cars.

Motor vehicle dealers are the bridge between automobile manufacturers and the U.S. consumer. Most dealerships offer one-stop shopping for customers who wish to buy, finance, and service their next car.

The retail automotive dealerships can offer rewarding career opportunities in any of three departments: new vehicle sales, used vehicle sales, and aftermarket sales. These departments involve a wide range of occupations, including those involving management, administrative support, sales, service, and repair. In addition to full-service dealerships, some motor vehicle dealers specialize in used vehicle sales only.

Sales is only one part of the automotive dealer—cars also must be serviced, and there are a host of potential opportunities in the repair field. Technical jobs can be extremely specific (such as tire repairers or automotive glass installers) or much more general—the automotive technician or auto body repairer. The work of automotive service technicians has evolved from simple mechanics to high technology. These days, integrated electronic systems and complex computers are high-tech, so auto technicians need to be electronic wizards—as well as having mechanical know-how. Automotive service technicians have developed into diagnostic, high-tech problem solvers. Technicians must have an increasingly broad base of knowledge about how vehicles' complex components work and interact, as well as the ability to work with electronic diagnostic equipment and computer-based technical reference materials. But repair jobs include far more than the technical experts: Service advisers, service managers, and shop managers all work on the "management" side of the auto service industry aisle.

However, that's only part of the auto industry picture. The industry also includes transportation jobs—taxi drivers, chauffeurs, bus or school bus drivers, route drivers, ambulance drivers, and various types of truck drivers. In addition, a host of other specialists are also involved to some degree in the automotive sector: the insurance specialists who work with auto owners (auto damage claims adjusters and appraisers), service station managers and attendants, vo-tech (vocational-technical) schoolteachers, automotive writers, and car museum directors.

Finally, there are the stars of the automotive world: the racing segment, including race car drivers, team mechanics, PR specialists and racing school instructors.

No matter what career path you choose in the automotive industry, there are many options and exciting opportunities to learn a wide range of skills. This may include everything from technical skills and how to use sophisticated diagnostic equipment, manuals, and databases to how to work in teams, offer efficient customer service, or run a small business.

DESIGN AND PRODUCTION

AUTOMOTIVE DESIGNER

CAREER PROFILE

Duties: Use artistic talent, computers, and information on product use, marketing, materials, and production methods to create designs that will make a car competitive in the marketplace

Alternate Title(s): Industrial Designer

Salary Range: $25,350 to $105,280+

Employment Prospects: Good

Advancement Prospects: Excellent

Best Geographical Location(s): Nearly one-third of all automotive designer jobs are located in Michigan

Prerequisites:

Education or Training—A bachelor's degree is required for most entry-level design positions

Experience—Some experience in art or design is helpful

Special Skills and Personality Traits—Creativity, practical knowledge, and artistic ability to be able to turn abstract ideas into formal designs

CAREER LADDER

```
┌─────────────────────────┐
│      Chief Designer      │
└─────────────────────────┘

┌─────────────────────────┐
│   Automotive Designer    │
└─────────────────────────┘

┌─────────────────────────┐
│     Design Assistant     │
└─────────────────────────┘
```

Position Description

Using artistic talent, computers, and information on product use, marketing, materials, and production methods, Automotive Designers create designs they hope will make the vehicle competitive in the marketplace. They use sketches and computer-aided design techniques to create computer models of proposed vehicles. These computer models eliminate the need for physical body mock-ups in the design process because they give designers complete information on how each piece of the vehicle will work with others.

The first step in developing a new design or altering an existing one is to determine the needs of the client, the ultimate function for which the design is intended, and its appeal to customers. When creating a new look for a car, Automotive Designers often begin by researching the desired design characteristics, such as size, shape, weight, color, materials used, cost, ease of use, fit, and safety. Designers then prepare sketches (by hand or with the aid of a computer) to illustrate the vision for the design.

After consulting with the product development team, Automotive Designers create detailed designs using drawings, a structural model, computer simulations, or a full-scale prototype. Many industrial designers increasingly are using computer-aided industrial design (CAID) tools to create designs and machine-readable instructions that communicate with automated production tools. Computer models allow greater ease and flexibility in exploring a greater number of design alternatives, lowering design costs and cutting the time it takes to deliver a product to market. Workers may repeatedly modify and redesign models until the models meet engineering, production, and marketing specifications. Automotive Designers working in parts and accessory production increasingly collaborate with manufacturers in the initial design stages to integrate motor vehicle parts and accessories into the design specifications for each vehicle.

Automotive Designers employed by large manufacturers generally work regular hours in well-lighted and comfortable settings, but occasionally they must work additional hours to meet deadlines.

Salaries

Average annual earnings for Automotive Designers, excluding deferred compensation, bonuses, royalties, and commissions, range from $39,240 to $67,430, depending on experience. The lowest 10 percent earn less than $25,350 while the highest 10 percent earn more than $105,280. Industrial designers in managerial, executive, or ownership positions earned substantially more—up to $600,000 annually. However, the $65,000 to $180,000 range is more typical.

Employment Prospects

Designers in the automotive field are expected to face keen competition for available positions. Because many talented individuals are attracted to this career, those with little or no formal education in design, or those who lack creativity and perseverance, will find it very difficult to establish and maintain a career in this field.

The employment of Automotive Designers is expected to grow about as fast as average for all occupations through the year 2012. In addition to those that result from employment growth, many job openings will arise from the need to replace designers who leave the field. There will be increased demand for Automotive Designers due to continued emphasis on product quality and safety, the demand for new cars that are easy and comfortable to use, the development of technology, and growing global competition among businesses.

Employment in the auto manufacturing industry is expected to grow with demand for cars and parts, but jobs will be lost due to downsizing and productivity increases. The growing intensity of international and domestic competition has increased cost pressures on manufacturers. In response, they have sought to improve productivity and quality through the application of high-tech production techniques, including computers and programmable equipment.

Growth in demand for domestically manufactured cars could be limited by a number of factors. A slowdown in the growth of the driving-age population as the smaller post-baby-boom generation comes of age may curb demand for cars and trucks. Foreign motor vehicle and parts producers will continue to control a substantial share of the U.S. market and, should they increasingly meet demand with imported vehicles and parts instead of products manufactured in U.S. transplant factories, domestic motor vehicle and parts output will be lower. Other factors that may limit growth of domestic motor vehicle production include improvements in vehicle quality and durability, which extend longevity, and more stringent safety and environmental regulations, which increase the cost of producing and operating motor vehicles.

Employment in automotive manufacturing is sensitive to cyclical swings in the economy; a 10 to 20 percent change in employment from one year to the next is not unusual. During periods of economic prosperity, consumers are more willing and able to purchase expensive goods such as cars, which may require large down payments and extended loan payments. During recessions, however, consumers are more likely to delay such purchases. Automation and continued global competition, however, are expected to produce job growth for Automotive Designers. These workers will increasingly be relied upon for further innovation in reducing costs and enhancing competitive advantage.

Advancement Prospects

Beginning Automotive Designers usually receive on-the-job training, and normally need one to three years of training before they can advance to higher-level positions. Experienced Automotive Designers in large firms may advance to chief designer, design department head, or other supervisory positions. Some Automotive Designers become teachers in design schools and colleges and universities.

Education and Training

A bachelor's degree is required for most entry-level design positions. Formal training for Automotive Designers is available in two- and three-year professional schools that award certificates or associate degrees in design. Graduates of two-year programs normally qualify as assistants to designers. The bachelor of fine arts (B.F.A.) degree is granted at four-year colleges and universities. The curriculum in these schools includes art and art history, principles of design, designing and sketching, and specialized studies.

Because computer-aided design is increasingly common, many employers expect new designers to be familiar with its use as a design tool.

The National Association of Schools of Art and Design currently accredits about 200 postsecondary institutions with programs in art and design; most of these schools award a degree in art. Some award degrees in industrial, interior, textile, graphic, or fashion design. Many schools do not allow formal entry into a bachelor's degree program until a student has successfully finished a year of basic art and design courses. Applicants may be required to submit sketches and other examples of their artistic ability.

Experience, Skills, and Personality Traits

Automotive Designers combine artistic talent with research on product use, customer needs, marketing, materials, and production methods to create the most functional and appealing design that will be competitive with others in the marketplace. Creativity is crucial in this field; Automotive Designers must have a strong sense of the aesthetic—an eye for color and detail, a sense of balance and proportion, and an appreciation of beauty. Despite the advancement of computer-aided design, sketching ability remains an important advantage.

Individuals in the design field must be creative, imaginative, persistent, and able to communicate their ideas in writing, visually, and verbally. Because tastes in style and fashion can change quickly, designers need to be well-read, open to new ideas and influences, and quick to react to changing trends. Problem-solving skills and the ability to work independently and under pressure are important traits. People in this field need self- discipline to start projects on their own, to budget their time, and to meet deadlines and production schedules.

Unions and Associations

Automotive Designers can belong to a number of professional organizations, including the Industrial Designers Society of America. Some salaried Automotive Designers also belong to a union, such as the United Auto Workers.

Tips for Entry

1. A good portfolio—a collection of examples of a person's best work—often is the deciding factor in getting a job.
2. Visit industry association Web sites to check out job postings for designers, such as the Web site of the Industrial Designers Society of America: http://www.idsa.org/employment.htm.
3. Mail a résumé to top automotive companies where you would like to work.
4. Attend professional conferences and check out job boards there.
5. Check Internet job listings at http://automotive@ thingamajob.com.
6. Visit your college's career counseling office for help in identifying companies where you would like to work.

MECHANICAL ENGINEER

CAREER PROFILE

Duties: Design improvements for engines, transmissions, and other working parts

Alternate Title(s): Automotive Mechanical Engineer

Salary Range: $42,190 to $94,110

Employment Prospects: Fair

Advancement Prospects: Excellent

Best Geographical Location(s): Most jobs in the automotive field are located in Michigan, although automotive plants in other parts of the country also hire Mechanical Engineers

Prerequisites:

Education or Training—A bachelor's degree in mechanical engineering is required for most entry-level jobs

Experience—A solid background in math and science is helpful

Special Skills and Personality Traits—Creative, inquisitive, analytical, and detail-oriented

Licensure/Certification—All 50 states require licensure for engineers who offer their services directly to the public

CAREER LADDER

```
┌─────────────────────────────────────┐
│   Mechanical Engineering Manager     │
└─────────────────────────────────────┘

┌─────────────────────────────────────┐
│       Mechanical Engineer            │
└─────────────────────────────────────┘

┌─────────────────────────────────────┐
│  Mechanical Engineering Technician   │
└─────────────────────────────────────┘
```

Position Description

Mechanical Engineers design improvements for engines, transmissions, and other working parts; mechanical engineering is one of the broadest engineering disciplines. Mechanical Engineers apply the theories and principles of science and mathematics to research and develop economical solutions to technical problems. They design products, machinery to build those products, and the systems that ensure the quality of the products and efficiency of the workforce and manufacturing process.

Mechanical Engineers consider many factors when developing a new product. For example, in developing an industrial robot, engineers determine precisely what function the robot needs to perform, design and test the robot's components, fit the components together in an integrated plan, and evaluate the design's overall effectiveness, cost, reliability, and safety.

Mechanical Engineers are the largest professional occupation in the automotive industry, and play an integral role in all stages of auto manufacturing. Mechanical Engineers oversee the building and testing of the engine, transmission, brakes, suspension, and other mechanical and electrical components. Using computers and assorted models, instruments, and tools, Mechanical Engineers simulate different parts of a car to determine whether each part meets cost, safety, performance, and quality specifications.

Mechanical Engineers use computers to accurately and efficiently perform computations and help model and simulate new designs. Mechanical Engineers use Computer-Aided Design (CAD) and Computer-Aided Manufacturing (CAM) for design data processing and to develop alternative designs. New computer and communications systems have improved the design process, enabling Mechanical Engineers to produce and analyze various product designs much more rapidly than in the past and to collaborate on designs with other engineers throughout the world.

Most automotive Mechanical Engineers work in office buildings, industrial plants, and production sites, where they monitor or direct operations or solve on-site problems Many work a standard 40-hour week, although sometimes deadlines or design problems bring extra pressure to a job. When this happens, Mechanical Engineers may work longer hours and experience considerable stress.

Salaries

The average annual salary of a Mechanical Engineer in the automotive industry ranges from $63,910 to $66,040. The lowest 10 percent earn less than $42,190, and the highest 10 percent earn more than $94,110. According to a 2001 salary survey by the National Association of Colleges and Employers, bachelor's degree candidates in mechanical engineering received starting offers averaging $48,426 a year, master's degree candidates had offers averaging $55,994, and Ph.D. candidates were initially offered $72,096.

Employment Prospects

Employment of Mechanical Engineers is projected to grow more slowly than the average for all occupations through 2012. Although overall manufacturing employment is expected to grow slowly, employment of Mechanical Engineers in auto manufacturing should increase more rapidly as the demand for improved cars grows and industrial machinery and processes become increasingly complex. In addition, the automotive industry is less likely to lay off Mechanical Engineers, since most work on long-term research and development projects or in other activities continue even during economic slowdowns.

The number of bachelor's degrees awarded in engineering began declining in 1987 and has continued to stay at about the same level through much of the 1990s. The total number of graduates from mechanical engineering programs is not expected to increase significantly. Although only a relatively small proportion of Mechanical Engineers leave the profession each year, many job openings will arise from replacement needs as Mechanical Engineers transfer to management, sales, or other professional occupations.

Advancement Prospects

Beginning mechanical engineering graduates usually work under the supervision of experienced engineers and may receive additional seminar-type training. As new Mechanical Engineers get more experience, they are assigned more difficult projects with greater independence to develop designs, solve problems, and make decisions. Mechanical

Engineers may advance to become technical specialists or to supervise a staff or team of engineers and technicians. Some may eventually become engineering managers.

It is important for Mechanical Engineers to continue their education throughout their careers, because their value to their employer depends on their knowledge of the latest technology. By keeping current in their field, Mechanical Engineers are able to deliver the best solutions and greatest value to their employers. Mechanical Engineers who have not kept current in their field may find themselves passed over for promotions

Education and Training

A bachelor's degree in engineering is required for entry-level mechanical engineering jobs. Most engineering programs involve a concentration of study in mechanical engineering, along with courses in both mathematics and science. Most programs include a design course, sometimes accompanied by a computer or laboratory class, or both. Graduate training is essential for many research and development programs, but is not required for most entry-level mechanical engineering jobs.

About 330 colleges and universities offer bachelor's degree programs in engineering that are accredited by the Accreditation Board for Engineering and Technology (ABET). ABET accreditation is based on an examination of an engineering program's student achievement, program improvement, faculty, curricular content, facilities, and institutional commitment. Some programs emphasize industrial practices, preparing students for a job in industry, whereas others are more theoretical and are designed to prepare students for graduate work. Therefore, students should investigate curricula and check accreditations carefully before selecting a college.

Admissions requirements for undergraduate engineering schools include a solid background in mathematics (algebra, geometry, trigonometry, and calculus) and sciences (biology, chemistry, and physics), and courses in English, social studies, humanities, and computers.

Bachelor's degree programs in mechanical engineering typically are designed to last four years, but many students find that it takes between four and five years to complete their studies. In a typical four-year college curriculum, students spend the first two years studying mathematics, basic sciences, introductory engineering, humanities, and social sciences. Students interested in mechanical engineering spend the last two years taking mostly engineering courses with a concentration in mechanical engineering.

Some programs offer a general engineering curriculum; students then specialize in graduate school or on the job. Some engineering schools and two-year colleges have agreements in which the two-year college provides the initial engineering education, and the engineering school automatically admits students for their last two years. In addition, a few engineering schools have arrangements in which a student spends three years in a liberal arts college studying pre-engineering subjects and two years in an engineering school studying core subjects, receiving a bachelor's degree from each school.

Some colleges and universities offer five-year master's degree programs; others offer five- or even six-year cooperative plans that combine classroom study and practical work, permitting students to gain valuable experience and finance part of their education.

Special Requirements

All 50 states and the District of Columbia require licensure for engineers who offer their services directly to the public. Engineers who are licensed are called Professional Engineers (PE). This licensure generally requires a degree from an ABET-accredited engineering program, four years of relevant work experience, and successful completion of a state examination. Recent graduates can start the licensing process by taking the examination in two stages. The initial Fundamentals of Engineering (FE) examination can be taken upon graduation; engineers who pass this examination are called Engineers in Training (EIT) or Engineer Interns (EI). The EIT certification is usually valid for 10 years.

After acquiring suitable work experience, EITs can take the second examination, the Principles and Practice of Engineering Exam. Several states have imposed mandatory continuing education requirements for relicensure, but most states recognize licensure from other states. Many Mechanical Engineers are licensed as PEs.

Experience, Skills, and Personality Traits

Mechanical Engineers should be creative, inquisitive, analytical, and detail-oriented. They should be able to work as part of a team and to communicate well both orally and in writing.

Unions and Associations

Mechanical Engineers can belong to a number of professional organizations, including the American Society of Mechanical Engineers; some belong to a union, such as the United Auto Workers.

Tips for Entry

1. Visit Web sites to check out job postings for Mechanical Engineers, such as the job board on the Web site of the American Society of Mechanical Engineers (www.asme.org/jobs).

2. Mail a résumé to top automotive companies where you would like to work.

3. Attend professional conferences and check out job boards there.

4. Visit your college's career counseling office for help in identifying companies where you would like to work.

5. Use your contacts. The easiest way to network is to ask someone you already know for the name of someone else. When you call, say, "So-and-so suggested I call you."

6. Develop electronic networking skills. Visit chat groups or message boards that pertain to your career area. Take special interest in those run by professional associations.

ELECTRICAL ENGINEER

CAREER PROFILE

Duties: Design automotive electrical systems, including the ignition system and accessories and industrial robot control systems used to assemble the vehicle

Alternate Title(s): Electronics Engineer; Automotive Electrical Engineer; Automotive Electronics Engineer

Salary Range: $46,210 to $104,500+

Employment Prospects: Good

Advancement Prospects: Excellent

Best Geographical Location(s): Most jobs in the automotive field are located in Michigan, although automotive plants in other parts of the country also hire electrical engineers

Prerequisites:

Education or Training—A bachelor's degree is required for most entry-level jobs

Experience—A solid background in math and science is helpful

Special Skills and Personality Traits—Creative, inquisitive, analytical, good computer skills, and detail-oriented

Licensure/Certification—All 50 states require licensure for engineers who offer their services directly to the public

CAREER LADDER

```
┌─────────────────────────────────────┐
│   Electrical Engineering Manager     │
└─────────────────────────────────────┘

┌─────────────────────────────────────┐
│      Electrical Engineer             │
└─────────────────────────────────────┘

┌─────────────────────────────────────┐
│  Electrical Engineering Technician   │
└─────────────────────────────────────┘
```

Position Description

Automotive Electrical Engineers design, develop, test, and supervise the manufacture of a vehicle's electrical system, including the ignition system and accessories, and industrial robot control systems used to assemble the vehicle. Electrical Engineers also design new products, write performance requirements, develop maintenance schedules, test equipment, solve operating problems, and estimate the time and cost of engineering projects.

Engineers are the largest professional occupation in the automotive industry, and play an integral role in all stages of auto manufacturing. Using computers and assorted models, instruments, and tools, Electrical Engineers simulate electrical systems of the vehicle to determine whether each part meets cost, safety, performance, and quality specifications.

Electrical Engineers use computers to accurately and efficiently perform computations and permit the modeling and simulation of new designs. Computer-Aided Design (CAD) and Computer-Aided Manufacturing (CAM) are used for design data processing and for developing alternative designs. New computer and communications systems have improved the design process, enabling Electrical Engineers to produce and analyze various product designs much more rapidly than in the past and to collaborate on designs with other engineers throughout the world.

Most automotive Electrical Engineers work in office buildings, industrial plants, and production sites, where they monitor or direct operations or solve on-site problems. Many work a standard 40-hour week, although sometimes deadlines or design problems mean that Electrical Engineers may work longer hours and experience considerable stress.

Salaries

The average annual salary for Electrical Engineers is between $69,640 and $72,090; the lowest 10 percent earn less than $46,210, and the highest 10 percent earn more than $104,500. Bachelor's degree candidates in electrical and electronics engineering typically receive starting offers averaging $51,910 a year; master's degree candidates average $63,812; and Ph.D. candidates average $79,241.

Employment Prospects

Electrical engineering graduates should have favorable job opportunities. Although overall manufacturing employment is expected to grow slowly, employment of Electrical Engineers in auto manufacturing should increase more rapidly as the demand for improved cars grows and industrial machinery and processes become increasingly complex. The number of job openings resulting from employment growth and the need to replace Electrical Engineers who transfer to other occupations or leave the labor force is expected to be in rough balance with the supply of graduates. The need for automotive manufacturers to invest heavily in research and development to remain competitive will provide openings for graduates who have learned the latest technologies. In addition, the automotive industry is less likely to lay off Electrical Engineers, since most work on long-term research and development projects or in other activities that continue even during economic slowdowns.

Employment of Electrical Engineers is projected to grow more slowly than the average for all occupations though 2012. The number of bachelor's degrees awarded in engineering began declining in 1987 and has continued to stay at about the same level through much of the 1990s, and the total number of graduates from electrical engineering programs is not expected to increase significantly. Although only a relatively small proportion of Electrical Engineers leave the profession each year, many job openings will arise from replacement needs. More typically, openings occur when Electrical Engineers transfer to management, sales, or other professional occupations.

Advancement Prospects

Beginning electrical engineering graduates usually work under the supervision of experienced engineers. As new Electrical Engineers become more experienced, they are assigned more difficult projects with greater independence to develop designs, solve problems, and make decisions. Electrical Engineers may advance to become technical specialists or to supervise a staff or team of engineers and technicians. Some may eventually become engineering managers.

To remain competitive, it is important for Electrical Engineers to continue their education throughout their careers, because their value to their employer depends on their knowledge of the latest technology. By keeping up to date, Electrical Engineers are able to come up with the best solutions to problems. Electrical Engineers who have not kept current in their field may find themselves passed over for promotions.

Education and Training

A bachelor's degree in engineering is required for entry-level electrical engineering jobs. Most electrical engineering programs involve a concentration of study in electrical engineering, along with courses in both mathematics and science. Most programs also add a design course, sometimes accompanied by a computer class or laboratory class, or both.

Graduate training is essential for many research and development programs, but is not required for the majority of entry-level electrical engineering jobs in the automotive industry.

About 330 colleges and universities offer bachelor's degree programs in engineering that are accredited by the Accreditation Board for Engineering and Technology (ABET). ABET accreditation is based on an examination of an engineering program's student achievement, program improvement, faculty, curricular content, facilities, and institutional commitment. Some programs emphasize industrial practices, preparing students for a job in industry, whereas others are more theoretical and are designed to prepare students for graduate work. Therefore, students interested in working in the automotive field should investigate curricula and check accreditations carefully before selecting a college.

Admissions requirements for undergraduate engineering schools include a solid background in mathematics (algebra, geometry, trigonometry, and calculus) and sciences (biology, chemistry, and physics), and courses in English, social studies, humanities, and computers.

Bachelor's degree programs in electrical engineering typically are designed to last four years, but many students find that it takes between four and five years to complete their studies. In a typical four-year college curriculum, the first two years are spent studying mathematics, basic sciences, introductory engineering, humanities, and social sciences. Students interested in electrical engineering spend the last two years taking engineering courses with a concentration in electrical engineering.

Some programs offer a general engineering curriculum; students then specialize in graduate school or on the job. Some engineering schools and two-year colleges have agreements in which the two-year college provides the initial engineering education, and the engineering school automatically admits students for their last two years. In addition, a few engineering schools have arrangements in which a student spends three years in a liberal arts college studying pre-engineering subjects and two years in an engineering school studying core subjects, receiving a bachelor's degree from each school.

Some colleges and universities offer five-year master's degree programs; others offer five- or even six-year cooperative plans that combine classroom study and practical work, permitting students to gain valuable experience and finance part of their education.

Special Requirements

All 50 states and the District of Columbia require licensure for engineers who offer their services directly to the public. Engineers who are licensed are called Professional Engineers (PE). This licensure generally requires a degree from an ABET-accredited engineering program, four years of relevant work experience, and successful completion of a state examination. Recent graduates can start the licensing process by taking the examination in two stages. The initial Fundamentals of Engineering (FE) examination can be taken upon graduation; engineers who pass this examination are called Engineers in Training (EIT) or Engineer Interns (EI). The EIT certification is usually valid for 10 years.

After acquiring suitable work experience, EITs can take the second examination, the Principles and Practice of Engineering Exam. Several states have imposed mandatory continuing education requirements for relicensure, but most states recognize licensure from other states. Many Electrical Engineers are licensed as PEs.

Experience, Skills, and Personality Traits

Electrical Engineers should be creative, inquisitive, analytical, and detail-oriented, with good computer skills. They should be able to work as part of a team and to communicate well both orally and in writing.

Unions and Associations

Electrical engineers can belong to a number of professional organizations, including the Institute of Electrical and Electronics Engineers or the Institute of Industrial Engineers, Inc.; a few also belong to a union, such as the United Auto Workers.

Tips for Entry

1. Visit Web sites to check out job postings for Electrical Engineers, such as the Web site of the Institute of Electrical and Electronics Engineers (www.ieee.org).
2. Mail a résumé to top automotive companies where you would like to work.
3. Attend professional conferences (such as the annual IEEE convention) and check out job boards there.
4. Check Internet job listings at www.engineering.com.
5. Visit your college's career counseling office for help in identifying companies where you would like to work.

INDUSTRIAL ENGINEER

CAREER PROFILE

Duties: Design automotive plant layout, including the arrangement of assembly line stations, material-moving equipment, work standards, and other production matters

Alternate Title(s): Quality Engineer

Salary Range: $40,760 to $91,090

Employment Prospects: Good

Advancement Prospects: Good

Best Geographical Location(s): Most jobs in the automotive field are located in Michigan, although automotive plants in other parts of the country also hire Industrial Engineers

Prerequisites:

Education or Training—A bachelor's degree is required for most entry-level jobs

Experience—A solid background in math and science is helpful

Special Skills and Personality Traits—Creative, inquisitive, analytical, good computer skills, and detail-oriented

Licensure/Certification—All 50 states require licensure for engineers who offer their services directly to the public

CAREER LADDER

```
┌─────────────────────────────────┐
│       Engineering Manager        │
└─────────────────────────────────┘

┌─────────────────────────────────┐
│       Industrial Engineer        │
└─────────────────────────────────┘

┌─────────────────────────────────┐
│   Industrial Engineer Technician │
└─────────────────────────────────┘
```

Position Description

Industrial Engineers (IEs) figure out how to do things better by designing engineering systems that improve quality and productivity. IEs make significant contributions to their employers by saving money while making the workplace better for fellow workers. They play an integral role in all stages of auto manufacturing, designing automotive plant layout, including the arrangement of assembly line stations, material-moving equipment, work standards, and other production matters.

Industrial Engineers discover a new way to assemble a product that will prevent worker injury, convert major production lines, represent the company in the design and construction of a new manufacturing plant, perform motion and time studies, implement lean manufacturing concepts, develop complete material handling systems for a new automobile, develop the conceptual layout of an automotive repair maintenance facility, and represent manufacturing and purchasing issues on a design team.

Industrial Engineers determine the most effective ways for an organization to use workers, machines, materials, information, and energy to make a product or to provide a service. They are the bridge between management goals and worksite performance. They are more concerned with increasing productivity through the management of people, methods of business organization, and technology than are engineers in other specialties, who generally work more with products or processes.

To solve organizational, production, and related problems most efficiently, Industrial Engineers carefully study the product and its requirements, use mathematical methods such as operations research to meet those requirements, and design manufacturing and information systems. They develop management control systems to help in financial planning and cost analysis, design production planning and control systems to coordinate activities and ensure product quality, and design or improve systems for the physical distribution of goods and services.

Industrial Engineers determine which plant location has the best combination of available raw materials, transportation facilities, and costs. They use computers for simulations and to control various activities and devices, such as assembly lines and robots. They also develop wage and salary administration systems and job evaluation programs.

Most Industrial Engineers work in office buildings, industrial plants, and production sites, where they monitor or direct operations or solve on-site problems. Many work a standard 40-hour week, although sometimes deadlines or design problems bring extra pressure to a job. When this happens, Industrial Engineers may work longer hours and experience considerable stress.

Salaries

Average annual salaries for Industrial Engineers range between $62,890 and $64,290. The lowest 10 percent earn less than $40,760, and the highest 10 percent earn more than $91,090. Bachelor's degree candidates in industrial engineering receive starting offers averaging about $48,320 a year; master's degree candidates average $56,265 a year; and Ph.D. candidates are initially offered $59,800. Top paying locations include Alaska (average $79,630), California ($72,720), and Washington, D.C. ($72,030).

Employment Prospects

Overall employment of Industrial Engineers is expected to grow about as fast as the average through 2012. Because the main function of Industrial Engineers is to make a higher-quality product as efficiently and as safely as possible, their services should be in demand in the automotive manufacturing sector as firms seek to reduce costs and increase productivity.

The number of bachelor's degrees awarded in engineering began declining in 1987 and has continued to stay at about the same level through much of the 1990s, and the total number of graduates from industrial engineering programs is not expected to increase significantly. Therefore, competition for jobs should not increase.

Advancement Prospects

Beginning industrial engineering graduates usually work under the supervision of experienced engineers. As new Industrial Engineers become more experienced, they are assigned more difficult projects with greater independence to develop designs, solve problems, and make decisions. Many Industrial Engineers move into management positions because the work is closely related.

Education and Training

A bachelor's degree in engineering is required for entry-level industrial engineering jobs. Most industrial engineering programs involve a concentration of study in industrial engineering, along with courses in both mathematics and science. Graduate training is not required for entry-level industrial engineering jobs in the automotive industry.

About 330 colleges and universities offer bachelor's degree programs in engineering that are accredited by the Accreditation Board for Engineering and Technology (ABET). ABET accreditation is based on an examination of an engineering program's student achievement, program improvement, faculty, curricular content, facilities, and institutional commitment. Some programs emphasize industrial practices, preparing students for a job in industry, whereas others are more theoretical and are designed to prepare students for graduate work. Therefore, students interested in working in the automotive field should investigate curricula and check accreditations carefully before selecting a college.

Admissions requirements for undergraduate engineering schools include a solid background in mathematics (algebra, geometry, trigonometry, and calculus) and sciences (biology, chemistry, and physics), and courses in English, social studies, humanities, and computers.

Bachelor's degree programs in industrial engineering typically are designed to last four years, but many students find that it takes between four and five years to complete their studies. In a typical four-year college curriculum, the first two years are spent studying mathematics, basic sciences, introductory engineering, humanities, and social sciences. Students interested in industrial engineering spend the last two years taking engineering courses with a concentration in industrial engineering.

Some programs offer a general engineering curriculum; students then specialize in graduate school or on the job. Other engineering schools and two-year colleges have agreements in which the two-year college provides the initial engineering education, and the engineering school automatically admits students for their last two years. In addition, a few engineering schools have arrangements in which a student spends three years in a liberal arts college studying pre-engineering subjects and two years in an engineering school studying core subjects, receiving a bachelor's degree from each school.

Some colleges and universities offer five-year master's degree programs; others offer five- or even six-year cooperative plans that combine classroom study and practical work, permitting students to gain valuable experience and finance part of their education.

Special Requirements

All 50 states and the District of Columbia require licensure for engineers. Licensed engineers are called Professional Engineers (PE); this generally requires a degree from an ABET-accredited engineering program, four years of relevant work experience, and successful completion of a state examination.

Recent graduates can start the licensing process by taking the examination in two stages. The initial Fundamentals of Engineering (FE) examination can be taken upon graduation; engineers who pass this examination are called Engineers in Training (EIT) or Engineer Interns (EI). The EIT certification is usually valid for 10 years.

After acquiring suitable work experience, EITs can take the second examination, the Principles and Practice of Engineering Exam. Several states have imposed mandatory continuing education requirements for relicensure, but most states recognize licensure from other states.

Experience, Skills, and Personality Traits

Industrial Engineers should be creative, inquisitive, analytical, and detail-oriented, with good computer skills. They need good time-management skills, mechanical aptitude, common sense, a strong desire for organization, resourcefulness, negotiation and leadership skills, and a passion for improvement.

Successful Industrial Engineers must be able to communicate effectively in order to sell their ideas. They must be able to manage multiple tasks.

Unions and Associations

Industrial Engineers may join a variety of professional organizations such as the Institute of Industrial Engineers; a few belong to a union such as the United Auto Workers.

Tips for Entry

1. Visit Web sites to check job postings for Industrial Engineers, such as the Web site of the Institute of Industrial Engineers (http://jobs.iienet.org).
2. Create a résumé and post it at the Web site of the Institute of Industrial Engineers.
3. Mail your résumé to top automotive companies where you would like to work.
4. Attend professional conferences (such as the Institute of Industrial Engineers annual convention) and check out job boards there.

CHEMICAL ENGINEER

CAREER PROFILE

Duties: Develop proper lubricants, gasoline, plastics, paint, and rubber to improve a car's appearance, weight, performance, and reliable operation; design processes used to manufacture cars

Alternate Title(s): Manufacturing Engineer; Project Engineer; Process Engineer; Product Development Engineer; Experimental Engineer; R&D Engineer

Salary Range: $48,450 to $107,520+

Employment Prospects: Fair

Advancement Prospects: Fair

Best Geographical Location(s): Most jobs in the automotive production field are located in Michigan, although automotive plants in other parts of the country also hire Chemical Engineers

Prerequisites:

Education or Training—A bachelor's degree is required for most entry-level jobs and continuing education is critical to keep abreast of the latest technology

Experience—A solid background in math, chemistry, and other sciences is helpful

Special Skills and Personality Traits—Creativity; inquisitiveness; analytical; detail-oriented; good communication skills

Licensure/Certification—All 50 states require licensure for engineers who offer their services directly to the public

CAREER LADDER

```
┌─────────────────────────────────────┐
│    Chemical Engineering Manager      │
└─────────────────────────────────────┘

┌─────────────────────────────────────┐
│         Chemical Engineer            │
└─────────────────────────────────────┘

┌─────────────────────────────────────┐
│   Chemical Engineering Technician    │
└─────────────────────────────────────┘
```

Position Description

Chemical Engineers in the automotive industry develop proper lubricants, gasoline, plastics, paint, and rubber to improve a car's appearance, weight, performance, and reliable operation, and design plants and processes used to manufacture cars. Chemical Engineers build a bridge between science and manufacturing, applying the principles of chemistry and engineering to solve problems involving the production or use of chemicals. They design equipment and develop processes for auto manufacturing, plan and test methods of manufacturing products and treating byproducts, and supervise production.

The knowledge and duties of Chemical Engineers overlap many fields. Chemical Engineers apply principles of chemistry, physics, mathematics, and mechanical and electrical engineering. Chemical Engineers also may specialize in the automotive industry in general, or in one field of technology, such as automotive plastics. They frequently specialize in a particular chemical process such as oxidation or polymerization. They must be aware of all aspects of chemical manufacturing and how it affects the environment, the safety of workers, and customers.

Because Chemical Engineers use computer technology to optimize all phases of research and production, they need to understand how to apply computer skills to chemical process analysis, automated control systems, and statistical quality control.

In addition to design and development, many Chemical Engineers work in testing, production, or maintenance. These engineers supervise production in factories, determine the causes of breakdowns, and test manufactured products to maintain quality. They also estimate the time and cost to complete projects.

Chemical Engineers use computers to produce and analyze designs, to simulate and test how a machine or system operates, and to generate specifications for parts. Using the Internet or other communications systems, Chemical Engineers can collaborate on designs with other engineers anywhere in the world. Many Chemical Engineers also use computers to monitor product quality and control process efficiency. Chemical Engineers may spend time writing reports and consulting with other engineers, as complex projects often require an interdisciplinary team of engineers.

Most Chemical Engineers work in office buildings, laboratories, or industrial plants, and some travel a great deal to other plants or worksites. Although many Chemical Engineers work a standard 40-hour week, sometimes deadlines or design problems may require longer hours.

Salaries

Starting salaries are significantly higher than those of college graduates in other fields. Average annual earnings of Chemical Engineers are $73,750, ranging from less than $48,450 to a high of more than $107,520. According to a 2003 salary survey by the National Association of Colleges and Employers, bachelor's degree candidates in chemical engineering received starting offers averaging $52,384 a year, master's degree candidates averaged $57,857, and Ph.D. candidates averaged $70,729.

Employment Prospects

Little or no growth in employment of Chemical Engineers is expected though 2012, according to the Bureau of Labor Statistics, and overall employment is expected to decline. However, although no new jobs due to growth are expected to be created, many openings will result from the need to replace Chemical Engineers who transfer to other occupations or leave the labor force.

Advancement Prospects

Beginning Chemical Engineers usually work under the supervision of experienced engineers and, in large companies, also may receive formal classroom or seminar-type training. As they gain knowledge and experience, they are assigned more difficult projects with greater independence to develop designs, solve problems, and make decisions.

Some Chemical Engineers move into chemical engineering management or into sales. (In sales, a chemical engineering background enables them to discuss technical aspects and assist in product planning, installation, and use.)

Chemical Engineers may advance to become technical specialists or to supervise a staff or team of engineers and technicians. Some may eventually become engineering managers or enter other managerial or sales jobs.

Many Chemical Engineers obtain graduate degrees in engineering or business administration to learn new technology and broaden their education. Many high-level executives in industry began their careers as engineers. It's important for Chemical Engineers to continue their education throughout their careers because much of their value to their employer depends on their knowledge of the latest technology. Engineers in high-technology areas, such as advanced chemistry, may find that technical knowledge becomes outdated rapidly.

By keeping current in their field, Chemical Engineers are able to deliver the best solutions and greatest value to their employers. Even those who continue their education are vulnerable to layoffs if the particular technology or product in which they have specialized becomes obsolete. On the other hand, it often is these high-technology areas that offer the greatest challenges, the most interesting work, and the highest salaries. Therefore, the choice of engineering specialty and employer involves an assessment not only of the potential rewards but also of the risk of technological obsolescence. Chemical Engineers who have not kept current in their field may find themselves passed over for promotions or vulnerable to layoffs, should they occur.

Education and Training

A bachelor's degree is required for most entry-level jobs in chemical engineering and continuing education is critical to keep abreast of the latest technology. College graduates with a degree in a physical science or mathematics occasionally may qualify for some engineering jobs, especially in specialties in high demand. Graduate training is essential for many research and development programs, but is not required for the majority of entry-level engineering jobs.

About 340 colleges and universities offer bachelor's degree programs in chemical engineering that are accredited by the Accreditation Board for Engineering and Technology (ABET). ABET accreditation is based on an examination of an engineering program's student achievement, program improvement, faculty, curricular content, facilities, and institutional commitment.

Programs of the same title may vary in content. For example, some programs emphasize industrial practices, preparing students for a job in industry, whereas others are more theoretical and are designed to prepare students for graduate work. Therefore, students should investigate curricula and check accreditations carefully before selecting a college.

Admissions requirements for undergraduate engineering schools include a solid background in mathematics (algebra, geometry, trigonometry, and calculus) and science (biology, chemistry, and physics), and courses in English, social studies, humanities, and computer and information technology. Bachelor's degree programs in chemical engineering typically are designed to last four years, but many students find that it takes between four and five to complete their studies. In a typical four-year college curriculum, the first two years are spent studying mathematics, basic sciences, introductory engineering, humanities, and social sciences. In the last two years, most courses are in engineering, usually with a concentration in chemical engineering.

Some engineering schools and two-year colleges have agreements whereby the two-year college provides the initial engineering education, and the engineering school automatically admits students for their last two years. In addition, a few engineering schools have arrangements whereby a student spends three years in a liberal arts college studying pre-engineering subjects and two years in an engineering school studying core subjects, and then receives a bachelor's degree from each school. Some colleges and universities offer five-year master's degree programs. Some five-year or even six-year cooperative plans combine classroom study and practical work, permitting students to gain valuable experience and to finance part of their education.

Special Requirements

All 50 states and the District of Columbia require licensure for engineers who offer their services directly to the public; licensed engineers are called Professional Engineers (PE). Many Chemical Engineers are licensed PEs.

This licensure generally requires a degree from an ABET-accredited engineering program, four years of relevant work experience, and successful completion of a state examination. Recent graduates can start the licensing process by taking the examination in two stages. The initial Fundamentals of Engineering examination can be taken upon graduation; engineers who pass this examination commonly are called engineers in training (EIT) or engineer interns. After acquiring suitable work experience, EITs can take the second examination (Principles and Practice of Engineering exam).

Several states have imposed mandatory continuing education requirements for relicensure. Most states recognize licensure from other states provided that the manner in which the initial license was obtained meets or exceeds their licensure requirements.

Experience, Skills, and Personality

Chemical Engineers should be creative, inquisitive, analytical, and detail-oriented. They should be able to work as part of a team and to communicate well, both orally and in writing. Communication abilities are important because Chemical Engineers often interact with specialists in a wide range of fields outside engineering.

Unions and Associations

Chemical Engineers may belong to professional associations such as the American Institute of Chemical Engineers or the American Chemical Society.

Tips for Entry

1. Contact placement and professional services firms (such as Kelly Services) for nationwide placement and contract positions.
2. Visit Web sites to check out positions for Chemical Engineers, such as the jobs listing on the Web site of the American Institute of Chemical Engineers (www.aiche.org) or the American Chemical Society (www.chemistry.org/portal/Chemistry).
3. Mail a résumé to top automotive companies where you would like to work.
4. Attend professional conferences and check out job boards there.
5. Visit your college's career counseling office for help in identifying companies where you would like to work.
6. Use your contacts. The easiest way to network is to ask someone you already know for the name of someone else. Then when you call, say, "Jane Doe suggested I call you."
7. Develop electronic networking skills. Visit chat groups or message boards that pertain to your career area. Take special interest in those run by professional associations.

ENGINEERING TECHNICIAN

CAREER PROFILE

Duties: Under supervision, prepare specifications for materials, devise and run tests to ensure product quality, and study ways to improve manufacturing efficiency

Alternate Title(s): Engineering Technologist, Automotive Engineering Technician

Salary Range: $27,440 to $66,170+

Employment Prospects: Good

Advancement Prospects: Good

Best Geographical Location(s): Most jobs in the automotive field are located in Michigan, although automotive plants in other parts of the country also hire engineering technicians

Prerequisites:

Education or Training—Associate degree in engineering or engineering technology, or extensive job training in engineering technology

Experience—A solid background in math and science is helpful

Special Skills and Personality Traits—Creativity, good communication skills, attention to detail

Licensure/Certification—Voluntary certification programs are available

CAREER LADDER

```
┌─────────────────────────────────────┐
│  Engineering Technician Supervisor   │
└─────────────────────────────────────┘

┌─────────────────────────────────────┐
│      Engineering Technician          │
└─────────────────────────────────────┘

┌─────────────────────────────────────┐
│           Entry Level                │
└─────────────────────────────────────┘
```

Position Description

Under the direction of automotive engineers, automotive Engineering Technicians prepare specifications for materials, devise and run tests to ensure product quality, and study ways to improve manufacturing efficiency. For example, testing may reveal how metal parts perform under conditions of heat, cold, and stress, and whether emissions control equipment meets environmental standards. Finally, prototype vehicles incorporating all the components are built and tested on test tracks, on road simulators, and in test chambers that can duplicate almost every driving condition, including crashes.

Engineering Technicians use the principles and theories of science, engineering, and mathematics to solve technical problems in research and development, manufacturing, construction, inspection, and maintenance. Their work is more limited in scope and more practically oriented than that of engineers.

Many Engineering Technicians help engineers, especially in research and development. They build or set up equipment, prepare and conduct experiments, collect data, calculate or record the results, and help engineers or scientists in other ways, such as making prototype versions of newly designed equipment. They also assist in design work, often using computer-aided design equipment. Others work in quality control, inspecting products and processes, conducting tests, or collecting data. They may assist in product design, development, or production.

Most Engineering Technicians specialize in certain areas, learning skills and working in the same disciplines as engineers, so job titles tend to follow the same structure as those of engineers:

- *Electrical and Electronics Engineering Technicians* help design, develop, test, and manufacture electrical and electronic equipment such as automobile electrical systems, industrial measuring or control devices, and onboard computers. They may work in product evaluation and testing, using measuring and diagnostic devices to adjust, test, and repair equipment. About 45 percent of Engineering Technicians are electrical and electronic engineering technicians.
- *Electromechanical Engineering Technicians* combine fundamental principles of mechanical engineering technology with knowledge of electrical and electronic circuits to design, develop, test, and manufacture electrical and computer-controlled mechanical systems.
- *Industrial Engineering Technicians* study the efficient use of personnel, materials, and machines in factories and repair shops. They prepare layouts of machinery and equipment, plan the flow of work, make statistical studies, and analyze production costs. Mechanical Engineering Technicians help mechanical engineers design, develop, test, and manufacture industrial machinery and vehicles themselves. They may assist in product tests by setting up instrumentation for auto crash tests, for example. They may make sketches and rough layouts, record data, make computations, analyze results, and write reports. When planning production, mechanical Engineering Technicians prepare layouts and drawings of the assembly process and of parts to be manufactured. They estimate labor costs, equipment life, and plant space. Some test and inspect machines and equipment in manufacturing departments or work with engineers to eliminate production problems.

Most Engineering Technicians work at least 40 hours a week in laboratories, offices, or manufacturing or industrial plants, or on construction sites. Some may be exposed to hazards from equipment, chemicals, or toxic materials.

Salaries

The average annual salary for electrical and electronics Engineering Technicians range between $43,650 and $45,150. The lowest 10 percent earn less than $27,660, and the highest 10 percent earn more than $66,170. The average annual salary for industrial Engineering Technicians ranges from $41,860 to $45,090. The average annual salary for mechanical Engineering Technicians is $41,890; the lowest-paid 10 percent earned less than $27,440 and the highest-paid 10 percent earned more than $61,640.

Employment Prospects

Opportunities will be best for students with an associate degree or extensive job training in engineering technology. As automotive technology becomes more sophisticated, employers continue to look for technicians who are skilled in new technology and require a minimum of additional job training. Overall employment of Engineering Technicians is expected to increase about as fast as the average for all occupations through 2012. As automotive production continues to grow, competitive pressures will force companies to improve and update manufacturing facilities and product designs more rapidly than in the past. However, the growing availability and use of advanced technologies, such as computer-aided design and drafting and computer simulation, will continue to increase productivity and limit job growth. In addition to growth, many job openings will stem from the need to replace technicians who retire or leave the labor force. Like engineers, employment of Engineering Technicians is influenced by local and national economic conditions. Increasing demand for more sophisticated electrical and electronic products will contribute to average growth in the job situation for electrical and electronics Engineering Technicians.

Advancement Prospects

Engineering Technicians usually begin by performing routine duties under the close supervision of an experienced technician, technologist, engineer, or scientist. As they gain experience, they are given more difficult assignments with only general supervision. Some Engineering Technicians eventually become supervisors.

Education and Training

Opportunities will be best for individuals with an associate degree or extensive job training in engineering technology. Because the type and quality of training programs vary considerably, prospective students should carefully investigate training programs before enrolling.

Although it may be possible to qualify for a few Engineering Technician jobs without formal training, most automotive employers prefer to hire someone with at least a two-year associate degree in engineering technology. Training is available at technical institutes, community colleges, extension divisions of colleges and universities, public and private vocational-technical schools, and the Armed Forces.

People with college courses in science, engineering, and mathematics may qualify for some positions, but they may need additional specialized training and experience.

Prospective engineering technicians should take as many high school science and math courses as possible to prepare for postsecondary programs in engineering technology. Most two-year associate degree programs accredited by the Technology Accreditation Commission of the Accreditation Board for Engineering and Technology (TAC/ABET) have minimum requirements of college algebra and trigonometry, and one or two basic science courses. Depending on the specialty, more math or science may be required.

The type of technical courses required also depends on the specialty. For example, prospective mechanical Engineering Technicians may take courses in fluid mechanics, thermodynamics, and mechanical design, while future electrical Engineering Technicians may take more classes in electric circuits, microprocessors, and digital electronics.

Although many publicly and privately operated schools provide technical training, the type and quality of programs vary considerably. Prospective students should be careful in selecting a program. Students should ask prospective employers about their preferences, and ask schools to provide information about the kinds of jobs obtained by graduates, the facilities and equipment, and faculty qualifications.

ABET-accredited programs usually offer an acceptable level of competence in the mathematics, science, and technical courses. Technical institutes offer intensive technical training through application and practice, but less theory and general education than community colleges. Many offer two-year associate degree programs and are similar to or part of a community college or state university system. Other technical institutes are run by private, for-profit organizations sometimes called proprietary schools. Their programs vary considerably in length and types of courses offered, although some are two-year associate degree programs. Community colleges offer curriculums that are similar to those in technical institutes, but that may include more theory and liberal arts.

Often there may be little or no difference between technical institute and community college programs, as both offer associate degrees. After completing the two-year program, some graduates get jobs as Engineering Technicians, while others continue their education at four-year colleges. However, there is a difference between an associate degree in pre-engineering and one in engineering technology. Students who enroll in a two-year pre-engineering program may find it very difficult to find work as an Engineering Technician should they decide not to enter a four-year engineering program, because pre-engineering programs usually focus less on hands-on applications and more on academic preparatory work. On the other hand, graduates of two-year engineering technology programs may not receive credit for many of the courses they have taken if they choose to transfer to a four-year engineering program. Colleges with these four-year programs usually do not offer Engineering Technician training, but college courses in science, engineering, and mathematics are useful in getting a job as an Engineering Technician. Many four-year colleges offer bachelor's degrees in engineering technology, but graduates of these programs often are hired to work as applied engineers, not technicians.

Area vocational-technical schools, another source of technical training, include postsecondary public institutions that serve local students and emphasize training needed by local employers. Most require a high school diploma or its equivalent for admission.

Other training in technical areas may be obtained in the Armed Forces, and many military technical training programs are highly regarded by employers. However, skills acquired in military programs are often narrowly focused, so they may not be useful in civilian industry, which often requires broader training. Therefore, some additional training may be needed, depending on the acquired skills and the kind of job.

Special Requirements

Although employers usually do not require Engineering Technicians to be certified, this can provide a competitive advantage. The National Institute for Certification in Engineering Technologies (NICET) has established a voluntary certification program for Engineering Technicians. Certification is available at various levels, each level combining a written examination in one of more than 30 specialties with a certain amount of job-related experience, a supervisory evaluation, and a recommendation.

Experience, Skills, and Personality Traits

Because many Engineering Technicians may help in design work, creativity is desirable. Good communication skills and the ability to work well with others is also important because these workers often are part of a team of engineers and other technicians. Engineering Technicians should also be detail-oriented and have good computer skills.

Unions and Associations

Engineering Technicians may choose to join a variety of professional groups such as the Junior Engineering Technical Society; a few may join a union such as the United Auto Workers.

Tips for Entry

1. Engineering Technician positions are often advertised in the classified section of the newspaper under "Mechanical" or "Professional."
2. Visit Web sites to check out job posting for Engineering Technicians.
3. Mail a résumé to top automotive companies where you would like to work.
4. Attend professional conferences and check out job boards there. Check out helpful Internet websites such as the Junior Engineering Technical Society (www.jets.org) or the National Institute for Certification in Engineering Technologies (www.nicet.org).
5. Visit your college's career counseling office for help in identifying companies where you would like to work.

INDUSTRIAL PRODUCTION MANAGER

CAREER PROFILE

Duties: Oversee production staff and equipment, ensure that production goals and quality standards are being met, and implement company policies

Alternate Title(s): Director of Production

Salary Range: $41,270 to $120,080

Employment Prospects: Fair

Advancement Prospects: Fair

Best Geographical Location(s): All parts of the country, but jobs are most plentiful in areas where automotive manufacturing is concentrated

Prerequisites:

Education or Training—A college degree is required

Experience—Experience in any type of business, especially in managing others, is helpful

Special Skills and Personality Traits—Good management skills and communication techniques, ability to work independently, attention to detail, good business skills

CAREER LADDER

```
┌─────────────────────────────────────┐
│      Plant Manager or               │
│  Vice President for Manufacturing   │
└─────────────────────────────────────┘

┌─────────────────────────────────────┐
│   Industrial Production Manager     │
└─────────────────────────────────────┘

┌─────────────────────────────────────┐
│      First-Line Supervisor          │
└─────────────────────────────────────┘
```

Position Description

Industrial Production Managers oversee first-line supervisors and managers of production and operating workers. These supervisors oversee inspectors, precision workers, machine setters and operators, assemblers, fabricators, and plant and system operators. They coordinate a variety of manufacturing processes and production activities, including scheduling, staffing, equipment, quality control, and inventory control.

Many manufacturing processes are highly automated; robots, computers, and programmable devices are an integral part of auto manufacturing. Throughout the manufacturing process, Industrial Production Managers emphasize teamwork and quality control. From initial planning and design to final assembly, numerous tests and inspections ensure that cars meet quality and safety standards. Modern manufacturing facilities integrate interchangeable tools on the assembly line so that they can quickly be changed to meet the needs of various models and specifications.

The primary mission of Industrial Production Managers lies in planning the production schedule and keeping track of budgetary limits and deadlines. Managers analyze the plant's personnel and capital resources to select the best way of meeting the production quota. Using mathematical formulas, Industrial Production Managers determine which machines will be used, whether new machines need to be purchased, whether overtime or extra shifts are necessary, and what the sequence of production will be. They monitor the production run to make sure that it stays on schedule and correct any problems that may arise.

Industrial Production Managers also must monitor product standards. If quality drops below the established standard, they must determine why standards are not being maintained and how to improve. If the problem relates to the quality of work, the manager may implement better training programs, reorganize the manufacturing process, or institute employee suggestion or involvement programs. If the cause is substandard materials, the manager works with the purchasing department to improve the quality of the product's components.

Because the work of many departments is interrelated, Industrial Production Managers work closely with heads of other departments such as sales, procurement, and logistics to plan and implement company goals. For example, the Industrial Production Manager works with the procurement department to make sure that plant inventories are maintained so that production delays can be avoided. A breakdown in communication between the Industrial Production Manager and the purchasing department can cause slowdowns and missed deadlines. Just-in-time production techniques have reduced inventory levels, making constant communication among the manager, suppliers, and purchasing departments even more important.

Computers play an integral part in this coordination, and are used to provide up-to-date information on inventory, the status of work in progress, and quality standards.

Industrial Production Managers usually report to the plant manager or the vice president for manufacturing, and may act as liaison between executives and first-line supervisors. In many plants, one Industrial Production Manager is responsible for all aspects of production. In large plants, there are managers in charge of each operation, such as machining, assembly, or finishing.

Most Industrial Production Managers divide their time between production areas and their offices, which are often located near production areas. They usually spend time meeting with subordinates or other department managers, analyzing production data, and writing and reviewing reports.

Most Industrial Production Managers work more than 40 hours a week, especially when production deadlines must be met. In facilities that operate 24 hours a day, they often work late shifts and may be called at any hour to deal with emergencies. This could mean going to the plant to resolve the problem, regardless of the hour, and staying until the situation is under control.

Restructuring has eliminated levels of management and support staff, thus shifting more responsibilities to Industrial Production Managers and compounding this stress. Dealing with production workers as well as superiors when working under the pressure of production deadlines or emergency situations can be stressful.

Salaries

The average annual salary for Industrial Production Managers ranges between $70,510 and $76,710; the lowest 10 percent earn less than $41,270, and the highest 10 percent earn more than $120,080. Top-paying states include Connecticut ($91,570) and Michigan ($90,100).

Employment Prospects

Employment of Industrial Production Managers is expected to grow more slowly than the average for all occupations through 2012, according to the Bureau of Labor Statistics. However, a number of job openings will stem from the need to replace workers who transfer to other occupations or leave the labor force. Those with the best chance of being hired include applicants with a college degree in industrial engineering, management, or business administration, and particularly those with an undergraduate engineering degree and a master's degree in business administration or industrial management.

Although more cars are projected to be produced, growing productivity among Industrial Production Managers and the workers they supervise means fewer managers will be needed. Increasing use of computers for scheduling, planning, and coordination will boost productivity. In addition, as the emphasis on quality in the production process has increased, some of the Industrial Production Manager's oversight responsibilities has shifted to supervisors and workers on the production line.

Because Industrial Production Managers are so essential to the efficient operation of a plant, however, they have not been greatly affected by recent efforts to flatten management structures. Nevertheless, this trend has led Industrial Production Managers to assume more responsibilities and has discouraged the creation of more jobs.

Advancement Prospects

Some Industrial Production Managers have worked their way up the ranks, starting as first-line supervisors, which can provide an intimate knowledge of the production process and the firm's organization. To be selected for promotion, however, they must obtain a college degree, demonstrate leadership qualities, and usually take company-sponsored courses in management skills and communication techniques.

In addition to formal training, Industrial Production Managers must keep informed of new production technologies and management practices. Many belong to professional organizations and attend trade shows at which new equipment is displayed; they also attend industry conferences and conventions at which changes in production methods and technological advances are discussed.

Industrial Production Managers with a proven record of superior performance may advance to plant manager or vice president for manufacturing; others transfer to jobs with more responsibilities at larger firms. Opportunities also exist for consultants.

Education and Training

A college degree is required, even for those who have worked their way up through the ranks. Although there is no standard preparation for this position, a college degree in industrial engineering, management, or business administration, or an undergraduate engineering degree and a master's degree in business administration or industrial management, is a good beginning.

Many Industrial Production Managers have a college degree in business administration, management, industrial technology, or industrial engineering. Others have a master's degree in industrial management or business administration (MBA). Some are former production-line supervisors who have been promoted.

Although many employers prefer candidates with a business or engineering background, some companies hire well-rounded liberal arts graduates. As production operations become more sophisticated, more and more employers are looking for candidates with graduate degrees in industrial management or business administration. Combined with an undergraduate degree in engineering, either of these graduate degrees is considered particularly good preparation.

Managers who do not have graduate degrees often take courses in decision sciences, which provide them with techniques and mathematical formulas that can be used to maximize efficiency.

Those who enter the field directly from college or graduate school often are unfamiliar with the firm's production process. As a result, they may spend their first few months on the job in the company's training program. These programs familiarize trainees with the production line, company policies, and the requirements of the job. In larger companies, they also may include assignments to other departments. A number of companies hire college graduates as first-line supervisors and later promote them.

Experience, Skills, and Personality Traits

Employers also are likely to seek candidates who have excellent communication skills and who are personable, flexible, and eager to enhance their knowledge and skills through ongoing training. Companies place great importance on a candidate's interpersonal skills, because the job requires the ability to compromise, persuade, and negotiate. Successful Industrial Production Managers must be well-rounded and have excellent communication skills.

Unions and Associations

Industrial Production Managers do not belong to unions but may choose to join various professional organizations such as the American Management Association or the National Management Association.

Tips for Entry

1. Mail a résumé to top automotive companies where you would like to work.
2. Attend professional conferences and check job boards there.
3. Check Internet job listings, such as the American Management Association at www.amanet.org; the National Management Association (www.nma1.org); Manufacturing.net (www.manufacturing.net); or the Alliance for Innovative Manufacturing (www.stanford.edu/group/AIM).
4. Visit your college's career counseling office for help in identifying companies where you would like to work.
5. Use your contacts. The easiest way to network is to ask someone you already know for the name of someone else. When you call, say, "So-and-so suggested I call you."
6. Develop your networking skills. Visit chat groups or message boards that pertain to your career area. Take special interest in those run by professional associations.

ASSEMBLER/FABRICATOR

CAREER PROFILE

Duties: Put together various parts to form subassemblies, and then put the subassemblies together to build a complete motor vehicle

Alternate Title(s): None

Salary Range: $9.41 to $21.07 per hour

Employment Prospects: Fair

Advancement Prospects: Fair

Best Geographical Location(s): Most jobs in the automotive field are located in Michigan, although automotive plants in other parts of the country also hire assemblers

Prerequisites:

Education or Training—A high school diploma is preferred for most positions; applicants need specialized training for some assembly jobs

Experience—Typically, new Assemblers and Fabricators are entry-level employees, but any type of mechanical experience is helpful

Special Skills and Personality Traits—Attention to detail, ability to work accurately and quickly, good eyesight and color vision, manual dexterity, and the ability to carry out complex, repetitive tasks quickly

CAREER LADDER

```
┌─────────────────────────────┐
│        Supervisor           │
│  or Quality Control Expert  │
└─────────────────────────────┘

┌─────────────────────────────┐
│     Assembler/Fabricator    │
└─────────────────────────────┘

┌─────────────────────────────┐
│         Entry Level         │
└─────────────────────────────┘
```

Position Description

Assemblers and Fabricators produce auto engines and electrical and electronic components from manufactured parts or subassemblies. Some may perform other routine tasks such as mounting and inflating tires, adjusting brakes, and adding gas, oil, brake fluid, and coolant to the assembled car on the production line.

Assemblers may work on subassemblies or the final assembly of a car or its components. For example, electrical and electronic equipment Assemblers put together or modify automotive systems, radio test equipment, onboard computers, machine-tool numerical controls, and prototypes of these and other products. Electromechanical equipment Assemblers prepare and test equipment or devices. Coil winders, tapers, and finishers wind wire coil used in electric motors. Engine and other machine Assemblers construct, assemble, or rebuild car engines. Structural

metal Fabricators and fitters align and fit structural metal parts according to detailed specifications prior to welding or riveting.

Assemblers and Fabricators who help develop products read and interpret engineering specifications from text, drawings, and computer-aided drafting systems, and may use different tools and precision measuring instruments. Some experienced Assemblers work with engineers and technicians, assembling prototypes or test products.

As technology changes, so too does the manufacturing process. For example, flexible manufacturing systems include the manufacturing applications of robotics, computers, programmable motion control, and various sensing technologies. These systems change the way in which cars are made, and affect auto manufacturing jobs. The concept of cellular manufacturing, for example, emphasizes working together within teams of workers over the old assembly-line process. Team Assemblers perform all of the assembly tasks assigned to their teams, rotating through the different tasks, rather than specializing in a single task. They also may decide how the work is to be assigned and how different tasks are to be performed. Some aspects of team assembly, such as rotating tasks, are becoming more common to all assembly and fabrication occupations. As the U.S. manufacturing sector continues to evolve in the face of growing international competition and changing technology, the nature of assembly and fabrication will also change.

Working conditions for automotive Assemblers and Fabricators vary from plant to plant. Conditions may be noisy, and many Assemblers may have to sit or stand for long periods. Assemblers usually work in rooms that are clean, well-lit, and dust-free, but some electrical and electronics Assemblers encounter soldering fumes, although ventilation systems and fans normally minimize this problem.

Most full-time Assemblers work a 40-hour week, although overtime and shiftwork is fairly common in the automotive industry. Work schedules of Assemblers may vary at plants with more than one shift.

Salaries

Earnings vary by industry, geographic region, skill, educational level, and complexity. Average hourly earnings of team Assemblers range from $11.14 to $12.10; the lowest 10 percent earn less than $7.49, and the highest 10 percent earn $18.01. Average hourly earnings of electrical and electronic equipment Assemblers range from $11.28 to $12.20; the lowest 10 percent earn less than $7.85, and the highest 10 percent earn more than $17.77. Average hourly earnings are $15.58 for engine and other machine assemblers; $11.48 for coil winders, tapers, and finishers; $11.87 for fiberglass laminators and finishers; $12.79 for timing device Assemblers, calibrators, and adjusters; $12.52 for electromechanical equipment Assemblers; and $13.55 for all other Assemblers.

Employment Prospects

Employment is expected to decline through the year 2012, reflecting increasing automation and the shift of assembly to countries with lower labor costs. As manufacturers strive for greater precision and productivity, automated machinery will be more often used to perform work more economically or efficiently. Recent advancements have made robotics more affordable, which should continue raising the productivity of assembly workers and cutting the number of jobs.

Still, there will be job openings as workers leave the industry. The effects of automation will be felt more acutely among some types of Assemblers and Fabricators than among others. Flexible manufacturing systems are expensive, and a large volume of repetitive work is required to justify their purchase. Also, where the assembly parts involved are irregular in size or location, it is harder to design a robot to handle these jobs. On the other hand, automation increasingly will be used in the precision assembly of electronic goods. Many companies have components assembled in countries where labor costs are lower, which cuts down on Assembler jobs in the United States.

Advancement Prospects

As Assemblers and Fabricators become more experienced, they may progress to jobs that require more skill and responsibility. Experienced Assemblers may become product repairers if they have learned the many assembly operations and understand the construction of a product. These workers fix assembled articles that operators or inspectors have identified as defective. Assemblers also can advance to quality control jobs or be promoted to supervisor. In some companies, Assemblers can become trainees for one of the skilled trades. Those with a background in math, science, and computers may advance to programmers or operators of more highly automated production equipment. Experienced Assemblers and Fabricators also may become members of research and development teams, working with engineers and other project designers to design, develop, build prototypes, and test new product models.

Education and Training

New Assemblers and Fabricators are normally entry-level employees. A high school diploma is preferred for most positions; applicants need specialized training for some assembly jobs. For example, employers may require that applicants for electrical or electronic Assembler jobs be technical school graduates or have military training. Other positions require only on-the-job training, including employer-sponsored classroom instruction in the assembly duties that employees may be required to perform.

Experience, Skills, and Personality Traits

The ability to do work accurately and quickly and to follow detailed instructions are key job requirements. Good eyesight (with or without glasses) is necessary for Assemblers and Fabricators who work with small parts. Plants that make electrical and electronic products may test applicants for color vision, because many of their products contain many different-colored wires. Manual dexterity and the ability to carry out complex, repetitive tasks quickly and methodically also are important skills.

Unions and Associations

Many Assemblers and Fabricators are members of labor unions, including the International Association of Machinists and Aerospace Workers; the United Electrical, Radio and Machine Workers of America; the United Automobile, Aerospace and Agricultural Implement Workers of America;

the International Brotherhood of Electrical Workers; and the United Steelworkers of America.

Tips for Entry

1. Visit your school's career counseling office for help in identifying companies where you would like to work.

2. Use your contacts. The easiest way to network is to ask someone you already know for the name of someone else. When you call, say, "So-and-so suggested I call you."

3. Mail a résumé to companies where you would like to work.

WELDER/SOLDERER/BRAZER

CAREER PROFILE

Duties: Although robots perform most of the welding, soldering, and brazing, workers still are needed for some welding and for maintenance and repair duties

Alternate Title(s): None

Salary Range: $9.53 to $22.06 per hour

Employment Prospects: Excellent

Advancement Prospects: Excellent

Best Geographical Location(s): Most jobs in the automotive field are located in Michigan, although automotive plants in other parts of the country also hire welders

Prerequisites:

Education or Training—A few weeks of on-the-job training for low-skilled positions to several years of combined school and on-the-job training for highly skilled jobs

Experience—Experience in welding or soldering, especially in the Armed Forces, can be helpful

Special Skills and Personality Traits—Good eyesight, attention to detail, good eye-hand coordination

Licensure/Certification—Some schools and the American Welding Society offer certification in welding

CAREER LADDER

```
┌─────────────────────────────────────┐
│  Welding Supervisor or Inspector     │
└─────────────────────────────────────┘

┌─────────────────────────────────────┐
│  Welder/Solderer/Brazer              │
└─────────────────────────────────────┘

┌─────────────────────────────────────┐
│  Apprentice Welder/Solderer/Brazer   │
└─────────────────────────────────────┘
```

Position Description

Welding is the most common way of permanently joining metal parts, by applying heat to metal pieces, melting and fusing them to form a permanent bond. Welders use many types of welding equipment. They may weld manually or semiautomatically, using machinery to help in performing welding tasks.

Arc welding is the most common type of welding, in which one metal clip carrying a strong electrical current is attached to any part of the piece being welded; a second clip is connected to a thin welding rod. When the rod touches the piece, it creates a powerful electrical circuit and massive heat that causes both the piece and the steel core of the rod to melt together, cooling quickly to form a solid bond. During welding, the flux that surrounds the rod's core vaporizes, forming an inert gas that protects the weld from elements that might weaken it.

Like arc welding, soldering and brazing use metal to join two pieces of metal. However, the metal added during the process has melting point lower than that of the piece, so only the added metal is melted, not the piece itself.

Soldering uses metals with a melting point below 800 degrees F.; brazing uses metals with a melting point above 800 degrees F. Because soldering and brazing do not melt the piece, these processes normally do not create distortions or weaknesses that can occur with welding. Soldering is commonly used to join electrical, electronic, and other small metal parts. Brazing produces a stronger joint than does soldering, and often is used to join metals other than steel, such as brass parts.

Skilled welding, soldering, and brazing workers generally plan work from drawings or specifications, or use their knowledge of fluxes and base metals to analyze parts. These workers then select and set up welding equipment and examine welds to make sure they meet specifications.

Other Welders perform more routine jobs that already have been planned and laid out and do not require extensive knowledge of welding techniques.

Automated welding is used in an increasing number of production processes, in which a machine or robot does the welding while monitored by a welding machine operator.

Welding, soldering, and brazing machine setters, operators, and tenders follow specified layouts, work orders, or blueprints. Operators must load parts correctly and constantly monitor the machine to ensure it produces the desired bond.

The work of arc, plasma, and oxy-gas cutters is closely related to that of Welders, but instead of joining metals, cutters use the heat from an electric arc, a stream of ionized gas, or burning gases to cut and trim metal objects to specific dimensions. Some operate and monitor cutting machines similar to those used by welding machine operators. Plasma cutting has been increasing in popularity because, unlike other methods, it can cut a wide variety of metals, including stainless steel, aluminum, and titanium.

Welding, soldering, and brazing workers often are exposed to a number of potential hazards, including the intense light created by the arc, hazardous fumes, and burns. They wear safety shoes, goggles, hoods with protective lenses, and other devices designed to prevent burns and eye injuries and to protect them from falling objects. They normally work in well-ventilated areas to limit their exposure to fumes.

Automated welding, soldering, and brazing machine operators are not exposed to as many dangers, and a face shield or goggles usually provide adequate protection. Welders and cutters may work outdoors, often in inclement weather, or indoors, sometimes in a confined area designed to contain sparks and glare. When outdoors, they may work on a scaffold or platform high off the ground. They may be required to lift heavy objects and work on shifts in a variety of awkward positions, having to make welds while bending, stooping, or working overhead.

About half of Welders, Solderers, and Brazers work a 40 hour week, but overtime is common, and some Welders work up to 70 hours per week. Welders also may work in shifts as long as 12 hours. Some Welders, Solderers, Brazers, and machine operators work on shifts in automotive factories that operate 24 hours a day.

Salaries

Average hourly earnings of Welders, cutters, Solderers, and Brazers range from $14.25 to $15.06; the lowest 10 percent earn less than $9.53 an hour, while the top 10 percent earn more than $22.06. Average hourly earnings of welding, soldering, and brazing machine setters, operators, and tenders range from $13.99 to $15.18; the lowest 10 percent earn less than $9.40, while the top 10 percent earn more than $23.89. Top-paying states include Michigan

(average $19.61/hour), Nevada ($17.32), and Massachusetts ($17.13).

Employment Prospects

Job prospects should be excellent for skilled candidates. Employment of welding, soldering, and brazing workers is expected to grow about as fast as the average for all occupations over the 2002–12 period. In addition, many openings will occur as workers retire or quit. A strong economy will keep demand for Welders high, but a downturn affecting auto manufacturing can result in employee layoffs in this group.

No matter how sound the economy, the pressures to improve productivity and hold down labor costs are leading many companies to become more automated, choosing computer-controlled and robotically controlled welding machinery. This may affect the demand for low-skilled manual welding, soldering, and brazing workers, because the jobs that are currently being automated are the simple, repetitive ones. The growing use of automation, however, should increase demand for highly skilled welding, soldering, and brazing machine setters, operators, and tenders.

Technology is helping to improve welding, creating more uses for welding in the workplace and expanding employment opportunities. For example, new ways are being developed to bond dissimilar materials and nonmetallic materials, such as plastics, composites, and new alloys. Also, laser beam and electron beam welding, new fluxes, and other new technologies and techniques are improving the results of welding, making it applicable to a wider assortment of jobs. Improvements in technology also have boosted welding productivity, making it more competitive with other methods of joining metals.

Advancement Prospects

Welders can advance to more skilled welding jobs with additional training and experience. For example, they may become welding supervisors, inspectors, or instructors. Some experienced Welders open their own repair shops.

Education and Training

Training for welding, soldering, and brazing workers can range from a few weeks of school or on-the-job training for low-skilled positions to several years of combined school and on-the-job training for highly skilled jobs. Formal training is available in high schools, vocational schools, and postsecondary institutions, such as vocational-technical institutes, community colleges, and private welding schools. The Armed Forces operate welding schools as well. Some employers provide training.

Courses in blueprint reading, shop mathematics, mechanical drawing, physics, chemistry, and metallurgy are helpful. Computer skills are becoming more important, especially for welding, soldering, and brazing machine operators, who are becoming responsible for the programming of computer-controlled machines and robots.

Special Requirements

Some Welders are certified by attending an independent testing lab or technical school to weld a test specimen to specific codes and standards required by the employer. Certification is also offered by the American Welding Society, which offers certification programs to meet a variety of needs.

Testing procedures are based on the standards and codes set by one of several industry associations with which the employer may be affiliated. If the welding inspector at the examining institution determines that the worker has performed according to the employer's guidelines, the inspector will then certify the Welder being tested as able to work with a particular welding procedure.

Experience, Skills, and Personality Traits

Welding, soldering, and brazing workers need good eyesight, eye-hand coordination, and manual dexterity, and should be able to concentrate on detailed work and be able to bend, stoop, and work in awkward positions.

Unions and Associations

Many Welders belong to unions such as the International Association of Machinists and Aerospace Workers; the International Brotherhood of Boilermakers, Iron Ship Builders, Blacksmiths, Forgers and Helpers; the International Union, United Automobile, Aerospace and Agricultural Implement Workers of America; the United Association of Journeymen and Apprentices of the Plumbing and Pipe Fitting Industry of the United States and Canada; and the United Electrical, Radio, and Machine Workers of America. Welders also may belong to the American Welding Society.

Tips for Entry

1. Visit your school's career counseling office for help in identifying companies where you would like to work.
2. Use your contacts. The easiest way to network is to ask someone you already know for the name of someone else. When you call, say, "So-and-so suggested I call you."
3. Visit the jobs listing or post your résumé on the Web site of the American Welding Society at www.aws.org/jobfind.

MACHINIST

Duties: Produce precision metal parts that meet precise specifications

Alternate Title(s): None

Salary Range: $9.78 to $23.36 per hour

Employment Prospects: Good

Advancement Prospects: Good

Best Geographical Location(s): Most jobs in the automotive field are located in Michigan, although automotive plants in other parts of the country also hire machinists

Prerequisites:

Education or Training—Apprenticeship programs, on-the-job training, and courses in high schools, vocational schools, or community or technical colleges

Experience—Experience with machine tools is helpful

Special Skills and Personality Traits—Mechanical ability, independence, and attention to detail

Shop Supervisor

Machinist

Entry Level

Position Description

Machinists produce precision metal parts using tools such as lathes, milling machines, and spindles. Although they may produce large quantities of one part, precision Machinists often produce small batches or one-of-a-kind items. They use their knowledge of the working properties of metals and their skill with machine tools to plan and carry out the operations needed to make machined products that meet precise specifications.

Before they make a part, Machinists must carefully plan and prepare the operation, reviewing blueprints or written specifications for a job. They calculate where to cut or bore into the piece of metal that is being shaped, how fast to feed the metal into the machine, and how much metal to remove. After selecting tools and materials for the job, they plan the sequence of cutting and finishing operations, and mark the metal stock to show where cuts should be made. Next, they position the metal stock on the machine tool, set the controls, and make the cuts. During the machining process, they must constantly monitor the feed and speed of the machine.

Machinists also ensure that the workpiece is being properly lubricated and cooled, because the machining of metal products generates a significant amount of heat. The temperature of the workpiece is a key concern because most

metals expand when heated; Machinists must adjust the size of their cuts relative to the temperature. Some rarer, but increasingly popular, metals, such as titanium, are created at extremely high temperatures.

Machinists also adjust cutting speeds to compensate for vibrations, which can decrease the accuracy of cuts, particularly on newer high-speed spindles and lathes. Some production Machinists may produce large quantities of one part, especially parts requiring the use of complex operations and great precision. Production Machinists work with complex computer numerically controlled (CNC) cutting machines, often consulting with computer-control programmers to determine how the automated equipment will cut a part. The programmer determines the path of the cut, and the Machinist determines the type of cutting tool, the speed of the cutting tool, and the feed rate.

After the production process is designed, relatively simple and repetitive operations normally are performed by machine setters, operators, and tenders.

Other Machinists do maintenance work, repairing or making new parts for existing machinery. To repair a broken part, maintenance Machinists may refer to blueprints and perform the same machining operations that were needed to create the original part.

Most machine shops of today are relatively clean, well-lit, and ventilated. Many computer-controlled machines are totally enclosed, minimizing the exposure of workers to noise, dust, and the lubricants used to cool workpieces during machining. Nevertheless, working around machine tools can be dangerous, and Machinists wear protective equipment such as safety glasses to shield against bits of flying metal and earplugs to protect their hearing.

The job requires stamina, because Machinists stand most of the day and, at times, may need to lift moderately heavy workpieces. Most Machinists work a 40-hour week, including evening and weekend shifts, as companies justify investments in more expensive machinery by extending hours of operation. Overtime is common during peak production periods.

Salaries

Average hourly earnings of Machinists range from $15.91 to $16.30; the lowest 10 percent earn less than $9.78 per hour, while the top 10 percent earn more than $23.36 per hour. Top-paying states are Washington D.C. (average $26.43/hour), Hawaii ($23.02), and Alaska ($20.68).

Employment Prospects

Despite projected slower-than-average employment growth, job opportunities for Machinists should continue to be excellent, according to the Bureau of Labor Statistics. Many young people may prefer to attend college or may not wish to enter production-related occupations, leaving fewer workers with the skills and knowledge to fill Machinist jobs. However, Machinist jobs are expected to grow more slowly than the average for all occupations over the 2002–12 period as new technology allows fewer Machinists to accomplish the same amount of work previously performed by more workers.

Still, technology is not expected to affect Machinist jobs as significantly as that of most other production occupations because many of the unique operations they perform cannot be efficiently automated. Due to modern production techniques, employers prefer workers such as Machinists, who have a wide range of skills and are capable of performing almost any task in a machine shop. In addition, firms are likely to keep their most skilled workers to operate and maintain expensive new machinery.

Employment levels in this occupation are influenced by economic cycles. As the demand for machined goods falls, Machinists involved in production may be laid off or forced to work fewer hours.

Advancement Prospects

Experienced Machinists may become computer-control programmers and operators, and some are promoted to supervisory or administrative positions in their firms. A few open their own shops.

Education and Training

Machinists train in high schools, vocational schools, or community or technical colleges, in apprenticeship programs, and on the job. High school or vocational school programs should include courses in mathematics, blueprint reading, metalworking, and drafting.

Apprenticeship classes are taught in cooperation with local community or vocational colleges, and combine shop training with related classroom instruction. In shop training, apprentices work almost full time, and are supervised by an experienced Machinist while learning to operate various machine tools. Classroom instruction includes math, physics, blueprint reading, mechanical drawing, and quality and safety practices.

A growing number of Machinists learn the trade at two-year associate degree programs at community or technical colleges. Graduates of these programs still need significant on-the-job experience before they are fully qualified.

As new automated machines are introduced, Machinists normally receive additional training to update their skills. This training usually is provided by a representative of the equipment manufacturer or a local technical school. Some employers offer tuition reimbursement for job-related courses.

Special Requirements

A number of training facilities and colleges have recently begun offering courses incorporating national skills standards developed by the National Institute of Metalworking Skills (NIMS). After completing such a curriculum and passing a performance requirement and written exam, a NIMS credential is granted to trainees, providing formal recognition of competency in a metalworking field. Completing a recognized certification program provides a Machinist with better career opportunities.

Experience, Skills, and Personality Traits

Machinists should be mechanically inclined, able to work independently, and able to do highly accurate work that requires concentration and physical effort.

Unions and Associations

Many Machinists are members of labor unions, including the International Association of Machinists and Aerospace Workers; the United Electrical, Radio and Machine Workers of America; the United Automobile, Aerospace and Agricultural Implement Workers of America; and the United Steelworkers of America.

Tips for Entry

1. Visit your school's career counseling office for help in identifying companies where you would like to work.
2. Use your contacts. The easiest way to network is to ask someone you already know for the name of someone else. When you call, say, "So-and-so suggested I call you."
3. Check newspaper classified ads under "Automotive" or "Technical."

TOOL AND DIE MAKER

CAREER PROFILE

Duties: Produce tools, dies, and special guiding and holding devices used in machines

Alternate Title(s): None

Salary Range: $13.19 to $30.83 per hour

Employment Prospects: Excellent

Advancement Prospects: Good

Best Geographical Location(s): All parts of the country, but jobs are most plentiful in areas where automotive manufacturing is concentrated

Prerequisites:

Education or Training—Most Tool and Die Makers train for four or five years in apprenticeships or post-secondary programs; employers typically recommend apprenticeship training

Experience—Basic knowledge of machines; many entrants have previously worked as machinists or machine setters

Special Skills and Personality Traits—Patience, attention to detail; good eyesight; mechanical ability; able to work and solve problems independently; good concentration; good computer skills

CAREER LADDER

```
┌─────────────────────────────┐
│        Shop Foreman         │
└─────────────────────────────┘

┌─────────────────────────────┐
│      Tool and Die Maker     │
└─────────────────────────────┘

┌─────────────────────────────┐
│  Tool and Die Maker Trainee │
│     or Machine Operator     │
└─────────────────────────────┘
```

Position Description

Tool and Die Makers are among the most highly skilled production workers in the automotive industry, creating tools, dies, and special guiding and holding devices that allow machines to manufacture automotive parts.

Tool Makers craft precision tools that are used to cut, shape, and form metal, and produce jigs and fixtures (devices that hold metal while it is bored, stamped, or drilled), gauges, and other measuring devices.

Die Makers construct metal forms called "dies" that are used to shape metal, and make metal molds for diecasting and molding plastics, ceramics, and composite materials. In addition to developing, designing, and producing new tools and dies, these workers also may repair worn or damaged tools, dies, gauges, jigs, and fixtures.

Tool and Die Makers use different machine tools and precision measuring instruments, and they also must understand the hardness and heat tolerance of a wide variety of common metals and alloys. They are experts in machining operations, mathematics, and blueprint reading, and are considered to be highly specialized machinists.

Using a blueprint as a guide, Tool and Die Makers plan the sequence of operations necessary to manufacture the item, and then measure and mark the pieces of metal that will be cut to form parts of the final product. At this point, they cut, drill, or bore the part as required, checking to make sure that the final product meets specifications. Finally, they assemble the parts and file, grind, or polish surfaces as required.

Modern technology is changing the ways in which Tool and Die Makers perform their jobs. For example, these workers often use computer-aided design (CAD) to develop products and parts, electronically developing drawings for the required tools and dies. Numerical tool and process control programmers use computer-aided manufacturing (CAM) programs to convert electronic drawings into computer programs containing a sequence of cutting tool operations.

Once these programs are developed, computer numerically controlled (CNC) machines follow the instructions in the program to produce the part. (Although computer-controlled machine tool operators or machinists usually operate CNC machines, Tool and Die Makers are trained in both operating CNC machines and writing CNC programs, and they can handle either job.)

Next, Tool and Die Makers assemble the different parts into a functioning machine, filing, grinding, and adjusting the different parts until they fit properly together. Finally, they run tests using the tools or dies they have made to ensure the manufactured parts meet specifications.

Tool and Die Makers usually work in toolrooms, which are quieter than the production floor because there are fewer machines being used at once. The rooms are kept clean and cool to minimize heat-related expansion of metal workpieces and to make room for the growing number of computer-operated machines. For safety reasons, machines have guards and shields; many computer-controlled machines are totally enclosed, which lessens the risk of noise, dust, and lubricants. Tool and Die Makers also must wear protective equipment, such as safety glasses to shield against bits of flying metal, earplugs to protect against noise, and gloves and masks to reduce exposure to hazardous lubricants and cleaners. Tool and Die Makers traditionally work just one shift a day, but overtime and weekend work are common, especially during peak production periods.

Salaries

The average hourly earnings of Tool and Die Makers range from $20.67 to $21.10; the lowest 10 percent earn less than $13.19 per hour, while the top 10 percent earn more than $30.83 per hour. Top-paying states are Michigan (average $24.74/hour), Oregon ($22.88), and Indiana ($22.55).

Employment Prospects

Applicants with the appropriate skills and background should enjoy excellent opportunities for Tool and Die Maker jobs—there are more job openings than there are workers being trained. In fact, automotive employers report problems in attracting well-trained applicants. One of the primary factors limiting the number of people entering the field is that many young people with the educational and personal qualifications necessary to learn tool and die making may prefer to attend college or may not want to enter production-related occupations.

Despite excellent job opportunities, there will be little or no change in the employment of Tool and Die Makers through 2012, according to the Bureau of Labor Statistics, because advancements in automation are improving worker productivity, thus limiting employment. On the other hand, Tool and Die Makers still play a key role in the operation of automotive factories. As companies invest in new equipment, modify production techniques, and implement prod-uct design changes more rapidly, they will continue to rely heavily on skilled Tool and Die Makers for retooling.

Advancement Prospects

As Tool and Die Makers become more experienced, they may progress to jobs that require more skill and responsibility or be promoted to shop supervisor. Those with a background in math, science, and computers may become operators of highly automated production equipment. Experienced Tool and Die Makers may join research and development teams, working with engineers and other project designers to produce and test new product models.

Education and Training

Most Tool and Die Makers train for four or five years in apprenticeships or postsecondary programs; employers typically recommend apprenticeship training. The best way to learn all aspects of tool and die making is a formal apprenticeship program that combines classroom instruction and job experience. More and more Tool and Die Makers receive most of their formal classroom training from community and technical colleges, sometimes in conjunction with an apprenticeship program.

Tool and Die Maker trainees learn to operate milling machines, lathes, grinders, spindles, and other machine tools, and how to use hand tools for fitting and assembling gauges, and other mechanical and metal-forming equipment. In addition, they study metalworking processes (such as heat treating and plating). Classroom training usually includes mechanical drawing, tool designing, tool programming, blueprint reading, and mathematics (algebra, geometry, trigonometry, and basic statistics).

Workers who become Tool and Die Makers without completing formal apprenticeships usually acquire their skills in a combination of informal on-the-job training and classroom instruction at a vocational school or community college. They often begin as machine operators and gradually take on more difficult assignments. Many machinists become Tool and Die Makers.

Experience, Skills, and Personality Traits

Because tools and dies must meet strict specifications, their work requires a great deal of patience, attention to detail, and good eyesight. Tool and Die Makers should be mechanically inclined, able to work and solve problems independently, and able to do work that requires concentration and physical effort. They also must have good computer skills to work with CAD technology and CNC machine tools.

Unions and Associations

Many Tool and Die Makers belong to labor unions, including the International Association of Machinists and Aerospace Workers; the United Electrical, Radio and Machine Workers of America; the United Automobile, Aerospace and

Agricultural Implement Workers of America; the United Steelworkers of America; the International Brotherhood of Boilermakers, Iron Ship Builders, Blacksmiths, Forgers and Helpers; and International Union, United Automobile, Aerospace and Agricultural Implement Workers of America.

Tips for Entry

1. Mail a résumé to top automotive companies where you would like to work.

2. Visit your school's career counseling office for help in identifying companies where you would like to work.

3. Use your contacts. The easiest way to network is to ask someone you already know for the name of someone else. When you call, say, "So-and-so suggested I call you."

4. Check the newspaper classified ads under "Automotive" or "Manufacturing."

COMPUTER-CONTROL OPERATOR

CAREER PROFILE

Duties: Use computer-controlled machines or robots that can be programmed to automatically manufacture car parts of different dimensions

Alternate Title(s): CNC Operator; Computer-Controlled Machine Tool Operator; Numerical Tool and Process Control Programmer

Salary Range: $9.23 to $21.35 per hour

Employment Prospects: Excellent

Advancement Prospects: Excellent

Best Geographical Location(s): All parts of the country, but jobs are most plentiful in areas where automotive manufacturing is concentrated

Prerequisites:

Education or Training—High school diploma, apprenticeship programs, informal on-the-job training, and vocational or postsecondary schools

Experience—Basic knowledge of computers and electronics; many entrants have previously worked as machinists or machine setters, operators, and tenders

Special Skills and Personality Traits—Mechanical aptitude; independence; attention to detail

CAREER LADDER

```
┌─────────────────────────────┐
│   Computer Programmer       │
│   or Supervisor             │
└─────────────────────────────┘

┌─────────────────────────────┐
│  Computer-Control Operator  │
└─────────────────────────────┘

┌─────────────────────────────┐
│   Apprentice Computer-      │
│   Control Operator          │
└─────────────────────────────┘
```

Position Description

Computer-Control Operators use computer numerically controlled (CNC) machines to cut and shape automobile parts. CNC machines include metal-machining tools such as lathes, multi-axis spindles, and milling machines, but the functions formerly performed by human operators are performed by a computer-control module. CNC machines cut away material from a solid block of metal, plastic, or glass (known as a workpiece) to form a finished part.

Computer-Control Operators normally produce large quantities of one part, although they may produce small batches or one-of-a-kind items. They use their knowledge of metals to design and carry out the operations needed to make machined products that meet precise specifications. First, workers review three-dimensional computerized blueprints of the part, calculating where to cut or bore into the workpiece, how fast to feed the metal into the machine, and how much metal to remove. Then they select tools and

material for the job and plan the sequence of cutting and finishing operations. After programmers turn the planned machining operations into a set of instructions that are translated into a computer program for the machine to follow, CNC operators perform the necessary machining operations. During the machining process, Computer-Control Operators constantly monitor the readouts from the CNC control module to identify problems.

CNC operators detect some problems by listening for specific sounds made during the machining process, such as of a dull cutting tool. The defective part is then removed and replaced. Machine tools rotate at high speeds, which can cause vibrations, causing the machine tools to make minor cutting errors. Computer-Control Operators listen for vibrations and then adjust the cutting speed to compensate. In older, slower machine tools, the cutting speed would be reduced to eliminate the vibrations, but the amount of time needed to finish the product would increase. In newer, high-speed CNC machines, increasing the cutting speed normally eliminates the vibrations and reduces production time. CNC operators also ensure that the workpiece is being properly lubricated and cooled, because the machining of metal products generates a significant amount of heat.

Most machine shops are clean, well-lit, and ventilated, and many computer-controlled machines are totally enclosed, minimizing the exposure of workers to noise, dust, and lubricants. Nevertheless, working around high-speed machine tools can be dangerous. Operators wear protective equipment such as safety glasses to shield against bits of flying metal and earplugs to dampen machinery noise, and must handle carefully hazardous coolants and lubricants.

Most Computer-Control Operators work a 40-hour week, with many evening and weekend shifts as companies justify investments in more expensive machinery by extending hours of operation. Overtime is common during peak production periods.

Salaries
Average hourly earnings of computer-controlled machine tool operators range between $14.14 and $14.74; the lowest 10 percent earn less than $9.23 an hour, whereas the top 10 percent earn more than $21.35 an hour. Top-paying states are Connecticut (average $17.35/hour), Kansas ($16.91), and New Jersey ($16.64).

Employment Prospects
Job opportunities will be excellent, according to the Bureau of Labor Statistics, as employers are expected to continue to have difficulty finding qualified workers. In addition to those jobs that result from employment growth, many job openings will arise from the need to replace operators who leave the field. There will be great demand for operators due to continued emphasis on product quality and safety; the demand for new cars that are easy and comfortable to use; the development of technology; and growing global competition among businesses.

Advancement Prospects
Experienced CNC operators may become CNC programmers, and some are promoted to supervisory or administrative positions in their firms. A few open their own shops.

Education and Training
Computer-Control Operators train in apprenticeship programs, informally on the job, and in secondary, vocational, or postsecondary schools. Due to a shortage of qualified applicants, many employers teach introductory courses that provide a basic understanding of metalworking machines, safety, and blueprint reading. A basic knowledge of computers and electronics also is helpful. Experience with machine tools is extremely important. In fact, many entrants to these occupations have previously worked as machinists or machine setters, operators, and tenders.

High school or vocational school courses in mathematics, blueprint reading, computer programming, metalworking, and drafting are recommended. Apprenticeship programs consist of shop training, where apprentices learn filing, hand-tapping, dowel fitting, and machine tool operation and receive classroom instruction in math, physics, programming, blueprint reading, CAD software, safety, and shop practices.

Skilled Computer-Control Operators need to understand the machining process, including the complex physics that occurs at the cutting point. Thus, most training programs teach CNC operators to perform operations on manual machines prior to operating CNC machines. A growing number of Computer-Control Operators receive most of their formal training from community or technical colleges. Less-skilled CNC operators may have only 12 weeks of classroom training prior to working on the shop floor.

To boost the skill level of all metalworkers and to create a more uniform standard of competence, a number of training facilities and colleges have recently begun implementing curriculums incorporating national skills standards developed by the National Institute of Metalworking Skills (NIMS). After completing such a curriculum and passing a performance requirement and written exam, a NIMS credential is granted to trainees, providing formal recognition of competency in a metalworking field. Completing a formal certification program opens the way to better career opportunities.

Experience, Skills, and Personality Traits
People interested in becoming Computer-Control Operators should be mechanically inclined and able to work independently and do highly accurate work

Unions and Associations
Computer-Control Operators may belong to labor unions such as the International Association of Machinists and Aerospace Workers; the United Electrical, Radio and Machine Workers of America; the United Automobile, Aerospace and Agricultural Implement Workers of America; and the United Steelworkers of America.

Tips for Entry
1. Mail a résumé to top automotive companies where you would like to work.
2. Visit your school's career counseling office for help in identifying companies where you would like to work.
3. Use your contacts. The easiest way to network is to ask someone you already know for the name of someone else. When you call, say, "So-and-so suggested I call you."
4. Check the newspaper classified ads under "Automotive" or "Manufacturing."

COMPUTER-CONTROL PROGRAMMER

CAREER PROFILE

Duties: Program computer-controlled machines or robots to automatically manufacture car parts of different dimensions

Alternate Title(s): Numerical Tool and Process Control Programmer; CNC Programmer

Salary Range: $12.01 to $27.60 per hour

Employment Prospects: Excellent

Advancement Prospects: Excellent

Best Geographical Location(s): All parts of the country, but jobs are most plentiful in areas where automotive manufacturing is concentrated, such as Michigan

Prerequisites:

Education or Training—High school diploma, apprenticeship programs, informal on-the-job training, and vocational or postsecondary schools

Experience—Basic knowledge of computers and electronics

Special Skills and Personality Traits—Computer skills; independence; attention to detail

CAREER LADDER

```
┌─────────────────────────────────────┐
│             Supervisor               │
└─────────────────────────────────────┘

┌─────────────────────────────────────┐
│   Computer-Control Programmer        │
└─────────────────────────────────────┘

┌─────────────────────────────────────┐
│        Apprentice Programmer         │
└─────────────────────────────────────┘
```

Position Description

Computer-Control Programmers program computers that direct a variety of computer numerically controlled (CNC) machines to cut and shape automobile parts from a solid block of metal, plastic, or glass (known as a workpiece) to form a finished part.

Computer-Control Programmers use their knowledge of metals and their skill with CNC programming to design and carry out the operations needed to make machined products that meet precise specifications.

First, workers review three-dimensional computerized blueprints of the part, calculating where to cut or bore into the workpiece, how fast to feed the metal into the machine, and how much metal to remove. Then, Computer-Control Programmers turn the planned machining operations into a set of instructions that are translated into a computer program for the machine to follow. The program is then saved onto a computer.

Computer-Control Programmers check new programs to make sure that the machinery will function properly and that specifications are met. Because a problem with the program could damage expensive machinery and tools, computer simulations may be used to check the program. If errors are found, the program must be fixed and retested until the problem is resolved. Growing links between computer-aided design (CAD) software and CNC machine tools means that designs can be automatically translated into instructions for the computer controller on the machine tool. This new computer-automated manufacturing (CAM) technology enables workers to easily modify programs for use on other jobs with similar specifications. Unique, modified CNC programs are saved for every different machine that performs a task.

Computer-Control Programmers work in offices that typically are near the shop floor and are usually clean, well-lit, and quiet, although they occasionally need to enter the shop floor to monitor CNC machining operations, where they encounter more hazards and must exercise safety precautions. Most Computer-Control Programmers work a 40-hour week. Overtime is common during peak production periods.

Salaries

The average hourly earnings of numerical tool and process control programmers range between $18.43 and $19.24; the lowest 10 percent earn less than $12.01 an hour, while the top 10 percent earn more than $27.60 an hour. Top-paying states include New Jersey (average $23.01/hour), Washington ($22.56), and Connecticut ($22.37)

Employment Prospects

Job opportunities will be excellent, as employers are expected to continue to have difficulty finding qualified workers. In addition to those that result from employment growth, many job openings will arise from the need to replace programmers who leave the field. There will be great demand for programmers due to continued emphasis on product quality and safety; the demand for new cars that are easy and comfortable to use; the development of technology; and growing global competition among businesses.

Advancement Prospects

Programmers may be promoted to supervisory or administrative positions in their firms; a few open their own shops.

Education and Training

Computer-Control Programmers train in apprenticeship programs, informally on the job, and in secondary, vocational, or postsecondary schools. Due to a shortage of qualified applicants, many employers teach introductory courses that provide a basic understanding of metalworking machines, safety, and blueprint reading. A basic knowledge of computers and electronics also is helpful. Experience with machine tools is extremely important. In fact, many entrants to these occupations have previously worked as machinists or machine setters, operators, and tenders.

High school or vocational school courses in mathematics, blueprint reading, computer programming, metalworking, and drafting are recommended. Skilled Computer Control Programmers need to understand the machining process, including the complex physics that occurs at the cutting point. Thus, most training programs teach CNC programmers to perform operations on manual machines prior to operating CNC machines. A growing number of Computer-Control Programmers receive most of their formal training from community or technical colleges.

Qualifications for Computer-Control Programmers vary widely depending upon the complexity of the job. Employers often prefer skilled machinists or those with technical school training. For those entering CNC programming directly, a basic knowledge of computers and electronics is necessary, and experience with machine tools is extremely helpful. Classroom training includes an introduction to computer numerical control, the basics of programming, and more complex topics, such as computer-aided manufacturing. Trainees start writing simple programs under the direction of an experienced programmer. Although machinery manufacturers are trying to standardize programming languages, there are numerous languages in use. Because of this, Computer-Control Programmers should be able to learn new programming languages. As new automation is introduced, Computer-Control Programmers normally receive extra training to update their skills. This training usually is provided by a representative of the equipment manufacturer or a local technical school. Many employers offer tuition reimbursement for job-related courses.

Experience, Skills, and Personality Traits

People interested in becoming Computer-Control Programmers should be mechanically inclined and able to work independently and do highly accurate work.

Unions and Associations

Computer-Control Programmers may belong to labor unions such as the International Association of Machinists and Aerospace Workers; the United Electrical, Radio and Machine Workers of America; the United Automobile, Aerospace and Agricultural Implement Workers of America; and the United Steelworkers of America.

Tips for Entry

1. Mail a résumé to top automotive companies where you would like to work.
2. Visit your school's career counseling office for help in identifying companies where you would like to work.
3. Use your contacts. The easiest way to network is to ask someone you already know for the name of someone else. When you call, say, "So-and-so suggested I call you."
4. Check the newspaper classified ads under "Automotive" or "Manufacturing."

AUTO COMPANY EXECUTIVE

CAREER PROFILE

Duties: Establishes price, size and weight, fuel economy, and safety and pollution control features of new cars

Alternate Title(s): Vice Chair; Chairman of the Board of Management; Chairman/CEO, Executive Vice President; Vice President

Salary Range: $83,200 to $204,970+

Employment Prospects: Fair

Advancement Prospects: Fair.

Best Geographical Location(s): Opportunities are greatest in those areas where auto manufacturing industries are located, such as Michigan

Prerequisites:

Education or Training—Four-year college degree in business administration or liberal arts

Experience—Business, marketing, advertising, or engineering experience helpful

Special Skills and Personality Traits—Leadership; self-confidence; motivation; decisiveness; flexibility; sound business judgment; good communication and people skills; determination

CAREER LADDER

```
┌─────────────────────────────┐
│   Auto Company Executive     │
│      of Larger Firm          │
└─────────────────────────────┘

┌─────────────────────────────┐
│   Auto Company Executive     │
└─────────────────────────────┘

┌─────────────────────────────┐
│   Auto Company Manager       │
└─────────────────────────────┘
```

Position Description

Auto Company Executives establish the "big picture" that is to be followed in the design of a new vehicle, including market appeal, price, size and weight, fuel economy, and safety and pollution control features. Car companies have specific goals and objectives that they strive to meet, and it is the job of the Auto Company Executive to figure out strategies and formulate policies to ensure that these objectives are met.

Although Auto Company Executives may have many different titles (chief executive officer, chief operating officer, board chair, president, vice president), all of these Auto Company Executives formulate policies and direct the operations of their corporations. The auto company's goals and policies are established by the chief executive officer in collaboration with other top Auto Company Executives, who are overseen by a board of directors. In a large car company,

the chief executive officer meets frequently with subordinate executives to ensure that operations are conducted in accordance with these policies.

The chief executive officer of a corporation retains overall accountability; however, a chief operating officer may be delegated several responsibilities, including the authority to oversee executives who direct the activities of various departments and implement the organization's policies on a day-to-day basis.

The nature of other high-level executives' responsibilities depends upon the size of the organization. In large organizations, the duties of such executives are highly specialized. Some managers, for instance, are responsible for the overall performance of one aspect of the organization, such as manufacturing, marketing, sales, purchasing, finance, personnel, training, administrative services, computer and information systems, transportation, or legal services.

Top Auto Company Executives typically have spacious offices and numerous support staff, and general managers in large auto manufacturing firms usually have comfortable offices close to those of the top executives to whom they report. Long hours, including evenings and weekends, are standard for most top Auto Company Executives and general managers, although their schedules may be flexible. Substantial travel between international, national, regional, and local offices to monitor operations and meet with customers, staff, and other executives often is required. Many Auto Company Executives also attend meetings and conferences sponsored by various associations. The conferences provide an opportunity to meet with prospective customers and contractors and allow managers and Auto Company Executives to keep abreast of technological and managerial innovations.

Salaries

Top Auto Company Executives are among the highest-paid of all auto manufacturing employees, and long hours, considerable travel, and intense pressure to succeed are common. However, salary levels vary substantially depending upon the level of managerial responsibility, length of service, and size and location of the firm. Average annual earnings of Auto Company Executives range from $83,200 to far more than $204,970.

Employment Prospects

Auto Company Executive jobs are usually filled through internal promotion and with the aid of headhunter firms, rather than via Internet postings. Numerous openings will occur each year as Auto Company Executives transfer to other positions, start their own businesses, or retire. However, many Auto Company Executives who leave their jobs transfer to other executive positions, which tends to limit the number of job openings for new entrants.

Experienced Auto Company Executives with strong leadership qualities and the ability to improve the efficiency or competitive position of the car manufacturer will have the best opportunities. In an increasingly global economy, experience in international economics, marketing, information systems, and knowledge of several languages also may be helpful.

Employment of top Auto Company Executives, including chief executives and general and operations managers of car manufacturers, is expected to grow about as fast as the average for all occupations through 2012. Because top managers are essential to the success of any organization, they should be more immune to automation and corporate restructuring—factors that are expected to adversely affect employment of lower-level managers. Projected employment growth of top Auto Company Executives reflects the projected change in industry employment over the 2002–12 period.

Advancement Prospects

Because many top Auto Company Executive positions are filled by promoting experienced, lower-level managers when an opening occurs, many top managers have been promoted from within the organization. Most auto companies prefer that their top executives have specialized backgrounds and, therefore, hire individuals who have been managers in other organizations.

Potential top Auto Company Executives demonstrate competence in their area of expertise and rise through their chosen discipline (such as engineering or marketing), and then compete for executive positions on the basis of leadership skills, education, and business and market savvy.

In large auto manufacturing companies, job transfers between local offices or subsidiaries are common for those on the executive career track. Top Auto Company Executives are under intense pressure to succeed, earning higher profits while making superior cars. Executives in charge of poorly performing organizations or departments usually find their jobs in jeopardy.

Auto Company Executives may advance quicker by participating in company training programs that teach company policy and operations. It is also a good idea to become familiar with the latest developments in management techniques at national or local training programs sponsored by various industry and trade associations. Lower-level executives with experience in a particular field (such as engineering) may attend executive development programs to facilitate their promotion to an even higher level. Participation in conferences and seminars can expand knowledge of national and international issues influencing the organization and can help the participants develop a network of useful contacts.

General managers may advance to top executive positions, such as executive vice president, in their own firm or they may take a corresponding position in another firm. They may even advance to peak corporate positions such as chief operating officer or chief executive officer. Chief executive officers often become members of the board of directors of one or more firms, typically as a director of their own firm and often as chair of its board of directors. Some top executives establish their own firms or become independent consultants.

Education and Training

The formal education and experience of top Auto Company Executives varies as widely as the nature of their responsibilities. Many top executives in the auto industry have a degree in business administration or liberal arts, often in engineering or marketing.

Experience, Skills, and Personality Traits

Top Auto Company Executives must have highly developed personal skills and an analytical mind able to quickly assess large amounts of information and data. In addition, top executives should be able to communicate clearly and persuasively. Other critical qualities include leadership, self-confidence, motivation, decisiveness, flexibility, sound business judgment, and determination.

Unions and Associations

Auto Company Executives may belong to professional groups such as the American Management Association, the Institute of Certified Professional Managers, or the National Management Association.

Tips for Entry

1. Auto Company Executives often find jobs by working with professional headhunters.

2. These jobs are usually filled through internal promotion and with the aid of headhunter firms, rather than via Web postings, but you can try contacting professional associations to network for job possibilities, such as the American Management Association (www.amanet.org); the Institute of Certified Professional Managers (http://cob.jmu.edu/icpm); or the National Management Association (www.nmal.org).

REPAIR AND RESTORATION

AUTOMOTIVE TECHNICIAN

CAREER PROFILE

Duties: Diagnose and repair cars; perform state inspections and vehicle emissions tests; maintain and perform preventive care

Alternate Title(s): Mechanic

Salary Range: $25,018 to $70,000+

Employment Prospects: Very good

Advancement Prospects: Very good

Best Geographical Location(s): All locations throughout the country have job possibilities for well-trained, experienced technicians

Prerequisites:

Education or Training—High school or postsecondary vocational school automotive service technician training program

Experience—Experience in car repairs

Special Skills and Personality Traits—Good diagnostic skills; attention to detail; mechanical ability; mathematics and computer skills

Licensure/Certification—Voluntary certification in one or more of the eight tests given by the National Institute for Automotive Service Excellence (ASE)

CAREER LADDER

```
┌─────────────────────────────────┐
│        Service Manager          │
│  or Master Automotive Technician │
└─────────────────────────────────┘

┌─────────────────────────────────┐
│      Automotive Technician      │
└─────────────────────────────────┘

┌─────────────────────────────────┐
│        Trainee Technician       │
└─────────────────────────────────┘
```

Position Description

The Automotive Technician is responsible for inspecting, maintaining, and repairing cars and light trucks. The ability to diagnose the source of a problem quickly and accurately requires good reasoning ability and a thorough knowledge of cars. In fact, many technicians consider diagnosing hard-to-find troubles one of their most challenging and satisfying duties.

Automotive Technicians have developed into high-tech problem solvers who must understand a car's complex components, working with electronic diagnostic equipment and computer-based technical reference materials. The increasing sophistication of automotive technology today means that technicians must use computerized shop equipment while maintaining their skill with traditional hand tools. By the year 2005, experts predict that 70 percent of new cars will be wired for the Internet and offer satellite-radio serv-

ice, cell-phone hookups, and built-in voice-recognition systems. Technicians must keep abreast of modern repair techniques for all these advanced components and systems.

About 840,000 Americans work as Automotive Technicians, mostly for retail and wholesale automotive dealers, independent automotive repair shops, or automotive service facilities at department, automotive, and home supply stores, according to the Bureau of Labor Statistics. Others work for gas stations; taxi and car leasing companies; or the government. About 18 percent of all service technicians are self-employed.

At the start of each job, Automotive Technicians get a description of the car's problem from the owner or the repair service manager. To locate the problem, technicians first test components and systems, and then isolate those that could not logically be the cause of the problem. Technicians may have to test-drive the car or use onboard and hand-held diagnostic computers or compression gauges to identify the source of the problem. In modern repair shops, service technicians compare the readouts from diagnostic testing devices to the standards provided by the manufacturer. The testing devices diagnose problems and make adjustments with precise calculations downloaded from large computerized databases. The computerized systems provide automatic updates to technical manuals and unlimited access to manufacturers' service information, technical service bulletins, and other information databases, which allow technicians to keep current on trouble spots and to learn new procedures.

Automotive Technicians are also responsible for routine service inspections, assessing and lubricating engines and other major components, and repairing or replacing worn parts before they cause problems that could damage critical components of the car. Technicians usually follow a checklist to ensure that every critical part is examined.

While shop owners provide large diagnostic equipment, technicians are expected to provide their own tools; many experienced workers have invested thousands of dollars in their own equipment. Some formal training programs have alliances with tool manufacturers that help entry-level technicians accumulate tools during their training period.

Salaries

Average hourly earnings of Automotive Technicians (including commission) range between $14.97 and $16.02 an hour. The lowest 10 percent may earn less than $8.29, and the highest 10 percent earn more than $25.54 an hour. Entry-level technicians earn an average of $25,018, and the most experienced master technicians can earn more than $70,000 a year.

On average, an Automotive Technician who works for local government and at new and used car dealers earn an average of $18.71 an hour. Employees at auto and home supply stores earn less (about $13.79). Those in small car repair shops earn about $14.03 an hour, while those at gas stations earn about $14.29 an hour.

Many experienced Automotive Technicians who work for car dealers and independent repair shops receive a flat rate commission related to the labor cost charged to the customer. Under this method, weekly earnings depend on the amount of work completed. Employers often guarantee commissioned technicians a minimum weekly salary. Top-paying states are Alaska (average $20.92/hour), Delaware (20.70), and Washington, D.C. ($19.21).

Employment Prospects

The growing complexity of automotive technology means more and more skilled workers will be required, contributing to the growth in demand for highly trained technicians. Opportunities should be very good for Automotive Technicians with excellent diagnostic and problem-solving skills and solid knowledge of electronics and mathematics.

While job opportunities are expected to be very good for those who complete automotive training programs in high school, vocational and technical schools, or community colleges, people without formal automotive training are likely to face stiff competition for entry-level jobs.

Most jobs will be found in car dealerships and independent repair shops, but new jobs also will be created in small retail operations that offer after-warranty repairs, such as oil changes, brake repair, air conditioner service, and other minor repairs that usually take less than four hours to complete.

Fewer national department store chains will provide auto repair services in large shops. Employment of Automotive Technicians in gasoline service stations will continue to decline, as fewer stations offer repair services. Most technicians can expect steady work, because changes in general economic conditions and developments in other industries have little effect on the car repair business.

Advancement Prospects

Beginners usually start as trainee technicians, mechanics' helpers, lubrication workers, or gas service station attendants, and gradually acquire and practice their skills by working with experienced mechanics and technicians. With a few months' experience, beginners can perform many routine service tasks and make simple repairs.

It usually takes two to five years of experience to become a fully trained Automotive Technician who can quickly perform the more difficult types of routine service and repairs. However, some graduates of automotive training programs are often able to earn promotion to this level after only a few months on the job. An additional one or two years' experience familiarizes mechanics and technicians with all types of repairs.

Experienced technicians with leadership ability may advance to shop supervisor, and those who work well with customers may become automotive repair service estimators or service managers. Some with solid financial backing may open their own independent repair shops.

Education and Training

Because of the complexity of new cars, employers today often require a high school diploma plus postsecondary training for technicians. Courses in automotive repair, electronics, physics, chemistry, English, computers, and mathematics provide a good educational background. While some service technicians still learn the trade by serving as an apprentice, today's sophisticated technology almost requires a formal training program in high school or postsecondary vocational school. Many high schools, community colleges, and public and private vocational and technical schools offer automotive service technician training programs.

Although high school programs are helpful, their quality is uneven. The better programs, such as the Automotive Youth

Education Service (AYES), provide students with a technician's certification and high school diploma. While others try to equip graduates with enough skills to get a job as a mechanic's helper or trainee mechanic, some schools offer an introduction to automotive technology and service that would be helpful only to consumers and hobbyists.

Traditional postsecondary programs usually offer combined classroom instruction and hands-on practice. Some trade and technical school programs provide concentrated training for six months to a year, depending on how many hours the student attends each week. Community college programs awarding an associate degree or certificate normally spread the training over two years, and supplement the automotive training with instruction in English, basic mathematics, computers, and other subjects. Some students earn repair certificates and opt to leave the program to begin their career before graduation. More recently, some programs have added classes in customer service and stress management to help technicians learn to deal with customers and parts vendors.

Many car manufacturers and their dealers sponsor two-year associate degree programs at postsecondary schools. The Accrediting Commission of Career Schools and Colleges of Technology (ACCSCT) currently certifies a number of automotive and diesel technology schools.

Education continues on the job; employers send service technicians to manufacturer training centers to learn how to repair new models or to receive special training in the repair of components, such as electronic fuel injection or air conditioners. Car dealers also may send promising beginners to manufacturer-sponsored mechanic training programs.

Special Requirements

Voluntary certification by the National Institute of Automotive Service Excellence (ASE) has become a standard credential for Automotive Technicians. Certification is available in eight different service areas, including electrical systems, engine repair, brake systems, suspension, heating, and air-conditioning. To be certified in each area, Automotive Technicians must have at least two years of experience and pass a written examination. Completion of an automotive training program in high school, vocational or trade school, or community or junior college may be substituted for one year of experience. In some cases, graduates of ASE-certified programs achieve certification in up to three specialties.

For certification as a master Automotive Technician, Automotive Technicians must be certified in all eight areas. Technicians must retake each examination at least every five years to maintain their certifications.

Experience, Skills, and Personality Traits

Automotive Technicians should have mechanical aptitude, strong analytical abilities, and an understanding of how cars work, in addition to good reading, mathematics, and computer skills. Persistence and attention to detail is important.

Technicians usually work indoors in clean, well-ventilated, well-lit repair shops, but some shops are drafty and noisy, so a high tolerance to noisy, dirty environments is important. Although technicians can fix some problems with simple adjustments, they often work with dirty and greasy parts or in awkward positions, lifting heavy parts and tools. Minor cuts, burns, and bruises are common, but technicians usually avoid serious accidents when the shop is kept clean and orderly and safety practices are observed.

Many Automotive Technicians can expect to work more than 40 hours a week; many of those working longer hours are self-employed. To satisfy customer service needs, some service shops offer evening and weekend service.

Unions and Associations

A few Automotive Technicians are members of labor unions such as the International Association of Machinists and Aerospace Workers; the International Union, United Automobile, Aerospace and Agricultural Implement Workers of America; the Sheet Metal Workers' International Association; and the International Brotherhood of Teamsters. They may belong to other associations, such as the Service Technicians Society or the National Institute for Automotive Service Excellence.

Tips for Entry

1. Try to obtain skills by working on your own cars, and by taking every relevant course available during high school or vocational school.
2. An internship or summer job at a dealer, repair shop, or service station can provide invaluable experience.
3. Check Web sites of local dealers and repair shops to spot job openings.
4. Check classifieds at Service Technicians Society jobsite: http://www.sts.sae.org/misc/classified.htm.
5. Positions should be advertised in the newspaper classified ad section under "trades: mechanical" or "auto."
6. Send your résumé and a cover letter to all the local dealers and repair shops in your area. Because there is always a demand for well-trained technicians, you may get called for an interview even if the job has not been advertised in the paper.
7. If you graduated from vocational or postsecondary school, find out if the school has a job placement service and work with them to land a position.

PARTS MANAGER

CAREER PROFILE

Duties: Responsible for operating a retail operation including staffing, scheduling, training and supervising staff, merchandising and inventory management, with customer service

Alternate Title(s): None

Salary Range: $13.23 to $28.23 per hour

Employment Prospects: Good

Advancement Prospects: Good

Best Geographical Location(s): All locations throughout the country have job possibilities for well-trained, experienced Parts Managers

Prerequisites:

Education or Training—High school diploma required; technical college, community college, or manufacturer-supported training program education helpful; two- or four-year degree programs in business, marketing, or another field or experience as auto technician also helpful

Experience—Prior automotive experience, demonstrated parts knowledge, and some retail sales experience

Special Skills and Personality Traits—A sound technical background; an ability to work with people; a keen sense of organization and attention to detail

Licensure/Certification—Voluntary certification by the National Institute for Automotive Service Excellence (ASE) in the Parts Specialist series

CAREER LADDER

```
┌─────────────────────────────────┐
│   General Manager or Dealer     │
└─────────────────────────────────┘

┌─────────────────────────────────┐
│         Parts Manager           │
└─────────────────────────────────┘

┌─────────────────────────────────┐
│  Assistant Parts Manager,       │
│      Manager Trainee,           │
│   or Counter Salesperson        │
└─────────────────────────────────┘
```

Position Description

The Parts Manager bears the overall responsibility for the parts department, and must hire, train, and supervise all department personnel. Controlling inventory, security, merchandising, and advertising are all responsibilities of the Parts Manager, as well as interacting with commercial customers. A well-run, efficient parts department is essential to a successful dealership or an auto parts store. The department supports dealership service and sales operations. Many large parts departments and auto part stores also aggressively sell parts and accessories to the public and to other dealers and independent repair shops.

Parts Managers run the parts department and keep the automotive parts inventory. Dealership parts managers display and promote sales of parts and accessories and deal with garages and other repair shops who need to buy parts. Auto parts store Parts Managers display and promote sales of parts and accessories to the public.

Salaries

Earnings vary depending on occupation, experience, and the dealer's geographic location and size, but average hourly wages for Parts Managers range between $13.23 an hour and $28.23 an hour.

Employment Prospects

Through 2012, population growth will increase demand for cars and jobs in car dealerships and auto parts stores.

Growth of the labor force and in the number of families in which both spouses need cars to drive to work will mean increased car sales and more jobs. As people earn more, they will be able to afford the luxury of owning several cars, which also should increase car parts sales. Perhaps, with this growth in car sales, more people keep their cars for many more years than in the past, which should also increase parts sales opportunities.

The trend toward dealership consolidation should have a minimal effect on car parts industry because of continued demand for cars and related services. Dealerships and auto parts stores will always need well-qualified people. In particular, as dealers try to become more efficient and flexible and more financially stable, they will place more emphasis on after-sales services such as car parts sales.

Advancement Prospects

Parts Managers can begin by working as a pick-up and delivery person, manager trainee, parts specialist, or shipping and receiving clerk, but often the best experience is acquired in the service department, where individuals learn about the frequency of repair and parts replacement of the cars and trucks sold by the dealership.

Opportunities as Parts Manager are best for people with college degrees and those with considerable automotive technician experience. However, as dealerships consolidate, the growth of managerial jobs will slow and competition for managerial positions will remain relatively keen.

Many Parts Managers advance by getting jobs in bigger dealerships, or moving from used car operations to new dealerships. Some Parts Managers move into other supervisory positions, such as service advisors or shop supervisors.

Education and Training

Although some individuals begin working in dealership parts departments right out of high school, others may decide first to seek training at technical colleges, community colleges, or manufacturer-supported training programs. Still others will come into the parts field after graduating from two- or four-year degree programs in business, marketing, or another field. A few auto technicians move into the parts field when openings occur.

Special Requirements

Voluntary certification by the National Institute of Automotive Service Excellence (ASE) has become a standard credential for many individuals in the auto repair industry.

In addition to certification in the eight different service areas of the auto repair series, Parts Managers can be certified in the parts specialist series (medium/heavy truck dealership parts specialist, medium/heavy truck aftermarket parts specialist [suspension and steering], and general motors parts consultant). To be certified in each area, Parts Managers must have at least two years of experience and pass a written examination. Completion of an automotive training program in high school, vocational or trade school, or community or junior college may be substituted for one year of experience. Parts Managers must retake each examination at least every five years to maintain their certifications.

Experience, Skills, and Personality Traits

This demanding job requires a person who is organized, personable, and comfortable managing employees and dealing directly with the public. Ideally, Parts Managers should have prior automotive experience, demonstrated parts knowledge, retail sales experience, and computer experience, since many parts departments have computerized inventories.

Unions and Associations

Relatively few Parts Managers in care dealerships are union members or are covered by union contracts, but Parts Managers may belong to the Automotive Aftermarket Industry Association (AAIA).

Tips for Entry

1. The best Parts Managers have automotive technician experience; try to obtain skills by working on your own cars and by taking every relevant course available during high school or vocational school.
2. An internship or summer job at a dealer, repair shop, or service station can provide invaluable experience.
3. Check Web sites of local dealers and repair shops to spot job openings.
4. Check classifieds at Service Technicians Society jobsite: http://www.sts.sae.org/misc/classified.htm
5. Positions should be advertised in the newspaper classified ad section under "Trades: mechanical" or "automotive."
6. Send your résumé and a cover letter to all the local dealers and repair shops in your area.
7. If you graduated from vocational or postsecondary school, find out if the school has a job placement service and work with them to land a position.

PARTS SPECIALIST

CAREER PROFILE

Duties: Supply car parts to technicians and repairers and sell replacement parts and accessories to the public

Alternate Title(s): Parts Salesperson, Parts Technician

Salary Range: $7.36 to $20.80 per hour

Employment Prospects: Good

Advancement Prospects: Good

Best Geographical Location(s): All locations throughout the country have job possibilities for well-trained, experienced Parts Specialists

Prerequisites:

Education or Training—High school diploma required; technical college, community college, or manufacturer-supported training program education, or experience as auto technician also helpful

Experience—Experience in sales and auto mechanics helpful

Special Skills and Personality Traits—Computer skills; independence; attention to detail; good math skills; strong communication skills

Licensure/Certification—Voluntary certification by the National Institute for Automotive Service Excellence (ASE) in the Parts Specialist Series

CAREER LADDER

```
┌─────────────────────────────┐
│       Parts Manager         │
└─────────────────────────────┘

┌─────────────────────────────┐
│      Parts Specialist       │
└─────────────────────────────┘

┌─────────────────────────────┐
│       Parts Helper,         │
│ Pickup and Delivery Person, │
│  or Shipping/Delivery Clerk │
└─────────────────────────────┘
```

Position Description

In support of the service and repair department, Parts Specialists supply vehicle parts to technicians and repairers and sell replacement parts and accessories to the public. Some Parts Specialists choose to work in dealerships or independent repair shops; others may prefer working in a truck fleet, a jobber store, or a retail parts store.

Often, these jobs are primarily involved with direct sales at the parts counter. Not only must this person be able to relate to customers politely and professionally, but they are often called upon to troubleshoot problems and procedures for customers who are performing their own repairs. They must be able to suggest complementary products and make sure that the customer is introduced to the full product line.

In addition, the Parts Specialist must work directly with technicians and shop managers to expedite parts required by the service department. They are often required by their dealerships to acquire ASE certification.

They must understand retail operations, replenish stock when necessary, keep track of inventory, provide price quotes, and ensure that the customer is aware of complementary products that may serve their needs.

Car owners in the United States spend almost $150 billion every year to service, repair, and equip their vehicles. This means there are millions of parts and accessories that need to be ordered, shipped, inventoried, sold, and delivered. It is the job of the parts specialist to see that all this happens.

A well-run, efficient parts department is essential to a successful dealership. Not only does it support service and sales operations, but many large parts departments aggressively sell parts and accessories to the public and to other dealers and independent repair shops.

Salaries

Earnings vary depending on occupation, experience, and the dealer's or auto parts store's geographic location and size, but average hourly wages for Parts Specialists range from $11.78 to $13.04 an hour. The lowest 10 percent earn less than $7.36 an hour, and the highest 10 percent earn more than $20.80.

Employment Prospects

Parts Specialists can enter this field by becoming a pickup and delivery person, parts helper, or shipping and receiving clerk, but often the best experience is acquired in an auto dealer service department, or in an auto parts store, where individuals learn about the frequency of repair and parts replacement of the cars and trucks sold by the dealership or by the auto parts store. Because selling and ordering parts requires a relatively high level of technical knowledge of the car, some parts technicians begin their careers as apprentice technicians in the service department.

Advancement Prospects

With experience, Parts Specialists can move into positions with larger dealerships. Some Parts Specialists become parts managers.

Education and Training

Although many students get jobs right out of high school, others may decide to seek additional training through technical colleges, community colleges, or manufacturer-supported training programs. Still others will come into the parts field after graduating from two- or four-year degree programs in business, marketing, or another field. A few auto technicians move into the parts field when openings occur.

Special Requirements

Voluntary certification by the National Institute of Automotive Service Excellence (ASE) has become a standard credential for many individuals in the auto repair industry. In addition to certification in the eight different service areas of the auto repair series, Parts Specialists can be certified in the parts specialist series (medium/heavy truck dealership parts specialist, medium/heavy truck aftermarket parts specialist [suspension and steering], and General Motors parts consultant). To be certified in each area, Parts Specialists must have at least two years of experience and pass a written examination. Completion of an automotive training program in high school, vocational or trade school, or community or junior college may be substituted for one year of experience. Specialists must retake each examination at least every five years to maintain their certifications. Voluntary certification in one or more of the eight tests is given by the National Institute for Automotive Service Excellence (ASE).

Experience, Skills, and Personality Traits

A sound technical background, an ability to work with people, a keen sense of organization, and attention to detail are the key qualities of good parts employees. Parts Specialists also need strong communications skills to deal effectively with customers and coworkers and to access technical information from manuals or computers. Technical knowledge is also important, since Parts Specialists must be able to identify the proper parts for particular problems. Computer skills are essential in order to operate sophisticated inventory databases as well as manage invoicing systems. Parts Specialists also must be able to use math to help with problems involving measurements, conversions, and financial transactions.

Unions and Associations

Parts Specialists do not usually belong to unions, but they may belong to the Automotive Aftermarket Industry Association (AAIA).

Tips for Entry

1. Obtain mechanics skills by working on your own cars and by taking every relevant course available during high school or vocational school.
2. An internship or summer job at a dealer, repair shop, or service station can provide invaluable experience.
3. Check Web sites of local dealers and repair shops to spot job openings.
4. Check classifieds at Service Technicians Society jobsite: http://www.sts.sae.org/misc/classified.htm
5. Positions should be advertised in the newspaper classified ad section under "trades: mechanical" or "automotive."
6. Send your résumé and a cover letter to all the local dealers and repair shops in your area.
7. If you graduated from vocational or postsecondary school, find out if the school has a job placement service and work with them to land a position.

TRANSMISSION TECHNICIAN

CAREER PROFILE

Duties: Work on gear trains, couplings, hydraulic pumps, and other transmission parts

Alternate Title(s): Transmission Mechanic

Salary Range: $14,000 to $40,000

Employment Prospects: Very good

Advancement Prospects: Very good

Best Geographical Location(s): All locations throughout the country have job possibilities for well-trained, experienced technicians

Prerequisites:

Education or Training—High school or postsecondary vocational school automotive service technician training program

Experience—Experience in transmission repairs

Special Skills and Personality Traits—Good diagnostic skills; attention to detail; mechanical ability; mathematics; computer skills

Licensure/Certification—Voluntary certification in transmission systems by the National Institute for Automotive Service Excellence (ASE)

CAREER LADDER

```
┌─────────────────────────────────┐
│        Shop Supervisor          │
└─────────────────────────────────┘

┌─────────────────────────────────┐
│     Transmission Technician     │
└─────────────────────────────────┘

┌─────────────────────────────────┐
│ Transmission Technician Assistant │
└─────────────────────────────────┘
```

Position Description

Transmission Technicians work on gear trains, couplings, hydraulic pumps, and other transmission parts. Extensive knowledge of computer controls, diagnosis of electrical and hydraulic problems, and other specialized skills are needed to work on these complex components, which require use of some of the most sophisticated technology used in vehicles.

At the start of each job, Transmission Technicians get a description of the car's problem from the owner or the repair service manager. To locate the problem, technicians first test components and systems, and then isolate those that could not logically be the cause. Technicians may have to test-drive the car to identify the source of the problem. In modern repair shops, Transmission Technicians compare the readouts from diagnostic testing devices to the standards provided by the manufacturer. The testing devices diagnose problems and make adjustments with precise calculations downloaded from large computerized databases. The computerized systems provide automatic updates to technical manuals and unlimited access to manufacturers' service information, technical service bulletins, and other information databases, which allow technicians to keep current on trouble spots and to learn new procedures.

Transmission Technicians are also responsible for routine service inspections and repairing or replacing worn parts before they cause problems that could damage critical components of the car. Technicians usually follow a checklist to ensure that every critical part is examined.

While shop owners provide large diagnostic equipment, Transmission Technicians are expected to provide their own tools. Many experienced workers have invested thousands of dollars in their own equipment. Some formal training programs have alliances with tool manufacturers that help entry-level technicians accumulate tools during their training period. Some Transmission Technicians specialize in automatic transmissions/transaxles, and others also may work with manual transmissions/transaxles. Others may specialize in diagnosis and repair of clutches; driveshafts, halfshafts, and universal joints; rear axles; or four-wheel drive components.

Salaries

Average hourly earnings of Transmission Technicians (including commission) range between $10 and $19 an hour. The lowest 10 percent may earn less than $8, and the highest 10 percent earn more than $24 an hour. On average, a Transmission Technician working for new and used car dealers earn an average of $17 an hour. Employees at auto and home supply stores earn less (about $12.35). The average annual salary for a Transmission Technician in 2001 was about $32,620; entry-level Transmission Technicians earn an average of $25,018.

Employment Prospects

As automotive technology becomes more complex, more skilled workers will be required, contributing to the growth in demand for highly trained Transmission Technicians. Opportunities should be very good for Transmission Technicians with excellent diagnostic and problem-solving skills and solid knowledge of electronics and mathematics.

While job opportunities are expected to be very good for those who complete automotive training programs in high school, vocational and technical schools, or community colleges, people without formal automotive training are likely to face stiff competition for entry-level jobs.

Most jobs will be found in specialty transmission shops, franchises, or car dealerships; most Transmission Technicians can expect steady work, because changes in general economic conditions and developments in other industries have little effect on the car repair business.

Advancement Prospects

Beginners usually start as trainee Transmission Technicians or mechanics' helpers, and gradually acquire skills by working with experienced technicians. It usually takes several years of experience to become a fully trained Transmission Technician who can quickly perform the more difficult types of routine service and repairs. However, some graduates of automotive training programs are often able to earn promotion to this level after only a few months on the job.

Experienced Transmission Technicians with leadership ability may advance to shop supervisor of specialty transmission shops, and those who work well with customers may become service estimators or service managers at a specialty transmission shop. Some with solid financial backing may open their own independent repair shops.

Education and Training

Employers today often require a high school diploma plus postsecondary training; courses in transmission repair, automotive repair, electronics, physics, chemistry, English, com-puters, and mathematics provide a good educational background. While some Transmission Technicians still learn the trade by serving as an apprentice, today's sophisticated technology almost requires a formal training program in high school or postsecondary vocational school. Many high schools, community colleges, and public and private vocational and technical schools offer Transmission Technician training programs.

Education continues on the job; employers send Transmission Technicians to manufacturer training centers to learn how to repair new models or to receive special training in the repair of components or training in the use of new equipment and diagnostic tools. Car dealers also may send promising beginners to manufacturer-sponsored mechanic training programs.

Special Requirements

Voluntary certification by the National Institute of Automotive Service Excellence (ASE) has become a standard credential for Transmission Technicians who pass the ASE certification test in automatic transmission/transaxle and/or manual drive train and axles, and have at least two years of experience in transmission repair. Completion of an automotive training program in high school, vocational or trade school, or community or junior college may be substituted for one year of experience. Transmission Technicians must retake each examination at least every five years to maintain their certification.

Experience, Skills, and Personality Traits

Transmission Technicians should have mechanical aptitude, strong analytical abilities, and an understanding of how transmissions work, in addition to good reading, mathematics, and computer skills. Persistence and attention to detail are important.

Transmission Technicians usually work indoors in clean, well-ventilated, well-lit repair shops, but some shops are drafty and noisy, so a high tolerance to noisy, dirty environments is important. Although technicians can fix some problems with simple adjustments, they often work with dirty and greasy parts or in awkward positions, lifting heavy parts and tools. Minor cuts, burns, and bruises are common, but technicians usually avoid serious accidents when the shop is kept clean and orderly and safety practices are observed.

Many Transmission Technicians can expect to work more than 40 hours a week; many of those working longer hours are self-employed. To satisfy customer service needs, some service shops offer evening and weekend service.

Unions and Associations

Some Transmission Technicians are members of labor unions such as the International Association of Machinists and Aerospace Workers; the International Union, United

Automobile, Aerospace and Agricultural Implement Workers of America; the Sheet Metal Workers' International Association; and the International Brotherhood of Teamsters.

Tips for Entry

1. Hands-on experience is important; try to improve your skills by working on your own cars and by taking every relevant course available during high school or vocational school.
2. An internship or summer job at a dealer, repair shop, or service station can provide invaluable experience.
3. Check Web sites of local transmission shops to spot job openings.
4. Check classified ads at Internet websites such as the Service Technicians Society site at: www.sts.sae.org/misc/classified.htm
5. Positions should be advertised in the newspaper classified ad section under "trades: mechanical" or "auto."
6. Send your résumé and a cover letter to all the local dealers and transmission repair shops in your area. Because there is always a demand for well-trained technicians, you may get called for an interview even if the job hasn't been advertised in the paper.
7. If you graduated from vocational or postsecondary school, find out if the school has a job placement service and work with them to get a job.

SERVICE ADVISER

CAREER PROFILE

Duties: Handle the administrative and customer relations part of the service department

Alternate Title(s): None

Salary Range: $17.96 to $21.66 per hour

Employment Prospects: Good

Advancement Prospects: Good

Best Geographical Location(s): All locations throughout the country have job possibilities for well-trained, experienced Service Advisers

Prerequisites:

Education or Training—High school diploma required; technical college, community college, or manufacturer-supported training program education helpful

Experience—Prior experience as automotive technician vital

Special Skills and Personality Traits—Sound technical background; an ability to work with people; a keen sense of organization; attention to detail

Licensure/Certification—Voluntary certification by the National Institute for Automotive Service Excellence (ASE) in customer service personnel

CAREER LADDER

```
┌─────────────────────────┐
│    Service Manager      │
└─────────────────────────┘

┌─────────────────────────┐
│    Service Adviser      │
└─────────────────────────┘

┌─────────────────────────┐
│    Auto Technician      │
└─────────────────────────┘
```

Position Description

The service department provides car repair services and sells accessories and replacement parts. Most service only cars and small trucks, but a small number service large trucks, buses, and tractor-trailers. Some dealerships also have body shops to do collision repair, refinishing, and painting. The work of the service department has a major influence on customers' satisfaction and willingness to purchase future cars from the dealership.

Service Advisers handle the administrative and customer relations functions of the service department. They meet customers, write repair orders, estimate the cost and time needed to do each job, handle customer complaints, and help bring new business into the service department. In addition to having a broad understanding of auto mechanics, Service Advisers must also be able to work with both the public and the shop technicians in a courteous, professional manner. They call customers when technicians discover new problems while doing the work, and explain to customers the work performed and the charges associated with the repairs.

Salaries

Earnings vary depending on occupation, experience, and the dealer's geographic location and size, but average hourly wages for Service Advisers range from $17.96 to $21.66 per hour.

Employment Prospects

Through 2012, population growth will increase demand for cars and their repairs. As the labor force grows, along with the number of families in which both spouses need cars to drive, there will be increased business in car sales and repairs. As people earn more, they will be able to afford the luxury of owning several cars.

Opportunities in service and repair management should be plentiful, especially for people who complete formal automotive service technician training. Most persons who enter service and repair occupations may expect steady work because changes in economic conditions have little effect on this part of the dealership's business. In the same respect, the trend toward dealership consolidation should have little effect on the car repair industry because of continued demand for cars and related services. Dealerships will always need well-qualified people to work in the service department. As dealers try to become more efficient and flexible and more financially stable, they will place more emphasis on service and repairs.

Advancement Prospects

Workers need years of experience in automotive service to advance to management positions in dealerships. Because automotive technology is getting more sophisticated all the time, dealerships increasingly prefer to hire graduates of postsecondary automotive training programs for management trainee positions. Graduates of such programs often earn promotion after only a few months on the job.

Education and Training

Most community and junior colleges and vocational and technical schools offer postsecondary automotive training programs leading to an associate's degree in automotive technology or auto body repair. They generally provide intense career preparation through a combination of classroom instruction and hands-on practice. Good reading and basic math skills also are required to study technical manuals, to keep abreast of new technology, and to learn new service and repair techniques. Additional courses in management or business are helpful.

Special Requirements

New certification for customer service personnel was first offered in spring 2003 by the National Institute for Automotive Service Excellence (ASE). The test measures product knowledge and people skills of service customer-contact personnel, and includes questions on communications (customer relations and internal relations); product knowledge (vehicle systems, service maintenance intervals, warranty service contracts, service bulletins, and vehicle identification); sales skills; and shop operations.

Experience, Skills, and Personality Traits

This position is a combination of automotive technician and customer service representative, and requires a person who is organized, personable, patient, tolerant, and comfortable interacting with automotive technicians and also dealing directly with the public.

Unions and Associations

Service Advisers do not generally belong to unions and are not usually covered by union contracts.

Tips for Entry

1. The best Service Advisers have automotive technician experience; try to obtain skills by working on your own cars and taking every relevant course available during high school or vocational school.
2. Check Web sites of local dealers and repair shops to spot job openings.
3. Positions should be advertised in the newspaper classified ad section under "trades: auto" or "general."
4. Send your résumé and a cover letter to all the local dealers and repair shops in your area.
5. If you graduated from vocational or postsecondary school, find out if the school has a job placement service and work with them to land a position.

SERVICE MANAGER

CAREER PROFILE

Duties: Oversee the entire service department and be responsible for the department's reputation, efficiency, and profitability

Alternate Title(s): None

Salary Range: $18 to $28 per hour

Employment Prospects: Excellent

Advancement Prospects: Excellent

Best Geographical Location(s): All locations throughout the country have job possibilities for well-trained, experienced Service Managers

Prerequisites:

Education or Training—High school diploma required; technical college, community college, or manufacturer-supported training program education helpful; two- or four-year degree programs in business also helpful

Experience—Prior experience as automotive technician vital; experience in supervising others helpful

Special Skills and Personality Traits—Sound technical background; ability to work with and manage people; a keen sense of organization; attention to detail

Licensure/Certification—Voluntary certification by the National Institute for Automotive Service Excellence (ASE) in customer service personnel

CAREER LADDER

```
┌─────────────────────────────┐
│  General Manager or Dealer  │
└─────────────────────────────┘

┌─────────────────────────────┐
│      Service Manager        │
└─────────────────────────────┘

┌─────────────────────────────┐
│      Service Adviser        │
└─────────────────────────────┘
```

Position Description

The service department provides car repair services and sells accessories and replacement parts. Most service only cars and small trucks, but a small number service large trucks, buses, and tractor-trailers. Some dealerships also have body shops to do collision repair, refinishing, and painting. The work of the service department has a major influence on customers' satisfaction and willingness to purchase future cars from the dealership.

The overall responsibility for the reputation, efficiency, and profitability of the service department rests with the Service Manager. He or she is responsible for controlling costs, building a loyal clientele, maintaining good employee relations, setting and obtaining sales and profit objectives, and maintaining service records. Service Managers also must make sure employees are properly trained and equipped for their duties. This is a demanding management position that may lead to fixed operations director (in charge of the service, parts, and body shop departments), general manager, or even dealer. Increasingly, service departments use computers to increase productivity and improve service workflow by scheduling customer appointments, troubleshooting technical problems, and locating service information and parts.

Salaries

Earnings vary depending on occupation, experience, and the dealer's geographic location and size, but average hourly wages for Service Managers range from $18 to $28.

Employment Prospects

Through 2012, population growth will increase demand for cars and their repairs. As the labor force grows and the number of families in which both spouses need cars to drive, there will be increased business in car sales and repairs. As people earn more, they will be able to afford the luxury of owning several cars.

Opportunities in service and repair management should be plentiful, especially for people who complete formal automotive service technician training. Most people who enter service and repair occupations may expect steady work because changes in economic conditions have little effect on this part of the dealership's business. In the same respect, the trend toward dealership consolidation should have little effect on the car repair industry because of continued demand for cars and related services. Dealerships will always need well-qualified people to work in the service department. As dealers try to become more efficient and flexible and more financially stable, they will place more emphasis on service and repairs.

Advancement Prospects

This demanding management position can lead to fixed operations director in charge of the service, parts and body shop departments, general manager, or even dealer. Workers need years of experience in automotive service to advance to service management positions. Because automotive technology is getting more sophisticated all the time, dealerships increasingly prefer to hire graduates of postsecondary automotive training programs for management trainee positions. Graduates of such programs often earn promotion after only a few months on the job.

Education and Training

Most community and junior colleges and vocational and technical schools offer postsecondary automotive training programs leading to an associate's degree in automotive technology or auto body repair. They generally provide intense career preparation through a combination of classroom instruction and hands-on practice. Good reading and basic math skills also are required to study technical manuals, to keep abreast of new technology, and to learn new service and repair techniques. Additional courses in management or business are helpful.

Special Requirements

New certification for customer service personnel was first offered in spring 2003 by the National Institute for Automotive Service Excellence (ASE). The test measures product knowledge and people skills of service customer-contact personnel, and includes questions on communications (customer relations and internal relations); product knowledge (vehicle systems, service maintenance intervals, warranty service contracts, service bulletins, and vehicle identification); sales skills; and shop operations.

Experience, Skills, and Personality Traits

This position is a combination of automotive technician and customer service representative, and requires a person who is organized, personable, patient, tolerant, and comfortable interacting with automotive technicians and also dealing directly with the public.

Unions and Associations

Service Managers do not generally belong to unions and are not usually covered by union contracts.

Tips for Entry

1. Check Web sites of local dealers and repair shops to spot job openings.
2. Check classifieds at the Service Technicians Society jobsite: http://www.sts.sae.org/misc/classified.htm.
3. Positions should be advertised in the newspaper classified ad section under "trades: mechanical" or "auto."
4. Send your résumé and a cover letter to all the local dealers and repair shops in your area.
5. If you graduated from vocational or postsecondary school, find out if the school has a job placement service and work with them to land a position.

SHOP MANAGER

CAREER PROFILE

Duties: Supervise and train other automotive technicians

Alternate Title(s): Shop Supervisor

Salary Range: $18,000 to $100,000

Employment Prospects: Good

Advancement Prospects: Good

Best Geographical Location(s): All locations throughout the country have job possibilities for well-trained, experienced Shop Managers

Prerequisites:

Education or Training—High school diploma required; technical college, community college, or manufacturer-supported training program education helpful

Experience—Experience in car repairs and management helpful

Special Skills and Personality Traits—Good diagnostic skills; an ability to manage people; attention to detail; mechanical ability; mathematics and computer skills

Licensure/Certification—Voluntary certification in one or more of the eight tests given by the National Institute for Automotive Service Excellence (ASE)

CAREER LADDER

```
┌─────────────────────────────────────┐
│  Shop Manager in Larger Dealership   │
│        or Service Manager            │
└─────────────────────────────────────┘

┌─────────────────────────────────────┐
│           Shop Manager               │
└─────────────────────────────────────┘

┌─────────────────────────────────────┐
│       Automotive Technician          │
│         or Service Adviser           │
└─────────────────────────────────────┘
```

Position Description

Shop Managers usually are among the most experienced service technicians who supervise and train other technicians to make sure that service work is performed properly. In this management position, the Shop Manager may assign the work to mechanics and directs the flow of cars through the shop.

The ability to manage other technicians and help diagnose the source of a problem quickly and accurately requires a combination of excellent management skills, good reasoning ability, and a thorough knowledge of cars. The increasing sophistication of automotive technology today means that Shop Managers must use computerized shop equipment while maintaining their skill with traditional hand tools.

Many Shop Managers work more than 40 hours a week, especially in those shops that, to satisfy customer service needs, offer evening and weekend service. Managers usually work indoors in clean, well-ventilated, well-lit repair shops, but some shops are drafty and noisy.

Salaries

Average hourly earnings of Shop Managers range between $15 and $25 an hour. The lowest 10 percent may earn less than $12, and the highest 10 percent earn more than $28 an hour. Annual salaries range from $18,000 to $100,000.

Employment Prospects

The growing complexity of automotive technology means more and more skilled workers will be required, and more employees will be hired to manage the shop. Opportunities should be very good for those with a combination of management skills and excellent diagnostic and problem-solving skills.

While job opportunities are expected to be very good for those who complete automotive training programs in high school, vocational and technical schools, or community colleges, people without formal automotive training are likely to face stiff competition for management jobs.

Most positions will be found in car dealerships and independent repair shops, although new management jobs also will be created in small retail operations that offer after-warranty repairs, such as oil changes, brake repair, air conditioner service, and other minor repairs that usually take less than four hours to complete.

Most Shop Managers can expect steady work, because changes in general economic conditions and developments in other industries have little effect on the car repair business.

Advancement Prospects

Shop Managers usually begin as auto technicians, and gradually acquire and practice their skills. It usually takes at least five years of experience to become ready to move into a shop management position, although some managers have many more years of experience as an automotive technician.

Experienced Shop Managers with leadership ability and who work well with customers may become service advisers or service managers. Some with solid financial backing may open their own independent repair shops.

Education and Training

Because of the complexity of new cars, employers today often require a high school diploma plus postsecondary training. Courses in business management, automotive repair, electronics, physics, chemistry, English, computers, and mathematics provide a good educational background. Many high schools, community colleges, and public and private vocational and technical schools offer automotive service technician training programs.

Special Requirements

Shop Managers may want to explore voluntary certification by the National Institute of Automotive Service Excellence (ASE), which has become a standard credential for automotive technicians. Certification is available in eight different service areas, including electrical/electronics systems, engine repair, engine performance, brakes, suspension and steering, heating/air-conditioning, automatic transmission/transaxles, and manual drive train and axles. New ASE tests for customer service personnel are also valuable. To be certified in each area, technicians must have at least two years of experience and pass a written examination. Completion of an automotive training program in high school, vocational or trade school, or community or junior college may be substituted for one year of experience.

Many Shop Managers have certification as a master automotive technician, which requires certification in all eight areas. The exams must be taken at least every five years to maintain certification.

Experience, Skills, and Personality Traits

Shop Managers should work well with others, feel comfortable in management positions, and have mechanical aptitude, strong analytical abilities, and an understanding of how cars work, in addition to good reading, mathematics, and computer skills. Persistence and attention to detail is important. A high tolerance to noisy, dirty environments is important.

Unions and Associations

Shop Managers do not usually belong to unions, but they may belong to other associations, such as the Service Technicians' Society or the National Institute for Automotive Service Excellence.

Tips for Entry

1. Since almost all Shop Managers begin by becoming an automotive technician, try to obtain skills by working on your own cars, and by taking every relevant course available during high school or vocational school.
2. An internship or summer job at a dealer, repair shop, or service station can provide invaluable experience.
3. Check Web sites of local dealers and repair shops to spot job openings.
4. Check classifieds at the Service Technicians Society jobsite: http://www.sts.sae.org/misc/classified.htm.
5. Positions should be advertised in the newspaper classified ad section under "trades: mechanical" or "auto."
6. Send your résumé and a cover letter to all the local dealers and repair shops in your area.
7. If you graduated from vocational or postsecondary school, find out if the school has a job placement service and work with them to land a position.

AUTOMOTIVE GLASS INSTALLER/REPAIRER

CAREER PROFILE

Duties: Remove and repair broken, cracked, or pitted windshields and window glass

Alternate Title(s): None

Salary Range: $8.03 to $20.55 per hour

Employment Prospects: Good

Advancement Prospects: Good

Best Geographical Location(s): All locations throughout the country have job possibilities for well-trained, experienced Automotive Glass Installer/Repairers

Prerequisites:

Education or Training—High school or postsecondary vocational school automotive service technician training program

Experience—Experience in car repairs helpful

Special Skills and Personality Traits—Attention to detail; good eye-hand coordination

CAREER LADDER

```
┌─────────────────────────────────────┐
│          Shop Manager               │
└─────────────────────────────────────┘

┌─────────────────────────────────────┐
│  Automotive Glass Installer/Repairer│
└─────────────────────────────────────┘

┌─────────────────────────────────────┐
│      Apprentice Automotive          │
│     Glass Installer/Repairer        │
└─────────────────────────────────────┘
```

Position Description

Automotive Glass Installers and Repairers remove broken, cracked, or pitted windshields and window glass. Automotive Glass Installers apply a moisture-proofing compound along the edges of the replacement glass, place it in the vehicle, and install rubber strips around the sides of the windshield or window to make it secure and weatherproof.

Using their knowledge of automotive construction and repair techniques, Automotive Glass Installers must develop appropriate methods for each job. They usually work alone, with only general directions from supervisors. In some shops, helpers or apprentices assist experienced Repairers.

Some Automotive Glass Installers will do on-site replacement and repair. They may go to a client's home, business, or dealership and complete their work at that location.

Salaries

Average hourly wages for Automotive Glass Installers and Repairers (including incentive pay) are between $13.06 and $13.61 an hour; the lowest 10 percent earn less than $8.03, and the highest 10 percent earn more than $20.55 an hour. Average hourly earnings in automotive repair shops where most Automotive Glass Installers and Repairers work are $12.51. Helpers and trainees usually earn from 30 to 60 percent of the earnings of skilled workers at an hourly rate, until they are skilled enough to be paid on an incentive basis. Top-paying states are Connecticut (average $21.30/hour), Minnesota ($18.26), and Ohio ($18.03).

Employment Prospects

Most Automotive Glass Installers work for automotive repair shops, car dealers, or independent automotive glass shops. Jobs for installers are expected to increase about as fast as the average for all occupations through the year 2012, according to the Bureau of Labor Statistics; opportunities should be best for those with formal training in automotive body repair and mechanics. Demand for qualified Automotive Glass Installers is expected to increase as the number of cars in operation continues to grow; as the number of cars increases, the number of cars damaged in accidents also will grow.

The need to replace experienced installers who transfer to other occupations, retire, or stop working for other reasons will account for most of the job openings. The car repair business is not very sensitive to changes in economic conditions, and experienced Automotive Glass Installers are rarely laid off. However, although major windshield damage must be repaired if a car is to be restored to safe operating condition, repair of minor chinks or chips can often be deferred during an economic slowdown.

Advancement Prospects

Some Automotive Glass Installers with leadership and business talents become service managers, shop managers, or auto technology teachers. Still others become automobile damage appraisers for insurance companies.

Education and Training

Most employers prefer to hire workers who have completed formal training programs in automotive windshield repair, supplementing their education with on-the-job training and short-term training sessions given by car, parts, or equipment manufacturers. Many high schools, vocational schools, private trade schools, and community colleges offer automotive glass installation as part of their automotive service programs.

Experience, Skills, and Personality Traits

A skilled Automotive Glass Installer must have patience, attention to detail, and good eye-hand coordination.

Unions and Associations

A few Automotive Glass Installers are members of unions, including the International Association of Machinists and Aerospace Workers; the International Union, United Automobile, Aerospace and Agricultural Implement Workers of America; the Sheet Metal Workers' International Association; and the International Brotherhood of Teamsters.

Tips for Entry

1. Check classified ads at the Service Technicians Society Web site: www.sts.sae.org/misc/classified.htm
2. An internship or summer job at a dealer, repair shop, or service station can provide invaluable experience.
3. Check Web sites of local dealers and repair shops to spot job openings.
4. Positions should be advertised in the newspaper classified ad section under "trades: mechanical" or "auto."
5. Send your résumé and a cover letter to all the local dealers and repair shops in your area.
6. If you graduated from vocational or postsecondary school, find out if the school has a job placement service and work with them to secure a position.

BODY REPAIR TECHNICIAN

CAREER PROFILE

Duties: Repair and straighten bent car bodies, remove dents, and replace crumpled parts that cannot be repaired

Alternate Title(s): None

Salary Range: $8.83 to $27.54 per hour

Employment Prospects: Excellent

Advancement Prospects: Good

Best Geographical Location(s): All locations throughout the country have job possibilities for well-trained, experienced Body Repair Technicians

Prerequisites:

Education or Training—High school diploma with on-the-job training

Experience—Experience in basic car repair helpful

Special Skills and Personality Traits—Good reading skills; basic math and computer skills; flair for color and form; artistic skills

Licensure/Certification—ASE Certification in Collision Repair & Refinishing

CAREER LADDER

Shop Manager

Body Repair Technician

Apprentice Body Repair Technician

Position Description

Automotive Body Repair Technicians straighten bent car bodies, remove dents, and replace crumpled parts that cannot be fixed. Although they repair all types of vehicles, they work primarily on cars and small trucks, although some repairers work on large trucks, buses, or tractor-trailers.

Body Repair Technicians use special equipment to restore damaged metal frames and body sections. They chain or clamp frames and sections to alignment machines that use hydraulic pressure to align damaged components. Designs built without frames must be restored to precise factory specifications for the vehicle to operate correctly. To do so, repairers use benchmark systems to make accurate measurements of how much each section is out of alignment and hydraulic machinery to return the vehicle to its original shape.

Body Repair Technicians remove badly damaged sections of body panels with a pneumatic metal-cutting gun or by other means, and weld in replacement sections. They remove less serious dents with a hydraulic jack or hand pry-ing bar or knock them out with hand tools or pneumatic hammers. Small dents and creases in the metal can be smoothed out by holding a small anvil against one side of the damaged area, while hammering the opposite side. Very small pits and dimples can be removed with pick hammers and punches in a process called "metal finishing."

Body Repair Technicians also repair or replace the plastic body parts are are used on more and more new models. They remove damaged panels and identify the properties of the plastic used on the vehicle. With most types of plastic, repairers can apply heat from a hot-air welding gun or by immersion in hot water and press the softened panel back into its original shape by hand. Badly damaged or hard-to-repair plastic parts are replaced.

Body Repair Technicians use plastic or solder to fill small dents that cannot be worked out of the plastic or metal panel. On metal panels, they file or grind the hardened filler to the original shape and clean the surface with a media blaster before painting. In many shops, automotive painters do the painting, but in small shops workers often do both body repairing and painting. A few Body Repair Technicians specialize in repairing fiberglass car bodies.

The advent of assembly-line repairs in large shops moves away from the one-vehicle, one-repairer method to a team approach, allowing Body Repair Technicians to specialize in one type of repair (such as frame straightening or fender repair).

Body repair work has variety and challenges. Using their broad knowledge of automotive construction and repair techniques, technicians must develop appropriate methods for each job. They usually work alone, with only general directions from supervisors. In some shops, helpers or apprentices assist experienced repairers.

Most Body Repair Technicians work 40 hours a week, although some (including self-employed repairers) work more than that. Repairers work in noisy body shops filled with the sounds of power tools and hammering against metal. Most shops are well ventilated to remove dust and paint fumes. Body Repair Technicians often work in awkward or cramped positions, and much of their work is strenuous and dirty. Hazards include cuts from sharp metal edges, burns from torches and heated metal, injuries from power tools, and fumes from paint. However, serious accidents usually are avoided when the shop is kept clean and orderly and safety practices are observed.

Salaries

Average hourly earnings of automotive Body Repair Technicians (including incentive pay) range from $15.93 to $17.19 an hour; the lowest 10 percent earn less than $8.83, and the highest 10 percent earn more than $27.54 an hour.

Most technicians who work for automotive dealers and repair shops are paid a predetermined amount for various tasks; earnings depend on the amount of work assigned to the repairer and how fast it is completed, although employers often guarantee workers a minimum weekly salary. Those who work for trucking companies, bus lines, and other organizations that maintain their own vehicles usually receive an hourly wage.

Helpers and trainees usually earn from 30 to 60 percent of the earnings of skilled workers at an hourly rate, until they are skilled enough to be paid on an incentive basis. Top-paying states are Colorado (average $23.83/hour), Alaska ($20.68), and Nevada ($20.52).

Employment Prospects

Most Body Repair Technicians work for automotive repair shops or car dealers; a few work for organizations that maintain their own motor vehicles, such as trucking companies. A small number work for wholesalers of cars, parts, and supplies. About one automotive Body Repair Technician out of eight is self-employed.

Jobs for Body Repair Technicians are expected to increase about as fast as the average for all occupations through the year 2012, according to the Bureau of Labor Statistics. Opportunities should be best for those with formal training in automotive body repair and mechanics. Demand for qualified Body Repair Technicians is expected to increase as the number of cars in operation continues to grow; as the number of cars increases, the number of cars damaged in accidents also will grow.

More and more new car designs have body parts made of steel alloys, aluminum, and plastics—materials that are harder to work with than traditional steel body parts. In addition, new, lighter-weight automotive designs are prone to greater collision damage than older, heavier designs and, consequently, more time is spent in repair.

The need to replace experienced repairers who transfer to other occupations, retire, or stop working for other reasons will account for the majority of job openings. The car repair business is not very sensitive to changes in economic conditions, and experienced body repairers are rarely laid off. However, although major body damage must be repaired if a car is to be restored to safe operating condition, repair of minor dents and crumpled fenders can often be deferred during an economic slowdown. During slowdowns, most employers will hire few new workers, some unprofitable body shops may go out of business, and some dealerships might consolidate body shops.

Advancement Prospects

Many Body Repair Technicians prefer to specialize—some in structural repair, others in painting and refinishing. Some technicians with leadership and business talents go on to own their own shops. Some become service managers, shop managers, or auto technology teachers if they have strong communication skills. Still others become automobile damage appraisers for insurance companies.

Education and Training

Most employers prefer to hire workers who have completed formal training programs in automotive body repair, supplementing their education with on-the-job training and short-term training sessions given by car, parts, or equipment manufacturers. Some degree of training is necessary because new technology has radically changed the car's structure, components, and materials, requiring employees to become proficient in new repair techniques and skills. For example, bodies of many newer cars are a combination of steel, aluminum, metal alloys, and plastics. Each of these materials requires somewhat different techniques to reshape parts and smooth out dents and small pits.

Many high schools, vocational schools, private trade schools, and community colleges offer automotive body repair training as part of their automotive service programs.

A fully skilled automotive Body Repair Technician must have good reading and basic mathematics and computer skills. Restoring cars to their original form requires a great deal of precision; body repairers must follow instructions and diagrams in technical manuals to make very precise three-dimensional measurements of the position of one body section relative to another.

It usually takes three to four years of on-the-job training to become skilled in all aspects of body repair. A new repairer starts out by helping experienced repairers remove damaged parts, sand body panels, and install repaired parts. They learn to remove small dents and make other minor repairs, progressing to more difficult tasks such as straightening and realigning body parts.

Continuing education is required as car parts, body materials, and electronics continue to become more complex. To keep up with these technological advances, repairers must continue to learn new skills and attend seminars and classes.

Special Requirements

Voluntary certification by the National Institute for Automotive Service Excellence (ASE) is the recognized standard of achievement for Automotive Body Repair Technicians. ASE offers a series of four exams for collision repair professionals twice a year. Repairers may take from one to four ASE Master Collision Repair & Refinish Exams. Repairers who pass at least one exam and have two years of hands-on work experience earn ASE certification. Completion of a postsecondary program in automotive body repair may be substituted for one year of work experience.

Those who pass all four exams become ASE master collision repair and refinish technicians. Automotive body repairers must retake the examination at least every five years to retain certification.

Experience, Skills, and Personality Traits

A skilled automotive Body Repair Technician must have good reading and basic mathematics and computer skills to follow instructions and diagrams in print and computer-based technical manuals. Technicians also should have artistic skills with a flair for color and form, and love working on cars.

Unions and Associations

Some automotive Body Repair Technicians are members of unions, including the International Association of Machinists and Aerospace Workers; the International Union, United Automobile, Aerospace and Agricultural Implement Workers of America; the Sheet Metal Workers' International Association; and the International Brotherhood of Teamsters. Most union Body Repair Technicians work for large car dealers, trucking companies, and bus lines.

Tips for Entry

1. Check classified ads at the Service Technicians Society Web site at www.sts.sae.org/misc/classified.htm.
2. Try to obtain skills by taking every body repair course available during high school or vocational school.
3. An internship or summer job at a dealer, repair shop, or service station can provide invaluable experience. Related work in the Armed Forces also may be helpful.
4. Check Web sites of local dealers and repair shops to spot job openings.
5. Positions should be advertised in the newspaper classified ad section under "trades: mechanical" or "auto."
6. Send your résumé and a cover letter to all the local dealers and repair shops in your area.
7. If you graduated from vocational or postsecondary school, find out if the school has a job placement service and work with them to secure a position.

DIESEL SERVICE TECHNICIAN

CAREER PROFILE

Duties: Repair and maintain the diesel engines in heavy trucks, buses, locomotives, bulldozers, cranes, road graders, farm tractors, combines, cars, light trucks, or boats

Alternate Title(s): Bus and Truck Mechanic, Diesel Engine Specialist

Salary Range: $10.84 to $25.15 per hour

Employment Prospects: Good

Advancement Prospects: Good

Best Geographical Location(s): All parts of the country, although towns and cities where trucking companies, bus lines, and other fleet owners have large operations are the best locations

Prerequisites:

Education or Training—High school diploma required; formal training in diesel mechanics at community and junior colleges and vocational and technical schools or the armed forces, highly recommended

Experience—Practical experience in car repair at a gasoline service station, in the armed forces, or as a hobby helpful

Special Skills and Personality Traits—Diagnostic skills; attention to detail; mechanical ability; mathematics and computer skills; problem-solving skills

Licensure/Certification—ASE certification is the recognized standard of achievement for Diesel Service Technicians

CAREER LADDER

```
┌─────────────────────────────────────┐
│  Shop Supervisor or Service Manager  │
│     or Self-Employed Technician      │
└─────────────────────────────────────┘

┌─────────────────────────────────────┐
│      Diesel Service Technician       │
└─────────────────────────────────────┘

┌─────────────────────────────────────┐
│  Apprentice Diesel Service Technician│
└─────────────────────────────────────┘
```

Position Description

Diesel Service Technicians repair and maintain the diesel engines that power transportation equipment such as heavy trucks, buses, and locomotives. Some Diesel Service Technicians and mechanics also work on heavy vehicles and mobile equipment such as bulldozers, cranes, road graders, farm tractors, and combines; a small number repair diesel-powered passenger automobiles, light trucks, or boats, and stationary power units.

Technicians who work for organizations that maintain their own vehicles spend most of their time doing preventive maintenance, eliminating unnecessary wear or damage to parts that could cause costly breakdowns. During a routine maintenance check, technicians repair or adjust all parts in brake systems, steering mechanisms, wheel bearings, and other important parts.

Typically Diesel Service Technicians handle all types of repairs from electrical systems to major engine repairs. Diesel maintenance is becoming increasingly complex, as more electronic components are used to control engine operation.

Diesel Service Technicians use a variety of tools in their work, including hand tools, power tools, machine tools such as lathes and grinding machines, welding and flame-cutting equipment to remove and repair exhaust systems, and jacks and hoists to lift and move large parts.

Diesel Service Technicians also use a variety of computerized testing equipment to pinpoint and analyze malfunctions in electrical systems and engines. In modern shops, Diesel Service Technicians use hand-held computers to diagnose problems and adjust engine functions, and they must keep up with new techniques and advanced materials as they are developed.

In large shops, Diesel Service Technicians generally receive their assignments from shop supervisors or service managers. Most supervisors and managers are experienced technicians who can help diagnose problems and maintain quality standards. Technicians may work as a team or be assisted by an apprentice or helper when doing heavy work, such as removing engines and transmissions.

Diesel Service Technicians usually provide their own tools (many experienced workers have thousands of dollars worth of equipment). Employers typically furnish expensive power tools, computerized engine analyzers, and other diagnostic equipment; but individual workers ordinarily accumulate hand tools with experience.

Diesel Service Technicians usually work indoors, although they occasionally make repairs to vehicles on the road. They may lift heavy parts and tools, handle greasy and dirty parts, and stand or lie in awkward positions to repair vehicles and equipment. Minor cuts, burns, and bruises are common, although serious accidents can usually be avoided if the shop is kept clean and orderly and safety procedures are followed. Although technicians normally work in well-lighted, heated, and ventilated areas, some shops are drafty and noisy. Some on-site repairs may be necessary on off-road equipment or stationary power units.

Salaries

Average hourly earnings of Diesel Service Technicians range from $16.81 to $17.27 an hour; the lowest 10 percent earn less than $10.84, and the highest 10 percent earn more than $25.15 an hour. Because many experienced Diesel Service Technicians who work for truck fleet dealers and independent repair shops receive a commission related to the labor cost charged to the customer, weekly earnings depend on the amount of work completed. Beginners usually earn from 50 to 75 percent of the rate of skilled workers; as they learn more, they receive increases until they reach the rates of skilled Diesel Service Technicians.

Most Diesel Service Technicians work a standard 40-hour week, although some work longer hours, particularly if they own their own businesses. A growing number of shops have expanded their hours to better perform repairs and routine service as a convenience to customers. Those who work for truck and bus firms providing service around the clock may work evenings, nights, and weekends; these technicians usually receive a higher rate of pay for working nontraditional hours. Top-paying states are Hawaii (average $22.90/hour), Alaska ($21.20), and Massachusetts ($20.21).

Employment Prospects

The job outlook should be steady because changes in economic conditions have little effect on the diesel repair business. During a financial downturn, however, some employers may be reluctant to hire new workers. Employment of Diesel Service Technicians is expected to grow as freight transportation by truck increases and more trucks are needed to keep up with the increasing volume of freight shipped nationwide. Because diesel engines are more durable and cost-effective than gas engines, more and more buses and trucks of all sizes will be run by diesels. In addition, Diesel Service Technicians will be needed to maintain and repair the growing number of school buses.

Opportunities should be good for those who complete formal training in diesel mechanics at community and junior colleges and vocational and technical schools or related duties in the armed forces. Applicants without formal training may face stiffer competition for entry-level jobs.

About 25 percent of Diesel Service Technicians work on buses, trucks, and other diesel-powered equipment for customers of vehicle and equipment dealers, automotive rental and leasing agencies, or independent automotive repair shops. Another 20 percent work for local and long-distance trucking companies, and another 19 percent maintain the buses, trucks, and other equipment of bus lines, public transit companies, school systems, or government offices. The rest maintain vehicles and other equipment for manufacturing, construction, or other companies. A relatively small number are self-employed.

Advancement Prospects

Experienced diesel mechanics with leadership ability may move into shop supervisor or service manager positions. Mechanics with sales ability may become sales representatives. Others open their own repair shops.

Education and Training

It is possible to become a diesel mechanic after years of on-the-job training, but employers often prefer to hire a graduate of a formal diesel engine training program, since these workers often have a head start in training. Many community colleges and trade and vocational schools offer programs in diesel repair. These programs, lasting six months to two years, lead to a certificate of completion or an associate degree.

Programs vary in the degree of hands-on equipment training they provide; some offer about 30 hours a week training on equipment, while others offer more lab or classroom instruction. Training provides a foundation in the latest diesel technology and instruction in the service and repair of the vehicles and equipment that technicians will encounter on the job. Training programs also improve the skills needed to interpret technical manuals and to communicate with coworkers and customers. In addition to the hands-on aspects of the training, many institutions teach communication skills, customer service, basic understanding of physics, and logical thought. Often employers work closely with representatives of training programs, providing instructors with the latest equipment, techniques, and tools, and offering jobs to graduates.

Unskilled beginners usually are assigned tasks such as cleaning parts, fueling and lubricating vehicles, and driving vehicles into and out of the shop. Beginners are then promoted to trainee positions as they gain experience and as job openings become available. In some shops, beginners with experience in car service start as trainee technicians. Most trainees perform routine service tasks and make minor repairs after a few months' experience. These workers begin to work on harder repair jobs as they prove their ability and competence.

After technicians master the repair and service of diesel engines, they learn to work on related components, such as brakes, transmissions, and electrical systems. Generally, technicians with at least three to four years of on-the-job experience will qualify as journeyman-level Diesel Service Technicians. Completion of a formal training program speeds advancement to the journeyman level.

Nearly all employers require completion of high school. Courses in automotive repair, electronics, English, mathematics, and physics provide a strong educational background for a career as a Diesel Service Technician.

In addition, technicians need a state commercial driver's license to test-drive trucks or buses on public roads.

Practical experience in car repair at a gasoline service station, in the armed forces, or as a hobby is also valuable. Employers often send experienced technicians and mechanics to special training classes conducted by manufacturers and vendors, in which workers learn the latest technology and repair techniques. Technicians receive updated technical manuals and service procedures outlining changes in techniques and standards for repair. It is essential for technicians to read, interpret, and comprehend service manuals to keep abreast of engineering changes.

Special Requirements

Voluntary certification by the National Institute for Automotive Service Excellence (ASE) is recognized as the standard of achievement for Diesel Service Technicians and mechanics. Technicians may be certified as master heavy-duty truck technicians or in specific areas of heavy-duty truck repair, such as gasoline engines; drive trains; brakes; suspension and steering; electrical and electronic systems; or preventive maintenance and inspection. For certification in each area, a technician must pass one or more of the ASE-administered exams and present proof of two years of relevant hands-on work experience. Two years of relevant formal training from a high school, vocational or trade school, or community or junior college program may be substituted for up to a year of the work experience requirement.

Technicians are retested every five years to remain certified and to ensure that they keep up with changing technology. Diesel Service Technicians may opt for ASE certification as school bus technicians, which recognizes technicians with the knowledge and skills required to diagnose, service, and repair different subsystems of school buses. The ASE School Bus Technician Test Series includes seven certification exams: Body Systems and Special Equipment; Diesel Engines; Drive Train; Brakes; Suspension and Steering; Electrical/Electronic Systems; and Air-Conditioning Systems and Controls. Whereas several of these tests parallel existing ASE truck tests, each one is designed to test knowledge of systems specific to school buses. In order to become ASE-certified in school bus repair, technicians must pass one or more of the exams and present proof of two years of relevant hands-on work experience. Technicians who pass all the tests become ASE-certified master school bus technicians.

Experience, Skills, and Personality Traits

Employers usually look for applicants with good diagnostic skills, attention to detail, mechanical ability, mathematics and computer skills, and strong problem-solving skills.

Unions and Associations

Many Diesel Service Technicians are members of labor unions, including the International Association of Machinists and Aerospace Workers; the Amalgamated Transit Union; the International Union, United Automobile, Aerospace and Agricultural Implement Workers of America; the Transport Workers Union of America; the Sheet Metal Workers' International Association; and the International Brotherhood of Teamsters.

Tips for Entry

1. Check job openings for Diesel Service Technicians with local employers such as trucking companies, truck dealers, or bus lines.
2. Contact locals of the unions mentioned above for news of job openings.
3. Look for job openings listed by the local office of your state employment service.

4. Check with the career counseling office of your vocational or two-year program.
5. Check the classifieds section of the newspaper under "trade" or "automotive."

6. Check classified ads at the Service Technicians Society Web site at www.sts.sae.org/misc/classified.htm.

SCHOOL BUS TECHNICIAN

CAREER PROFILE

Duties: Repair and maintain school buses

Alternate Title(s): Diesel Engine Specialist, Diesel Service Technician, Heavy Duty Truck Technician

Salary Range: $10.84 to $25.15 per hour

Employment Prospects: Good

Advancement Prospects: Good

Best Geographical Location(s): All parts of the country, especially larger towns and cities where school districts have large operations

Prerequisites:

Education or Training—High school diploma required; formal training in diesel mechanics at community and junior colleges and vocational and technical schools highly recommended

Experience—Practical experience in truck repair at a gasoline service station, for bus lines, or in the armed forces helpful

Special Skills and Personality Traits—Diagnostic skills; attention to detail; mechanical ability; mathematics and computer skills; problem-solving skills

Licensure/Certification—ASE certification is the recognized standard of achievement for School Bus Technicians

CAREER LADDER

```
┌─────────────────────────────┐
│      Shop Supervisor        │
│    or Service Manager       │
└─────────────────────────────┘

┌─────────────────────────────┐
│    School Bus Technician    │
└─────────────────────────────┘

┌─────────────────────────────┐
│ Apprentice School Bus Technician │
└─────────────────────────────┘
```

Position Description

School Bus Technicians repair and maintain the diesel or gasoline engines that power school buses. Technicians who work for organizations that maintain their own buses spend most of their time doing preventive maintenance, eliminating unnecessary wear or damage to parts that could cause costly breakdowns. During a routine maintenance check, technicians repair or adjust all parts in brake systems, steering mechanisms, wheel bearings, and other important parts.

Typically, School Bus Technicians handle all types of repairs from electrical systems to major engine repairs. Diesel maintenance is becoming increasingly complex, as more electronic components are used to control engine operation. Technicians use a variety of tools in their work, including hand tools, power tools, machine tools such as lathes and grinding machines, welding and flame-cutting equipment to remove and repair exhaust systems, and jacks and hoists to lift and move large parts.

School Bus Technicians also use a variety of computerized testing equipment to pinpoint and analyze malfunctions in electrical systems and engines. In modern shops, technicians use handheld computers to diagnose problems and adjust engine functions, and they must keep up with new techniques and advanced materials as they are developed.

In large shops, School Bus Technicians generally receive their assignments from shop supervisors or service managers. Most supervisors and managers are experienced technicians themselves who can help diagnose problems and maintain quality standards. Technicians may work as a team or be assisted by an apprentice or helper when doing heavy work, such as removing engines and transmissions.

School Bus Technicians usually provide their own tools (many experienced workers have thousands of dollars worth of equipment). Employers typically furnish expensive power tools, computerized engine analyzers, and other diagnostic equipment; but individual workers ordinarily accumulate hand tools with experience.

Technicians usually work indoors, although they occasionally make repairs to vehicles on the road. They may lift heavy parts and tools, handle greasy and dirty parts, and stand or lie in awkward positions to repair vehicles and equipment. Minor cuts, burns, and bruises are common, although serious accidents can usually be avoided if the shop is kept clean and orderly and safety procedures are followed. Although technicians normally work in well-lighted, heated, and ventilated areas, some shops are drafty and noisy.

Salaries

Average hourly earnings of School Bus Technicians range from $16.81 to $17.27 an hour; the lowest 10 percent earn less than $10.84, and the highest 10 percent earn more than $25.15 an hour. Beginners usually earn from 50 to 75 percent of the rate of skilled workers; as they learn more, they receive increases until they reach the rates of skilled service technicians.

Most School Bus Technicians work a standard 40-hour week, although some work longer hours. Technicians usually receive a higher rate of pay for working nontraditional hours.

Employment Prospects

The job outlook should be steady because changes in economic conditions have little effect on the school bus repair business. During a financial downturn, however, some employers may be reluctant to hire new workers. Opportunities should be good for those who complete formal training in diesel mechanics at community and junior colleges and vocational and technical schools. Applicants without formal training may face stiffer competition for entry-level jobs.

Advancement Prospects

Experienced School Bus Technicians with leadership ability may move into shop supervisor or service manager positions. Mechanics with sales ability may become sales representatives.

Education and Training

It is possible to become a School Bus Technician after years of on-the-job training, but employers often prefer to hire a graduate of a formal diesel engine training program, since these workers often have a head start in training. Many community colleges and trade and vocational schools offer programs in diesel repair. These programs, lasting six months to two years, lead to a certificate of completion or an associate degree.

Programs vary in the degree of hands-on equipment training they provide; some offer about 30 hours a week training on equipment, while others offer more lab or classroom instruction. Training provides a foundation in the latest diesel technology and instruction in the service and repair of the types of buses that technicians will encounter on the job. Training programs also improve the skills needed to interpret technical manuals and to communicate with coworkers and customers. In addition to the hands-on aspects of the training, many institutions teach communication skills, customer service, basic understanding of physics, and logical thought. Often employers work closely with representatives of training programs, providing instructors with the latest equipment, techniques, and tools, and offering jobs to graduates.

While most employers prefer to hire graduates of formal training programs, some School Bus Technicians continue to learn their skills on the job. Unskilled beginners usually are assigned tasks such as cleaning parts, fueling and lubricating vehicles, and driving buses into and out of the shop. Beginners are then promoted to trainee positions as they gain experience and as job openings become available. In some shops, beginners with experience in car service start as trainee technicians. Most trainees perform routine service tasks and make minor repairs after a few months' experience. These workers begin to work on harder repair jobs as they prove their ability and competence.

After School Bus Technicians master the repair and service of school bus engines, they learn to work on related components, such as brakes, transmissions, and electrical systems. Generally, technicians with at least three to four years of on-the-job experience will qualify as journeyman-level diesel technicians. Completion of a formal training program speeds advancement to the journeyman level.

Nearly all employers require completion of high school. Courses in automotive repair, electronics, English, mathematics, and physics provide a strong educational background for a career as a School Bus Technician.

Practical experience in car repair at a gasoline service station, in the armed forces, or as a hobby is also valuable. Employers often send experienced technicians to special training classes conducted by manufacturers, in which workers learn the latest technology and repair techniques. Technicians constantly receive updated technical manuals and service procedures outlining changes in techniques and standards for repair. It is essential for technicians to read, interpret, and comprehend service manuals and computer-based service information sources in order to keep abreast of engineering changes.

Special Requirements

Voluntary certification by the National Institute for Automotive Service Excellence (ASE) is recognized as the standard of achievement for School Bus Technicians, which recognizes technicians with the knowledge and skills required to diagnose, service, and repair different subsystems of school buses. The ASE School Bus Technician Test Series includes seven certification exams: Body Systems and Special Equipment; Diesel Engines; Drive Train; Brakes; Suspension and Steering; Electrical/Electronic Systems; and Air-Conditioning Systems and Controls. Each test is designed to test knowledge of systems specific to school buses. In order to become ASE-certified in school bus repair, technicians must pass one or more of the exams and present proof of two years of relevant hands-on work experience. Technicians who pass all the tests become ASE-certified master School Bus Technicians.

In addition, School Bus Technicians may need a state commercial driver's license to test-drive buses on public roads.

Experience, Skills, and Personality Traits

Employers usually look for applicants with good diagnostic skills, attention to detail, mechanical ability, mathematics and computer skills, and strong problem-solving skills.

Unions and Associations

Some School Bus Technicians are members of labor unions, including the International Association of Machinists and Aerospace Workers; the Amalgamated Transit Union; the International Union, United Automobile, Aerospace and Agricultural Implement Workers of America; the Transport Workers Union of America; the Sheet Metal Workers' International Association; and the International Brotherhood of Teamsters.

Tips for Entry

1. Check job openings for School Bus Technicians with local bus lines.
2. Contact locals of the unions mentioned above for news of job openings.
3. Look for job openings listed by the local office of your state employment service.
4. Check with the career counseling office of your vocational or two-year program.
5. Check the classifieds section of the newspaper under "trade" or "automotive."

MOBILE HEAVY EQUIPMENT TECHNICIAN

CAREER PROFILE

Duties: Keep construction equipment such as bulldozers, cranes, crawlers, draglines, graders, and excavators in working order

Alternate Title(s): Mobile Heavy Equipment Mechanic

Salary Range: $11.80 to $25.55 per hour

Employment Prospects: Good

Advancement Prospects: Good

Best Geographical Location(s): All parts of the country, especially agricultural areas and areas where equipment wholesale distribution and leasing firms, large construction firms, and mining companies have large operations

Prerequisites:

Education or Training—A high school diploma plus vocational or two-year formal diesel or heavy equipment mechanic training program

Experience—Experience working on diesel engines and heavy equipment acquired in the armed forces

Special Skills and Personality Traits—Good diagnostic skills; attention to detail; mechanical ability; mathematics and computer skills; strong problem-solving skills; flexibility; the capacity to learn new skills quickly

CAREER LADDER

```
┌─────────────────────────────────┐
│   Field Mobile Heavy Equipment  │
│   Technician or Shop Supervisor │
│    or Self-Employed Technician  │
└─────────────────────────────────┘

┌─────────────────────────────────┐
│  Mobile Heavy Equipment Technician │
└─────────────────────────────────┘

┌─────────────────────────────────┐
│     Apprentice Mobile Heavy     │
│       Equipment Technician      │
└─────────────────────────────────┘
```

Position Description

Mobile Heavy Equipment Technicians keep construction equipment such as bulldozers, cranes, crawlers, draglines, graders, excavators, and other equipment in working order. They typically work for equipment wholesale distribution and leasing firms, large construction and mining companies, local and federal governments, or other organizations operating and maintaining heavy machinery and equipment fleets. Mobile Heavy Equipment Technicians employed by the federal government may work on tanks and other armored equipment.

Heavy vehicles and mobile equipment are indispensable to many industrial activities, moving materials, tilling land, lifting beams, and digging earth to pave the way for development and production. Mobile Heavy Equipment Technicians repair and maintain engines and hydraulics, transmission, and electrical systems powering farm equipment, cranes, and bulldozers.

Mobile Heavy Equipment Technicians perform routine maintenance checks on diesel engines and fuel, brake, and transmission systems to ensure peak performance, safety, and longevity of the equipment. Maintenance checks and comments from equipment operators usually alert technicians to problems. With many types of modern heavy and mobile equipment, technicians can plug handheld diagnostic computers into onboard computers to diagnose many components needing adjustment or repair. After locating the problem, these technicians rely on their training and experience to use the best possible technique to solve the problem. If necessary, they may partially dismantle the component to examine parts for damage or excessive wear. Then, using handheld tools, they repair, replace, clean, and lubricate parts, as necessary.

After reassembling the component and testing it for safety, they put it back into the equipment and return the equipment to the field. In some cases, technicians calibrate systems by typing codes into the onboard computer.

Many types of heavy and mobile equipment use hydraulics to raise and lower movable parts, such as scoops, shovels, log forks, and scraper blades. When hydraulic components malfunction, technicians examine them for hydraulic fluid leaks, ruptured hoses, or worn gaskets on fluid reservoirs. Occasionally, the equipment requires extensive repairs, such as replacing a defective hydraulic pump.

Mobile Heavy Equipment Technicians perform a variety of other repairs, diagnosing electrical problems and replacing defective components, or repairing undercarriages and track assemblies. Occasionally, technicians weld broken equipment frames and structural parts, using electric or gas welders.

Many Mobile Heavy Equipment Technicians in large shops specialize in one or two types of repair; for example, a shop may have individual specialists in major engine repair, transmission work, electrical systems, and suspension or brake systems. They use a variety of tools, including power tools, machine tools such as lathes and grinding machines, welding and flame-cutting equipment to remove and repair exhaust systems, and jacks and hoists to lift and move large parts. They also use a variety of computerized testing equipment to pinpoint and analyze malfunctions in electrical systems and other essential systems, such as tachometers, dynamometers, ohmmeters, ammeters, and voltmeters.

Mobile Heavy Equipment Technicians usually work indoors, although many make repairs at the work site. They often lift heavy parts and tools, handle greasy and dirty parts, and stand or lie in awkward positions to repair vehicles and equipment. Minor cuts, burns, and bruises are common; but serious accidents are normally avoided when the shop is kept clean and safety practices are observed. Although technicians often work in well-lit, heated, and ventilated areas, some shops are drafty and noisy.

When heavy and mobile equipment breaks down at a construction site, it may be too difficult or expensive to bring it into a repair shop, so the shop often sends a field service technician to the site. Field service technicians work outdoors and spend much of their time away from the shop. More experienced service technicians specialize in field service, driving trucks specially equipped with replacement parts and tools.

Salaries

Average hourly rates for Mobile Heavy Equipment Technicians range from $17.69 and $18.07. The lowest 10 percent earn less than $11.80, and the highest 10 percent earn more than $25.55. Field technicians normally earn a higher wage than their counterparts, because they are required to make on-the-spot decisions necessary to serve their customers. Top-paying states are Alaska (average 24.80/hour), Hawaii ($22.58), and California ($22.25).

Employment Prospects

Opportunities for Mobile Heavy Equipment Technicians should be good for those who have completed formal training programs in diesel or heavy equipment mechanics, but people without formal training may experience more and more problems getting a job. Employment of Mobile Heavy Equipment Technicians is expected to grow slower than the average for all occupations through the year 2012; most job openings will occur as experienced technicians retire.

Many employers have a hard time finding candidates with formal postsecondary training to fill available technician openings because many young people with mechanic training prefer to work as automotive service technicians, diesel service technicians, or industrial machinery repairers, where they can make more money and have more job opportunities.

Increasing numbers of Mobile Heavy Equipment Technicians will be needed to support growth in the construction industry and among equipment dealers and leasing companies. Because of the nature of construction activity, demand for technicians follows the economic cycle; as the economy strengthens, construction activity increases and more mobile heavy equipment is needed to grade construction sites, excavate basements, and lay water and sewer lines. All of this increases the need for periodic service and repair. In addition, the construction and repair of highways and bridges also requires more technicians to service equipment.

As equipment becomes more complex, more and more repairs must be made by trained technicians. Construction and mining are particularly sensitive to changes in the level of economic activity; therefore, heavy and mobile equipment may be idled during downturns. In addition, winter is traditionally the slow season for construction, particularly in cold regions. Few technicians may be needed during periods when equipment is used less, although employers usually try to keep experienced workers through the slow times.

Advancement Prospects

Experienced Mobile Heavy Equipment Technicians may advance to field service jobs, where they earn more money and have more chance to tackle problems independently. Technicians with leadership ability may become shop supervisors or service managers. Some technicians open their own repair shops or invest in a franchise.

Education and Training

High school courses in automobile repair, physics, chemistry, and mathematics provide a strong foundation for a career as a Mobile Heavy Equipment Technician. Although many people qualify for technician jobs after years of on-the-job training, most employers prefer applicants to have completed a formal diesel or heavy equipment mechanic training program after graduating from high school.

Many community colleges and vocational schools offer programs in diesel technology; some tailor programs to heavy equipment mechanics, which focus on the basics of analysis and diagnostic techniques, electronics, and hydraulics. The increased use of electronics and computers makes training in the fundamentals of electronics essential for new heavy and mobile equipment mechanics. Some one-to two-year programs lead to a certificate of completion, whereas others lead to an associate degree in diesel or heavy equipment mechanics. These programs provide a foundation in the components of diesel and heavy equipment technology and enable trainee technicians to advance more quickly to the experienced worker level.

A combination of formal and on-the-job training prepares trainee technicians with the knowledge to efficiently service and repair equipment handled by a shop. Most beginners perform routine service tasks and make minor repairs after a few months' experience. They advance to harder jobs as they prove their ability and competence. After trainees master the repair and service of diesel engines, they learn to work on related components, such as brakes, transmissions, and electrical systems. Generally, a service technician with at least three to four years of on-the-job experience is accepted as fully qualified.

Many employers send trainee technicians to training sessions conducted by heavy equipment manufacturers. These sessions, which may last up to a week, provide intensive instruction in the repair of a manufacturer's equipment. Some sessions focus on particular components found in the manufacturer's equipment, such as diesel engines, transmissions, axles, and electrical systems. Other sessions focus on particular types of equipment, such as crawler-loaders and crawler-dozers. As they progress, trainees may periodically attend additional training sessions. When appropriate, experienced technicians attend training sessions to gain familiarity with new technology or equipment.

It is also essential for Mobile Heavy Equipment Technicians to be able to read and interpret service manuals and to be familiar with the use of computer-based service information to keep abreast of engineering changes. Because the technology used in heavy equipment is becoming more sophisticated, featuring electronic and computer-controlled components, training in electronics is essential for these technicians to make engine adjustments and diagnose problems. Training in the use of handheld computers also is necessary, because computers help technicians diagnose problems and adjust component functions.

Special Requirements

Voluntary certification by the National Institute for Automotive Service Excellence (ASE) is recognized as the standard of achievement for Mobile Heavy Equipment Technicians. Technicians may be certified as a master heavy-duty diesel technician or in one or more of six different areas of heavy-duty equipment repair: brakes, gasoline engines, diesel engines, drive trains, electrical systems, and suspension and steering. For certification in each area, technicians must pass a written examination and have at least two years' experience. High school, vocational or trade school, or community or junior college training in gasoline or diesel engine repair may substitute for up to one year's experience.

To remain certified and ensure that technicians keep up with changing technology, they must be retested every five years.

Experience, Skills, and Personality Traits

Employers usually look for applicants with good diagnostic skills, attention to detail, mechanical ability, mathematics and computer skills, and strong problem-solving skills. Employers seek people who understand the fundamentals of diesel engines, transmissions, electrical systems, and hydraulics. Additionally, the constant change in equipment technology makes it necessary for technicians to be flexible and have the capacity to learn new skills quickly.

Unions and Associations

About one-fourth of all service technicians and mechanics are members of unions including the International Association of Machinists and Aerospace Workers, the International Union of Operating Engineers, and the International Brotherhood of Teamsters.

Tips for Entry

1. Check job openings for Mobile Heavy Equipment Technicians with local employers such as construction companies or leasing companies.
2. Contact locals of the unions mentioned above for news of job openings.
3. Look for job openings listed by the local office of your state employment service.
4. Check with the career counseling office of your vocational or two-year program.
5. Check the classifieds section of the newspaper under: "trade" or "automotive."
6. Check classified ads at the Service Technicians Society Web site at www.sts.sae.org/misc/classified.htm.

FARM EQUIPMENT MECHANIC

CAREER PROFILE

Duties: Maintain and repair farm equipment such as tractors and manure spreaders as well as smaller lawn and garden tractors in suburban areas

Alternate Title(s): Farm Equipment Technician

Salary Range: $8.90 to $19.06 per hour

Employment Prospects: Good

Advancement Prospects: Good

Best Geographical Location(s): Rural parts of the country (especially the Midwest)

Prerequisites:

Education or Training—A high school diploma plus vocational or two-year formal diesel or heavy equipment mechanic training program

Experience—Experience working on diesel engines and heavy equipment acquired in the armed forces

Special Skills and Personality Traits—Good diagnostic skills; attention to detail; mechanical ability; mathematics and computer skills; strong problem-solving skills; flexibility and the capacity to learn new skills quickly

CAREER LADDER

```
┌─────────────────────────────┐
│   Shop Supervisor or        │
│   Self-Employed Mechanic    │
└─────────────────────────────┘

┌─────────────────────────────┐
│   Farm Equipment Mechanic   │
└─────────────────────────────┘

┌─────────────────────────────┐
│   Apprentice Farm           │
│   Equipment Mechanic        │
└─────────────────────────────┘
```

Position Description

Farm Equipment Mechanics service, maintain, and repair farm equipment as well as smaller lawn and garden tractors sold to suburban homeowners. What typically was a general repairer's job around the farm in the past has evolved into a specialized technical career.

Farmers have increasingly turned to farm equipment dealers to service and repair their equipment because the machinery has become far more complex. Modern equipment uses more electronics and hydraulics making it difficult to perform repairs without some specialized training.

Farm Equipment Mechanics work mostly on equipment brought into the shop for repair and adjustment. During planting and harvesting seasons, they may travel to farms to make emergency repairs to minimize delays in farm operations. Mechanics repair and maintain engines and hydraulic, transmission, and electrical systems powering farm equipment. They also perform routine maintenance checks on engines and fuel, brake, and transmission systems to ensure peak performance, safety, and longevity of the equipment.

Maintenance checks and comments from equipment operators usually alert mechanics to problems.

After locating the problem, Farm Equipment Mechanics rely on their training and experience to use the best possible technique to solve the problem. If necessary, they may partially dismantle the component to examine parts for damage or excessive wear. Then, using handheld tools, they repair, replace, clean, and lubricate parts, as necessary.

Some types of farm equipment use hydraulics to raise and lower movable parts, such as scoops or plows. When hydraulic components malfunction, Farm Equipment Mechanics examine them for hydraulic fluid leaks, ruptured hoses, or worn gaskets on fluid reservoirs. Occasionally, the equipment requires extensive repairs, such as replacing a defective hydraulic pump.

Farm Equipment Mechanics perform a variety of other repairs, diagnosing electrical problems and replacing defective components, or repairing undercarriages and track assemblies. Occasionally, mechanics weld broken equipment frames and structural parts, using electric or gas welders.

Farm Equipment Mechanics often lift heavy parts and tools, handle greasy and dirty parts, and stand or lie in awkward positions to repair vehicles and equipment. Minor cuts, burns, and bruises are common, but serious accidents are normally avoided when the shop is kept clean and safety practices are observed. Although mechanics usually work in well-lighted, heated, and ventilated areas, some shops are drafty and noisy.

When farm equipment breaks down at the farm, it may be too difficult or expensive to bring it into a repair shop, so the shop often sends a field service mechanic to the site. Field service mechanics work outdoors and spend much of their time away from the shop. More experienced mechanics specialize in field service, driving trucks specially equipped with replacement parts and tools.

The hours of work for Farm Equipment Mechanics vary according to the season of the year. During the busy planting and harvesting seasons, mechanics often work six or seven days a week, 10 to 12 hours daily. In slow winter months, however, mechanics may work fewer than 40 hours a week.

Salaries

Average hourly earnings of Farm Equipment Mechanics are $13.21 to $13.58. The lowest 10 percent earn less than $8.90, and the highest 10 percent earn more than $19.06 per hour. Top-paying states are Nevada (average $18.06/hour), New Jersey ($17.75), and Michigan ($17.60).

Employment Prospects

Opportunities for Farm Equipment Mechanics should be good for those who have completed formal training programs in diesel or heavy equipment mechanics, but people without formal training may experience more and more problems getting a job. Employment of Farm Equipment Mechanics is expected to grow slower than the average for all occupations through the year 2012; most job openings will occur as experienced mechanics retire.

Many employers have a hard time finding candidates with formal postsecondary training to fill available mechanic openings because many young people with mechanic training prefer to work as automotive service technicians, diesel service technicians, or industrial machinery repairers, where they can make more money and have more job opportunities.

Winter is traditionally the slow season for agriculture, particularly in cold regions. Few Farm Equipment Mechanics may be needed during periods when equipment is used less, although employers usually try to keep experienced workers through the slow times.

Advancement Prospects

Farm Equipment Mechanics with leadership ability may become shop supervisors or service managers. Some open their own repair shops or invest in a franchise.

Education and Training

High school courses in automobile repair, physics, chemistry, and mathematics provide a strong foundation for a career as a Farm Equipment Mechanic. Although many people qualify for mechanic jobs after years of on-the-job training, most employers prefer applicants to have completed a formal diesel or heavy equipment mechanic training program after graduating from high school.

Many community colleges and vocational schools offer programs in diesel technology; some tailor programs to heavy equipment mechanics, which focus on the basics of analysis and diagnostic techniques, electronics, and hydraulics. The increased use of electronics and computers makes training in the fundamentals of electronics essential for new Farm Equipment Mechanics. Some one- to two-year programs lead to a certificate of completion, whereas others lead to an associate degree in diesel or heavy equipment mechanics. These programs provide a foundation in the components of diesel and heavy equipment technology and enable trainee mechanics to advance more quickly to the experienced worker level.

A combination of formal and on-the-job training prepares trainee mechanics with the knowledge to efficiently service and repair equipment handled by a shop. Most beginners perform routine service tasks and make minor repairs after a few months' experience. They advance to harder jobs as they prove their ability and competence. After trainees master the repair and service of diesel engines, they learn to work on related components, such as brakes, transmissions, and electrical systems. Generally, a mechanic with at least three to four years of on-the-job experience is accepted as fully qualified.

Many employers send trainee mechanics to training sessions conducted by farm equipment manufacturers. These weeklong sessions provide intensive instruction in the repair of a manufacturer's equipment. Some sessions focus on particular components found in the manufacturer's equipment, such as diesel engines, transmissions, axles, and electrical systems. Other sessions focus on particular types of equipment, such as tractors or hay balers. As they progress, mechanics may periodically attend additional training sessions. When appropriate, experienced mechanics attend training sessions to gain familiarity with new technology or equipment.

It is also essential for Farm Equipment Mechanics to be able to read and interpret service manuals to keep abreast of engineering changes. Because the technology used in farm equipment is becoming more sophisticated, featuring electronic and computer-controlled components, training in electronics is essential for these mechanics to make engine adjustments and diagnose problems. Training in the use of handheld computers also is necessary because computers help technicians diagnose problems and adjust component functions.

Experience, Skills, and Personality Traits

Employers usually look for applicants with good diagnostic skills, attention to detail, mechanical ability, mathematics and computer skills, and strong problem-solving skills. Employers seek people who understand the fundamentals of diesel engines, transmissions, electrical systems, and hydraulics. Additionally, the constant change in equipment technology makes it necessary for Farm Equipment Mechanics to be flexible and have the capacity to learn new skills quickly.

Unions and Associations

About one-fourth of all Farm Equipment Mechanics are members of unions including the International Association of Machinists and Aerospace Workers, the International Union of Operating Engineers, and the International Brotherhood of Teamsters.

Tips for Entry

1. Check job openings for Farm Equipment Mechanics from local employers such as farm equipment dealers, hardware stores, or leasing companies.
2. Contact locals of the unions mentioned above for news of job openings.
3. Look for job openings listed by the local office of your state employment service.
4. Check with the career counseling office of your vocational or two-year program.
5. Check the classifieds section of the newspaper under: "agriculture" or "automotive."

ALTERNATIVE FUEL VEHICLE TECHNICIAN

CAREER PROFILE

Duties: Diagnose and repair vehicles that use alternative fuel; perform state inspections and vehicle emissions tests; maintain and perform preventive care

Alternate Title(s): None

Salary Range: $25,000 to $70,000

Employment Prospects: Fair

Advancement Prospects: Fair

Best Geographical Location(s): All locations throughout the country have job possibilities for well-trained in alternative fuels

Prerequisites:

Education or Training—High school or postsecondary vocational school automotive service technician training program, including classes in alternative fuels

Experience—Interest or experience in cars

Special Skills and Personality Traits—Good diagnostic skills; attention to detail; mechanical ability; mathematics and computer skills

Licensure/Certification—Voluntary certification in one or more of the eight tests given by the National Institute for Automotive Service Excellence (ASE)

CAREER LADDER

```
┌─────────────────────────────┐
│   Fleet Service Manager     │
│      or Shop Owner          │
└─────────────────────────────┘

┌─────────────────────────────┐
│ Alternative Fuel Vehicle Technician │
└─────────────────────────────┘

┌─────────────────────────────┐
│   Automotive Technician     │
└─────────────────────────────┘
```

Position Description

To decrease the country's dependence on foreign oil and to address concerns with increasing air pollution, the United States has begun to search for substitutes to gasoline and diesel fuels. There are already hundreds of thousands of alternative fuel vehicles on the road, and many large fleets have converted to alternative fuels.

Considerable market expansion has occurred in natural gas, propane, ethanol, and biodiesel, with more modest advances in battery-electric power. Electric vehicle (EV) technology has seen considerable growth in off-road applications such as airport equipment. With such a variety of technologies on the road, technicians need specialized training to offer quality service.

Alternative Fuel Vehicle (AFV) Technicians are specialists who also must have knowledge of and work on standard fuel vehicles, and be able to diagnose engine problems, and analyze and solve system malfunctions related to friction, hydraulics, pneumatics, and electronics. Most typically they work in fleet situations, where they are the alternative fuel specialist. Their daily job routine is very similar to that of a standard auto technician, except that Alternative Fuel Vehicle Technicians repair and maintain alternative fuel vehicles that run on substances such as methanol or electricity.

Salaries

Average hourly earnings of AFV Technicians (including commission) range between $10 and $19 an hour. The lowest 10 percent may earn less than $8, and the highest 10 percent earned more than $24 an hour. Entry-level technicians earn an average of $25,018 and the most experienced master

AFV Technicians can earn more than $70,000 a year. Many experienced technicians who work for car dealers and independent repair shops receive a flat rate commission related to the labor cost charged to the customer. Under this method, weekly earnings depend on the amount of work completed. Employers often guarantee commissioned AFV Technicians a minimum weekly salary.

Employment Prospects

The demand for technicians to service this growing number of vehicles is increasing, which translates into job security for the Alternative Fuel Vehicle Technician.

Advancement Prospects

The alternative fuels field is a developing career track, and for individuals with drive, there is almost no limit to options and advancement. Many technicians love the day-to-day challenge of repairing and maintaining alternative fuel vehicles and have a good career doing just that, but others may go on to become fleet service managers, shop owners, or even teachers.

Education and Training

Although some students get jobs right out of high school, others may decide to seek specialized training through a technical school with an alternative fuels program. Still others will expand their education into a two-year associates degree or a four-year bachelor's degree.

Because Alternative Fuel Vehicle Technicians are specialists who also must have knowledge of and work on standard fuel vehicles, mechanical skills are very important. Most of the technology found in alternative fuel vehicles are common to all vehicles. Like any auto technician, an AFV Technician needs diagnostic and mechanical skills, plus a grounding in electronics, physics, and applied mathematics. For that reason, even technical schools offering top-notch AFV training often are dominated by conventional classes in auto technology. But in addition, AFV service programs typically offer instruction in handling high-pressure gaseous fuels including natural gas and propane. Another commonly offered course covers the inspection of high-pressure fuel cylinders for damage or deterioration. AFV training providers also often offer courses in nonroad vehicles including airport equipment and material-handling equipment such as forklifts.

In most metropolitan areas, basic training in AFV service can be found without traveling very far. Local colleges and trade schools, along with a handful of state universities and privately operated schools, offer most of the AFV training.

Many training centers adopt a "train-the-trainer" model, in which students are usually on-staff instructors from colleges and large fleet operators. After being trained, they return home to share knowledge with their own staff. The train-the-trainer approach has been the foundation of the National Alternative Fuels Training Consortium (NAFTC), based at West Virginia University.

NAFTC develops standard, competency-based AFV training. Since its inception in 1992, NAFTC-trained instructors have trained more than 3,000 AFV Technicians around the country, and will soon train technicians abroad through Clean Cities International. NAFTC also maintains a network of AFV training facilities nationwide. Most are community colleges. More information about the NAFTC and its approved training centers is available at http://naftp.nrcce.wvu.edu.

Another list of highly AFV qualified training providers is available from the National Automotive Technicians Education Foundation (NATEF), which is a part of ASE—the National Institute for Automotive Service Excellence. NATEF evaluates training providers against a set of industry standards. To deserving providers it awards certification in Continuing Automotive Service Education (CASE). CASE-certified AFV training providers can be located at www.natef.org/certified.cfm.

In spite of its small size, the College of the Desert has earned a nationwide reputation as a leader in AFV Technician training. The school has worked closely with SunLine Transit, southern California's AFV-centric public transit agency, to establish service standards for hydrogen-powered buses. That experience helps develop service procedures for fuel cell cars of the future.

Training in the workings of CNG (compressed natural gas) vehicles, and in the design and maintenance of natural gas fueling stations, is offered by the Natural Gas Vehicle Institute (NGVI), based in Las Vegas (www.ngvi.com). Many classes are open to the public, while private training is offered to clients including fleet operators and transit agencies. Its technician training classes cover natural gas fueling systems in depth, but they do not include hands-on diagnosis of drivability problems. NGVI's training is officially endorsed by the Natural Gas Vehicle Coalition.

In addition, NATEF and the DOE (Department of Energy) have released *Alternative Fuels Vehicle Technician,* a video designed to highlight the growth potential in AFV service. The NATEF training video illustrates the driving forces behind the growing numbers of AFVs in use today, and how an automotive technician can locate opportunities in this new industry. It is available in 28- and 15-minute versions; information on obtaining a copy of *Alternative Fuels Vehicle Technician* is available at NATEF at (703) 713-0100.

Special Requirements

Voluntary certification by the National Institute of Automotive Service Excellence (ASE) has become a standard credential for Alternative Fuel Vehicle Technicians. Certification is available in a variety of service areas; to be certified in each area, technicians must have at least two years of experience and pass a written examination. Completion of an automotive training program in high school, vocational or trade school, or community or junior college may be substituted for one year of experience. Technicians must retake each examination at least every five years to maintain their certification. ASE-certified professionals usually wear blue and white ASE insignia and carry credentials listing their areas of expertise; employers often display their technicians' credentials in the customer waiting area.

Experience, Skills, and Personality Traits

AFV Technicians should have strong mechanical and diagnostic skills. Strong communications skills are crucial for talking with customers and coworkers. Independent thinking and learning skills are also useful to the Alternative Fuel Vehicle Technician, who must read and understand considerable amounts of technical information to keep up with emerging technology.

Unions and Associations

A few AFV Technicians are members of labor unions such as the International Association of Machinists and Aerospace Workers; the International Union, United Automobile, Aerospace and Agricultural Implement Workers of America; the Sheet Metal Workers' International Association; and the International Brotherhood of Teamsters. They may belong to other associations, such as the Service Technicians Society or the National Institute for Automotive Service Excellence.

Tips for Entry

1. Check classified ads at Internet Web sites such as the Service Technicians Society site at www.sts.sae.org/misc/classified.htm.
2. Try to obtain skills by working on your own cars, and by taking every relevant course available during high school or vocational school.
3. An internship or summer job at a dealer, repair shop, or service station can provide invaluable experience.
4. Check Web sites of local dealers and repair shops to spot job openings.
5. Positions should be advertised in the newspaper classified ad section under "trades: mechanical" or "auto."
6. Send your résumé and a cover letter to all the local dealers and repair shops in your area. Because there is always a demand for well-trained technicians, you may get called for an interview even if the job has not been advertised in the paper.
7. If you graduated from vocational or postsecondary school, find out if the school has a job placement service and work with them to secure a position.

TUNE-UP TECHNICIAN

CAREER PROFILE

Duties: Adjust the ignition timing and valves, and adjust or replace spark plugs and other parts to ensure efficient engine performance

Alternate Title(s): None

Salary Range: $8 to $15 per hour

Employment Prospects: Good

Advancement Prospects: Good

Best Geographical Location(s): All locations throughout the country have job possibilities for well-trained, experienced technicians

Prerequisites:

Education or Training—High school or postsecondary vocational school automotive service technician training program

Experience—Experience in car repairs

Special Skills and Personality Traits—Good diagnostic skills; attention to detail; mechanical ability; mathematics and computer skills

Licensure/Certification—Voluntary certification in the engine performance test given by the National Institute for Automotive Service Excellence (ASE)

CAREER LADDER

```
┌─────────────────────────────┐
│      Shop Supervisor        │
└─────────────────────────────┘

┌─────────────────────────────┐
│     Tune-up Technician      │
└─────────────────────────────┘

┌─────────────────────────────┐
│ Tune-up Technician Apprentice │
└─────────────────────────────┘
```

Position Description

Tune-up Technicians adjust the ignition timing and valves, and adjust or replace spark plugs and other parts to ensure efficient engine performance. They often use electronic test equipment, such as on-board diagnostic meters, to isolate and adjust malfunctions in fuel, ignition, and emissions control systems.

They will use manuals and computer-based reference sources to obtain specifications. Tune-up Technicians perform general engine diagnosis, and diagnose and repair ignition systems; fuel, air induction, and exhaust systems; emissions control systems; and engine electrical systems. They also perform engine-related maintenance services such as replacement of belts and filters.

These technicians typically work in specialty tune-up shops; most dealerships would be unlikely to hire an employee whose only job is tune-ups.

Salaries

Average hourly earnings of Tune up Technicians range between $8 and $15. The lowest 10 percent may earn less than $8, and the highest 10 percent earn more than $18 an hour.

Employment Prospects

Opportunities should be very good for Tune-up Technicians with excellent skills. While job opportunities are expected to be very good for those who complete automotive training programs in high school, vocational and technical schools, or community colleges, people without formal automotive training may face more competition.

Jobs can be found at larger car dealerships, but most jobs will be found in national franchise shops or retail operations that offer after-warranty repairs, such as oil changes, brake repair, air conditioner service, tune-ups, and other minor repairs that usually take less than four hours to complete. Fewer national department store chains will provide specialized auto repair services in large shops.

Still, most Tune-up Technicians can expect steady work, because changes in general economic conditions and developments in other industries have little effect on the car repair business.

Advancement Prospects

Beginners usually start as trainee Tune-up Technicians, mechanics' helpers, lubrication workers, or gas service station attendants, and gradually acquire and practice their skills by working with experienced technicians. Experienced Tune-up Technicians with leadership ability may advance to shop supervisor.

Education and Training

A high school diploma is almost always required, and postsecondary training is helpful. Courses in automotive repair, electronics, physics, chemistry, English, computers, and mathematics provide a good educational background. Many high schools, community colleges, and public and private vocational and technical schools offer a variety of automotive service training programs.

Education continues on the job; employers send Tune-up Technicians to manufacturer training centers to learn how to repair new models or to receive special training in the repair of components. Car dealers also may send promising beginners to manufacturer-sponsored mechanic training programs. Auto dealers, parts suppliers, and tool suppliers also may offer supplemental training courses to enable the technician to keep up with changing technology.

Special Requirements

Voluntary certification by the National Institute of Automotive Service Excellence (ASE) has become a standard credential for many automotive technicians. While certification is not required for Tune-up Technicians, the test in "engine performance" is helpful. To be certified in this area, technicians must have at least two years of experience and pass a written examination. Completion of an automotive training program in high school, vocational or trade school, or community or junior college may be substituted for one year of experience. Technicians must retake each examination at least every five years to maintain their certification.

Experience, Skills, and Personality Traits

Tune-up Technicians should have mechanical aptitude, analytical abilities, and an understanding of how cars work, in addition to good reading, mathematics, and computer skills. Persistence and attention to detail is important. Technicians usually work indoors in clean, well-ventilated, well-lit repair shops, but some shops are drafty and noisy, so a high tolerance to noisy, dirty environments is important. Minor cuts, burns, and bruises are common, but technicians usually avoid serious accidents when the shop is kept clean and orderly and safety practices are observed. Many Tune-Up Technicians work 40 hours a week; to satisfy customer service needs, some service shops offer evening and weekend service.

Unions and Associations

Some Tune-up Technicians belong to labor unions such as the International Association of Machinists and Aerospace Workers; the International Union, United Automobile, Aerospace and Agricultural Implement Workers of America; the Sheet Metal Workers' International Association; and the International Brotherhood of Teamsters.

Tips for Entry

1. Try to obtain skills by working on your own cars, and by taking every relevant course available during high school or vocational school.
2. An internship or summer job at a dealer, repair shop, or service station can provide invaluable experience.
3. Check Web sites of local dealers and repair shops to spot job openings.
4. Check classified ads at Internet Web sites such as the Service Technicians Society site at www.sts.sae.org/misc/classified.htm.
5. Positions should be advertised in the newspaper classified ad section under "trades: mechanical" or "auto."
6. Send your résumé and a cover letter to all the local dealers and repair shops in your area. Because there is always a demand for well-trained Tune-up Technicians, you may get called for an interview even if the job hasn't been advertised in the paper.
7. If you graduated from vocational or postsecondary school, find out if the school has a job placement service and work with them to land a position.

AIR-CONDITIONING TECHNICIAN

CAREER PROFILE

Duties: Install and repair air conditioners and service components, such as compressors, condensers, and controls

Alternate Title(s): Air-Conditioning Mechanic

Salary Range: $21,650 to $55,070

Employment Prospects: Very good

Advancement Prospects: Very good

Best Geographical Location(s): All locations throughout the country have job possibilities for well-trained, experienced Air-Conditioning Technicians (especially areas in warmer climates)

Prerequisites:

Education or Training—High school or postsecondary vocational school automotive service technician training program, and special training in federal and state regulations governing the handling and disposal of refrigerants

Experience—Experience in automotive air conditioning, engine cooling, and heating systems helpful

Special Skills and Personality Traits—Good diagnostic skills; attention to detail; mechanical ability; mathematics and computer skills

Licensure/Certification—Certification by a U.S. organization in refrigerant recovery and recycling approved by the Environmental Protection Agency is required; voluntary certification in heating and air-conditioning systems by the National Institute for Automotive Service Excellence (ASE)

CAREER LADDER

```
┌─────────────────────────────┐
│      Shop Supervisor         │
│     or Self-Employment       │
└─────────────────────────────┘

┌─────────────────────────────┐
│  Air-Conditioning Technician │
└─────────────────────────────┘

┌───────────────────────────────────┐
│ Air-Conditioning Technician Assistant │
└───────────────────────────────────┘
```

Position Description

Automotive Air-Conditioning Technicians install and repair air conditioners and service components, such as compressors, condensers, and controls. At the start of each job, technicians get a description of the car's problem from the owner or the repair service manager. To locate the problem, technicians first test components and systems, and then isolate those that could not logically be the cause of the problem. Technicians may have to test-drive the car to identify the source of the problem.

Air-Conditioning Technicians are also responsible for maintaining engine cooling systems and heating systems, routine service inspections, and repairing or replacing worn parts before they cause problems that could damage critical components of the car. Technicians usually follow a checklist to ensure that every critical part is examined. Also, they retrofit older air-conditioning systems to comply with current regulations.

While shop owners provide large diagnostic equipment, Air-Conditioning Technicians are expected to provide their own tools; many experienced workers have invested thousands of dollars in their own equipment. Some formal training programs have alliances with tool manufacturers that help entry-level technicians accumulate tools during their training period.

Salaries

Average hourly earnings of Air-Conditioning Technicians (including commission) range between $16.90 and $17.60 an hour. The lowest 10 percent may earn less than $10.41, and the highest 10 percent earned more than $26.48 an hour. On average, Air-Conditioning Technicians working for new and used car dealers earn an average of $17 an hour. Employees at auto and home supply stores earn less (about $12.35). The average annual salary for a technician in 2001 was about $32,620; entry-level technicians earn an average of $25,018.

Employment Prospects

As automotive technology becomes more complex, more skilled workers will be required, contributing to the growth in demand for highly trained Air-Conditioning Technicians. Opportunities should be very good for technicians with excellent diagnostic and problem-solving skills and solid knowledge of electronics and mathematics.

While job opportunities are expected to be very good for those who complete automotive training programs in high school, vocational and technical schools, or community colleges, people without formal automotive training are likely to face stiff competition for entry-level jobs.

Most jobs will be found in car dealerships and national or regional repair chains; most Air-Conditioning Technicians can expect steady work because changes in general economic conditions and developments in other industries have little effect on the car repair business.

Advancement Prospects

Beginners usually start as trainee Air-Conditioning Technicians or mechanics' helpers, and gradually acquire skills by working with experienced technicians. It usually takes several years of experience to become a fully trained Air-Conditioning Technician who can quickly perform the more difficult types of routine service and repairs. However, some graduates of automotive training programs are able to earn promotion to this level after only a few months on the job.

Experienced technicians with leadership ability may advance to shop supervisor, and those who work well with customers may become service estimators or service managers. Some with solid financial backing may open their own independent repair shops.

Education and Training

Employers today often require a high school diploma plus postsecondary training; courses in air-conditioning repair, automotive repair, electronics, physics, chemistry, English, computers, and mathematics provide a good educational background. While some technicians still learn the trade by serving as an apprentice, today's sophisticated technol-

ogy almost requires a formal training program in high school or postsecondary vocational school. Many high schools, community colleges, and public and private vocational and technical schools offer Air-Conditioning Technician training programs.

Education continues on the job; employers send technicians to manufacturer training centers to learn how to repair new equipment or to receive special training in the repair of components. Car dealers also may send promising beginners to manufacturer-sponsored mechanic training programs.

Air-Conditioning Technicians must also complete special training in federal and state regulations governing the handling and disposal of refrigerants.

Special Requirements

Air-Conditioning Technicians who service motor vehicle air conditioners must be trained and certified by a U.S. organization in refrigerant recovery and recycling approved by the U.S. Environmental Protection Agency (EPA). Training programs must cover the use of recycling equipment in compliance with industry standards, regulatory requirements, refrigerant containment, and the effects of ozone depletion. To be certified, technicians must pass a test demonstrating their knowledge in these areas.

The National Institute of Automotive Service Excellence (ASE) Refrigerant Recovery and Recycling Review and Quiz is an EPA-approved Section 609 Technician Certification Program. (See http://www.asecert.org/subchannels/pro_refrigerant_online.cfm.) Certification earned as a result of a passing score on the online quiz is only deemed as certification in the context of the EPA.

This credential is not the equivalent of technical certification from the main ASE testing and certification program, which has become a standard credential for Air-Conditioning Technicians who pass the ASE certification test in air-conditioning systems and have at least two years of experience in air-conditioning repair. Completion of an automotive training program in high school, vocational or trade school, or community or junior college may be substituted for one year of experience. Technicians must retake each examination at least every five years to maintain their certification.

Experience, Skills, and Personality Traits

Air-Conditioning Technicians should have mechanical aptitude, strong analytical abilities, and an understanding of how engine cooling and air cooling and heating systems work, in addition to good reading, mathematics, and computer skills. Persistence and attention to detail is important.

Technicians usually work indoors in clean, well-ventilated, will-lit repair shops, but some shops are drafty and noisy, so a high tolerance to noisy, dirty environments is important. Although technicians can fix some problems with simple adjustments, they often work with dirty and greasy parts or in awkward positions, lifting heavy parts and tools. Minor cuts, burns, and bruises are common, but technicians usually avoid serious accidents when the shop is kept clean and orderly and safety practices are observed.

Many technicians can expect to work more than 40 hours a week; many of those working longer hours are self-employed. To satisfy customer service needs, some service shops offer evening and weekend service.

Unions and Associations

A few Air-Conditioning Technicians are members of labor unions such as the International Association of Machinists and Aerospace Workers; the International Union, United Automobile, Aerospace and Agricultural Implement Workers of America; the Sheet Metal Workers' International Association; and the International Brotherhood of Teamsters.

Tips for Entry

1. Hands-on experience is important; try to improve your skills by working on your own cars and by taking every relevant course available during high school or vocational school.

2. An internship or summer job at a dealer, repair shop, or service station can provide invaluable experience.

3. Check Web sites of local dealers to spot job openings.

4. Check classified ads at Internet Web sites such as the Service Technicians Society site at www.sts.sae.org/misc/classified.htm.

5. Positions should be advertised in the newspaper classified ad section under "trades: mechanical" or "auto."

6. Send your résumé and a cover letter to all the local dealers in your area. Because there is always a demand for well-trained Air-Conditioning Technicians, you may get called for an interview even if the job hasn't been advertised in the paper.

7. If you graduated from vocational or postsecondary school, find out if the school has a job placement service and work with them to get a job.

ALIGNMENT TECHNICIAN

CAREER PROFILE

Duties: Align and balance wheels and repair steering mechanisms and suspension systems

Alternate Title(s): Front End Mechanic

Salary Range: $14,000 to $40,000

Employment Prospects: Very good

Advancement Prospects: Very good

Best Geographical Location(s): All locations throughout the country have job possibilities for well-trained, experienced Alignment Technicians

Prerequisites:

Education or Training—High school or postsecondary vocational school automotive service technician training program

Experience—Experience in car repairs

Special Skills and Personality Traits—Good diagnostic skills; attention to detail; mechanical ability; mathematics and computer skills

Licensure/Certification—Voluntary certification in suspension and steering systems by the National Institute for Automotive Service Excellence (ASE)

CAREER LADDER

```
┌─────────────────────────────────┐
│        Shop Supervisor          │
└─────────────────────────────────┘

┌─────────────────────────────────┐
│      Alignment Technician       │
└─────────────────────────────────┘

┌─────────────────────────────────┐
│  Alignment Technician Assistant │
└─────────────────────────────────┘
```

Position Description

Alignment Technicians align and balance wheels and repair steering mechanisms and suspension systems using special alignment equipment and wheel-balancing machines. They will work on steering racks and gear boxes, power steering systems, steering linkage components, spindles, ball joints, control arms springs, struts, and shock absorbers.

At the start of each job, the technician gets a description of the car's problem from the owner or the repair service manager. To locate the problem, the technician first tests components and then isolates those that could not logically be the cause of the problem. Technicians may have to test-drive the car to identify the source of the problem.

In modern repair shops, Alignment Technicians compare the readouts from diagnostic testing devices to the standards provided by the manufacturer. The testing devices can help diagnose problems and suggest adjustments with precise calculations downloaded from large computerized databases. The computerized systems provide automatic updates to technical manuals and unlimited access to manufacturers' service information, technical service bulletins, and other information databases, which allow technicians to keep current on trouble spots and to learn new procedures. Technicians are also responsible for routine service inspections and repairing or replacing worn parts before they cause problems.

While shop owners provide large diagnostic equipment, Alignment Technicians are expected to provide their own tools; many experienced workers have invested thousands of dollars in their own equipment. Some formal training programs have alliances with tool manufacturers that help entry-level technicians accumulate tools during their training period.

Salaries

Average hourly earnings of Alignment Technicians (including commission) range between $10 and $19 an hour. The lowest 10 percent may earn less than $8, and the highest 10 percent earn more than $24 an hour. Alignment Technicians working for new and used car dealers earn an average of $17 an hour. Employees at auto and home supply stores earn less (about $12.35). The average annual salary for an Alignment Technician is about $32,620; entry-level technicians earn an average of $25,018.

Employment Prospects

Opportunities should be very good for Alignment Technicians with excellent diagnostic and problem-solving skills and solid knowledge of electronics and mathematics, according to the Bureau of Labor Statistics. While job opportunities are expected to be very good for those who complete automotive training programs in high school, vocational and technical schools, or community colleges, people without formal automotive training are likely to face stiff competition for entry-level jobs.

Most jobs will be found in car dealerships and national franchise shops or retail operations that offer after-warranty repairs. Most technicians can expect steady work, because changes in general economic conditions and developments in other industries have little effect on the car repair business.

Advancement Prospects

Beginners usually start as trainee Alignment Technicians or mechanics' helpers, and gradually acquire skills by working with experienced technicians. It usually takes several years of experience to become a fully trained Alignment Technician who can quickly perform the more difficult types of routine service and repairs. However, some graduates of automotive training programs are able to earn promotion to this level after only a few months on the job.

Experienced technicians with leadership ability may advance to shop supervisor and those who work well with customers may become service estimators or service managers. Some with solid financial backing may open their own independent repair shops.

Education and Training

Employers today often require a high school diploma plus postsecondary training; courses in transmission repair, automotive repair, electronics, physics, chemistry, English, computers, and mathematics provide a good educational background. While some Alignment Technicians still learn the trade by serving as an apprentice, today's sophisticated technology almost requires a formal training program in high school or postsecondary vocational school.

Education continues on the job; employers send technicians to manufacturer training centers to learn how to repair new models or to receive special training in the repair of components. Car dealers also may send promising beginners to manufacturer-sponsored mechanic training programs.

Special Requirements

Voluntary certification by the National Institute of Automotive Service Excellence (ASE) has become a standard credential for Alignment Technicians who pass the relevant ASE certification test and have at least two years of experience in front-end repair. Completion of an automotive training program in high school, vocational or trade school, or community or junior college may be substituted for one year of experience. Technicians must retake each examination at least every five years to maintain their certification.

Experience, Skills, and Personality Traits

Alignment Technicians should have mechanical aptitude, strong analytical abilities, and an understanding of how cars steer and drive, in addition to good reading, mathematics, and computer skills. Persistence and attention to detail is important.

Technicians usually work indoors in clean, well-ventilated, well-lit repair shops, but some shops are drafty and noisy, so a high tolerance to noisy, dirty environments is important. Although technicians can fix some problems with simple adjustments, they often work with dirty and greasy parts or in awkward positions, lifting heavy parts and tools. Minor cuts, burns, and bruises are common, but technicians usually avoid serious accidents when the shop is kept clean and orderly and safety practices are observed.

Many technicians can expect to work more than 40 hours a week; many of those working longer hours are self-employed. To satisfy customer service needs, some service shops offer evening and weekend service.

Unions and Associations

A few Alignment Technicians are members of labor unions such as the International Association of Machinists and Aerospace Workers; the International Union, United Automobile, Aerospace and Agricultural Implement Workers of America; the Sheet Metal Workers' International Association; and the International Brotherhood of Teamsters.

Tips for Entry

1. Hands-on experience is important; try to improve your skills by working on your own cars and by taking every relevant course available during high school or vocational school.

2. An internship or summer job at a dealer, repair shop, or service station can provide invaluable experience.
3. Check Web sites of local dealers to spot job openings.
4. Check classified ads at Internet Web sites such as the Service Technicians Society site at www.sts.sae.org/misc/classified.htm.
5. Positions should be advertised in the newspaper classified ad section under "trades: mechanical" or "auto."
6. Send your résumé and a cover letter to all the local dealers in your area. Because there is always a demand for well-trained Alignment Technicians, you may get called for an interview even if the job hasn't been advertised in the paper.
7. If you graduated from vocational or postsecondary school, find out if the school has a job placement service and work with them to get a job.

BRAKE SPECIALIST

CAREER PROFILE

Duties: Diagnose and repair brake hydraulic systems, disc and drum brake components, power assist units, and antilock brake systems

Alternate Title(s): Brake Technician

Salary Range: $14,000 to $40,000

Employment Prospects: Very good

Advancement Prospects: Very good

Best Geographical Location(s): All locations throughout the country have job possibilities for well-trained, experienced Brake Specialists

Prerequisites:

Education or Training—High school or postsecondary vocational school automotive service technician training program

Experience—Experience in car repairs

Special Skills and Personality Traits—Good diagnostic skills; attention to detail; mechanical ability; mathematics and computer skills

Licensure/Certification—Voluntary certification in brake systems by the National Institute for Automotive Service Excellence (ASE)

CAREER LADDER

```
┌─────────────────────────────┐
│      Shop Supervisor        │
└─────────────────────────────┘

┌─────────────────────────────┐
│      Brake Specialist       │
└─────────────────────────────┘

┌─────────────────────────────┐
│  Brake Specialist Apprentice │
└─────────────────────────────┘
```

Position Description

Brake Specialists adjust brakes, replace brake linings and pads, and make other repairs on brake systems. Some technicians and mechanics specialize in both brake and front-end work. Brake Specialists measure and resurface disc and drums, adjust shoes, replace and repair calipers, master cylinders, and wheel cylinders, replace hoses and lines, bleed and flush hydraulic systems. They also diagnose and repair power brake units, antilock brake systems, wheel bearings and parking brakes, and traction control systems.

At the start of each job, the Brake Specialist gets a description of the car's braking problem from the owner or the repair service manager. To locate the problem, Brake Specialists first test components and then isolate those that could not logically be the cause of the problem; they may have to test-drive the car to identify the source of the problem.

In modern repair shops, Brake Specialists compare the readouts from diagnostic testing devices to the standards provided by the manufacturer. The testing devices diagnose problems and make adjustments with precise calculations downloaded from large computerized databases. The computerized systems provide automatic updates to technical manuals and unlimited access to manufacturers' service information, technical service bulletins, and other information databases, which allow Brake Specialists to keep current on trouble spots and to learn new procedures. Specialists are also responsible for routine service inspections, and repairing or replacing worn parts before they cause problems.

While shop owners provide large diagnostic equipment, Brake Specialists are expected to provide their own tools; many experienced workers have invested thousands of dollars in their own equipment. Some formal training programs have alliances with tool manufacturers that help entry-level technicians accumulate tools during their training period.

Salaries

Average hourly earnings of Brake Specialists (including commission) range between $10 and $19 an hour. The lowest 10 percent may earn less than $8, and the highest 10 percent earn more than $24 an hour. On average, Brake Specialists working for new and used car dealers earn an average of $17 an hour. Employees at auto and home supply stores or national franchises earn less (about $12.35). The average annual salary for a Brake Specialist is about $32,620; entry-level specialists earn an average of $25,018.

Employment Prospects

Opportunities should be very good for Brake Specialists with excellent diagnostic and problem-solving skills and solid knowledge of electronics and mathematics, according to the Bureau of Labor Statistics. While job opportunities are expected to be very good for those who complete automotive training programs in high school, vocational and technical schools, or community colleges, people without formal automotive training are likely to face stiff competition for entry-level jobs.

Most jobs will be found in car dealerships and national franchise brake repair shops; most Brake Specialists can expect steady work, because changes in general economic conditions and developments in other industries have little effect on the car repair business.

Advancement Prospects

Beginners usually start as trainee Brake Specialists or mechanics' helpers, and gradually acquire skills by working with experienced technicians. They may learn their jobs in considerably less time than other types of auto technician specialists because they do not need a complete knowledge of automotive repair in order to fix brakes.

Experienced Brake Specialists with leadership ability may advance to shop supervisor; those who work well with customers may become service estimators or service managers. Some with solid financial backing may open their own independent repair shops.

Education and Training

Employers today often require a high school diploma plus postsecondary training; courses in brake repair, general automotive repair, electronics, physics, chemistry, English, computers, and mathematics provide a good educational background. While some Brake Specialists still learn the trade by serving as an apprentice, many others attend a formal training program in high school or postsecondary vocational school.

Education continues on the job; employers send Brake Specialists to manufacturer training centers to learn how to repair new products or to receive special training in the repair of components. Car dealers also may send promising beginners to manufacturer-sponsored mechanic training programs.

Special Requirements

Voluntary certification by the National Institute of Automotive Service Excellence (ASE) has become a standard credential for Brake Specialists who pass the relevant ASE certification test and have at least two years of experience in brake repair. Completion of an automotive training program in high school, vocational or trade school, or community or junior college may be substituted for one year of experience. Specialists must retake each examination at least every five years to maintain their certification.

Experience, Skills, and Personality Traits

Brake Specialists should have mechanical aptitude, strong analytical abilities, and an understanding of how brake systems work, in addition to good reading, mathematics, and computer skills. Persistence and attention to detail are important.

Brake Specialists usually work indoors in clean, well-ventilated, well-lit repair shops, but some shops are drafty and noisy, so a high tolerance to noisy, dirty environments is important. Although specialists can fix some problems with simple adjustments, they often work with dirty and greasy parts or in awkward positions, lifting heavy parts and tools. Minor cuts, burns, and bruises are common, but specialists usually avoid serious accidents when the shop is kept clean and orderly and safety practices are observed.

Many Brake Specialists can expect to work more than 40 hours a week; many of those working longer hours are self-employed. To satisfy customer service needs, some service shops offer evening and weekend service.

Unions and Associations

A few Brake Specialists are members of labor unions such as the International Association of Machinists and Aerospace Workers; the International Union, United Automobile, Aerospace and Agricultural Implement Workers of America; the Sheet Metal Workers' International Association; and the International Brotherhood of Teamsters.

Tips for Entry

1. Hands-on experience is important; try to improve your skills by working on your own cars and by taking every relevant course available during high school or vocational school.
2. An internship or summer job at a dealer, repair shop, or service station can provide invaluable experience.
3. Check Web sites of local dealers to spot job openings.

4. Check classified ads at the Service Technicians Society Web site: www.sts.sae.org/misc/classified.htm.

5. Positions should be advertised in the newspaper classified ad section under "trades: mechanical" or "auto."

6. Send your résumé and a cover letter to all the local dealers in your area. Because there is always a demand for well-trained Brake Specialists, you may get called for an interview even if the job hasn't been advertised in the paper.

7. If you graduated from vocational or postsecondary school, find out if the school has a job placement service and work with them to get a job.

AUTOMOTIVE PAINTER

CAREER PROFILE

Duties: Refinish and repaint old and damaged cars, trucks, and buses in automotive body repair and paint shops

Alternate Title(s): None

Salary Range: $9.70 to $26.48 per hour

Employment Prospects: Excellent

Advancement Prospects: Good

Best Geographical Location(s): All locations throughout the country have job possibilities for well-trained, experienced Automotive Painters

Prerequisites:

Education or Training—High school diploma or post-secondary vocational school training program

Experience—Painting, car body repair work helpful

Special Skills and Personality Traits—Attention to detail, good sense of color

CAREER LADDER

```
┌──────────────────────────────┐
│     Shop Supervisor          │
│   or Self-Employment         │
└──────────────────────────────┘

┌──────────────────────────────┐
│     Automotive Painter       │
└──────────────────────────────┘

┌──────────────────────────────┐
│  Apprentice Automotive Painters │
└──────────────────────────────┘
```

Position Description

Automotive Painters refinish and repaint old and damaged cars, trucks, and buses in automotive body repair and paint shops. They are among the most highly skilled manual spray operators because they perform intricate, detailed work and mix paints to match the original color, a task that is especially difficult if the color has faded. They may work for auto body repair shops, car manufacturers, or car dealers.

To prepare a vehicle for painting, painters or their helpers prepare the car's surface, removing mirrors and trim and applying tape, plastic, or paper to surfaces that should not be painted (such as chrome trim, headlights, windows, and mirrors).

Next, they apply solvents to remove grease and dirt from the surfaces to be painted. Then they use power sanders and sandpaper to remove the original paint or rust, and then fill small dents and scratches with body filler.

They set up portable ventilators and exhaust units to remove the fumes from the painting area, setting up ladders and scaffolds to work on larger cars. Depending on the job, Automotive Painters may need to mix paints. Some customers request custom color; others need only part of the car painted, but need a custom paint because their existing paint is faded.

When the paint is chosen or mixed, painters choose the correct spray guns for the primers, paints, and sealers they will apply.

Using a spray gun to apply several coats of paint, the Automotive Painters apply lacquer, enamel, or water-based primers to cars with metal bodies, and flexible primers to newer cars with plastic body parts. Controlling the spray gun by hand, they apply successive coats until the finish of the repaired sections of the vehicle matches that of the original undamaged portions. To speed drying between coats, they may place the freshly painted vehicle under heat lamps or in a special infrared oven.

After each coat of primer dries, they sand the surface to remove any flaws and to improve the bond of the next coat. If there are blisters or streaks, Automotive Painters investigate the cause: They may need to thin the paint or adjust the spray nozzle to get the proper flow and thickness. Between coats of paint, painters may move cars to infrared ovens to speed the drying process or put heat lamps around the vehicles. Regardless of how they dry the paint, painters set and change the controls on the heating and exhaust units. Final sanding of the primers may be done by hand with a fine grade of sandpaper.

A sealer then is applied and allowed to dry, followed by the final topcoat. When lacquer is used, painters or their helpers usually polish the finished surface after the final coat has dried.

Some tasks require Automotive Painters to use paintbrushes instead of paint sprayers. For example, some areas cannot be reached with spray guns, and some lettering or designs may require hand painting. Other designs and logos are stenciled on. To apply any lettering or design, painters must carefully measure where the information will go. They may also need to read a blueprint to determine the proper location of the item.

Automotive Painters must maintain their equipment and work areas. They take apart sprayers and power equipment to clean and maintain them, and clean their hand tools with solvents, wire brushes, and cloths. In addition, painters clean their work areas to control dust particles that can settle on fresh paint.

Automotive Painters typically work indoors and may be exposed to dangerous fumes from paint and coating solutions. Although painting usually is done in special ventilated booths, many operators wear masks or respirators that cover their noses and mouths. In addition, the Clean Air Act of 1990 regulates emissions of volatile organic compounds from paints and other chemicals, which has led to increasing use of more sophisticated paint booths and fresh air systems that provide a safer work environment.

Automotive Painters have to stand for long periods of time and, when using a spray gun, they may have to bend, stoop, or crouch in uncomfortable positions to reach different parts of the article. Most painters work a normal 40-hour week, but self-employed Automotive Painters sometimes work more than 50 hours a week, depending on the number of vehicles customers want repainted.

Salaries

Average hourly earnings of Automotive Painters range from $9.70 to $26.48 an hour. Average hourly earnings of Automotive Painters is $15.86 in car repair shops and $23.23 in auto manufacturing.

Many Automotive Painters hired by car dealers and independent automotive repair shops receive a commission based on the labor cost charged to the customer. Under this method, earnings depend largely on the amount of work a painter does and how fast it is completed. Employers frequently guarantee commissioned painters a minimum weekly salary.

Helpers and trainees usually receive an hourly rate until they become sufficiently skilled to work on commission. Trucking companies, bus lines, and other organizations that repair and refinish their own cars usually pay by the hour.

Employment Prospects

Because the detailed work of refinishing cars in collision repair shops and car dealerships does not lend itself to automation, Automotive Painters who work in these places are expected to experience slightly faster growth than other professions. As the demand for refinishing continues to grow, slower productivity growth among these workers will lead to employment increases more in line with the growing demand for their services.

Automotive Painters can expect relatively steady work because cars damaged in accidents require repair and refinishing regardless of the state of the economy.

Advancement Prospects

Most painting and coating workers acquire their skills on the job, usually by watching and helping other experienced workers. Most transportation equipment painters start as helpers and gain their skills informally on the job. Becoming skilled in all aspects of automotive painting usually requires a year or two of on-the-job training.

Beginning helpers usually remove trim, clean, and sand surfaces to be painted, mask surfaces that they do not want painted, and polish finished work. As helpers gain experience, they progress to more complicated tasks, such as mixing paint to achieve a good match and using spray guns to apply primer coats or final coats to small areas.

For most Automotive Painters, advancement often comes in the form of higher wages as they gain experience and skills. Some experienced painters open their own paint shops. Experienced painters with leadership ability may become team leaders or supervisors. Those who acquire practical experience or college or other formal training may become sales or technical representatives for chemical or paint companies.

Education and Training

Most employers require applicants to have a high school degree or GED. Employers also prefer applicants who have taken courses in car painting. High school students interested in this occupation should take art classes, which may help students develop a good eye for color. Shop classes (especially auto body repair) also would be helpful.

Most Automotive Painters learn their skills on the job, beginning as helpers to experienced painters who help with simpler tasks, such as removing trim and sanding. As they gain experience and skill, trainees take on more complicated tasks, such as mixing and matching paints. It usually takes one to two years of on-the-job training to become a skilled car painter.

Some employers sponsor training programs to help their workers become more productive. This training is available from manufacturers of chemicals, paints, or equipment, or from other private sources, and may include safety and quality tips and knowledge of products, equipment, and general business practices. Some Automotive Painters are sent to technical schools to learn the intricacies of mixing and applying different types of paint.

Special Requirements

Voluntary certification by the National Institute for Automotive Service Excellence (ASE) is recognized as the standard of achievement for Automotive Painters. Painters can be certified in painting and refinishing as part of the Collision Repair and Refinishing Series of ASE tests by passing a written examination and have at least two years of experience in the field. High school, trade or vocational school, or community or junior college training in automotive painting and refinishing may substitute for up to one year of experience. To retain certification, Automotive Painters retake the exam at least every five years.

Experience, Skills, and Personality Traits
Automotive Painters should have keen eyesight, a good sense of color, attention to detail, and good eye-hand coordination. Employers look for painters who have an ability to do careful, precise work.

Unions and Associations
Many Automotive Painters belong to unions including the International Brotherhood of Painters and Allied Trades the Sheet Metal Workers International Association, or the International Brotherhood of Teamsters.

Tips for Entry
1. An internship or summer job at a dealer, auto body repair shop, or other work involving spray painting, can provide invaluable experience.
2. Check Web sites of local dealers and repair shops to spot job openings.
3. Check classifieds at the Service Technicians Society jobsite: www.sts.sae.org/misc/classified.htm.
4. Positions should be advertised in the newspaper classified ad section under "trades: mechanical" or "auto."
5. Send your résumé and a cover letter to all the local dealers and repair shops in your area.
6. If you graduated from vocational or postsecondary school, find out if the school has a job placement service and work with them to land a position.

TIRE REPAIRER

CAREER PROFILE

Duties: Repairs tires of motor vehicles

Alternate Title(s): Tire Technician

Salary Range: $7.28 to $15.25 per hour

Employment Prospects: Good

Advancement Prospects: Good

Best Geographical Location(s): All locations throughout the country have job possibilities for experienced Tire Repairers

Prerequisites:

Education or Training—High school diploma

Experience—Experience working on cars is helpful

Special Skills and Personality Traits—Hard-working; able to pay attention to details

CAREER LADDER

```
┌─────────────────────────────┐
│       Auto Technician        │
└─────────────────────────────┘

┌─────────────────────────────┐
│        Tire Repairer         │
└─────────────────────────────┘

┌─────────────────────────────┐
│         Entry Level          │
└─────────────────────────────┘
```

Position Description

A Tire Repairer fixes damaged tires of cars, buses, trucks, and other automotive vehicles by raising the vehicle, removing the wheel, and locating and fixing the problem with the tire. He or she may rotate tires to different positions on the vehicle, using a tire changing machine, hand tools, and tire balancing machine. Using a hydraulic jack, the Tire Repairer unbolts the wheel, using a lug wrench, and removes the wheel from the vehicle by hand. When repairing giant tires of heavy equipment, the Tire Repairer uses a power hoist. The Tire Repairer locates a puncture in a tubeless tire by visual inspection or by immersing the inflated tire in a water bath and watching for air bubbles to appear from the puncture.

The Tire Repairer then seals the puncture in a tubeless tire by inserting adhesive material and expanding the rubber plug into the puncture, using hand tools. Alternatively, he or she may dismount the tire and use an internal patch.

The Tire Repairer separates a tubed tire from the wheel, using a rubber mallet and metal bar or mechanical tire changer. Then, the Tire Repairer removes the inner tube from the tire and inspects the tire casing for defects, such as holes and tears. Next, the repairer glues a tire patch over the rupture in the tire casing, using rubber cement. The repairer inflates the inner tube and immerses it in water to locate a leak, buffs the defective area of the inner tube, using a scraper, and

patches the tube with an adhesive rubber patch or seals a rubber patch to the tube, using a hot vulcanizing plate.

The Tire Repairer then reassembles the tire onto the wheel, and places the wheel on a balancing machine to determine the counterweights required to balance the wheel. After mounting the required counterweights onto the rim of the wheel, the repairer cleans the sides of white wall tires and remounts the wheel onto the vehicle.

Tire Repairers also may respond to emergency calls to make repairs or replacements of damaged tires at a customer's home or on the road.

A Tire Repairer may be designated according to a specialty, such as a giant-tire repairer/changer or road service tire changer.

Salaries

Starting salaries usually are about $8,840 to $15,140 per year. Salaries may vary according to location and individual ability. Average pay ranges from $10.02 to $10.72 an hour. The lowest 10 percent earn $7.28 per hour; the highest 10 percent earn $15.25. Top-paying states are Michigan (average $14.04/hour), New York ($13.08), and New Jersey ($13).

Employment Prospects

Employment of these workers is expected to grow more slowly than the average through 2012, according to the U.S.

Bureau of Labor Statistics. Tire Repairers work in tire franchises (such as Goodyear) or in stores that specialize in selling and servicing tires (such as Sears).

Advancement Prospects

Tire Repairers may advance by getting a job in a larger dealer or franchise, or—after obtaining specialized education in auto mechanics—by becoming an auto technician.

Education and Training

There are no special educational requirements needed, since training takes place on the job.

Experience, Skills, and Personality Traits

Tire Repairers must be willing to work all hours and in any type of weather, although workers employed by large franchises typically work indoors. Tire Repairers should be hard workers with good attention to detail. The work is physically demanding.

Unions and Associations

A few Tire Repairers may belong to labor unions such as the International Union, United Automobile, Aerospace and Agricultural Implement Workers of America or the International Brotherhood of Teamsters. They may belong to other associations, such as the National Institute for Automotive Service Excellence and the Automotive Service Association.

Tips for Entry

1. Hands-on experience is important; try to improve your skills by working on your own cars, and by taking every relevant course available during high school or vocational school.
2. An internship or summer job at a dealer, tire repair shop, or service station can provide invaluable experience.
3. Check Web sites of local tire repair shops or car dealers to spot job openings.
4. Positions should be advertised in the newspaper classified ad section under "trades: mechanical" or "auto."
5. Send your résumé and a cover letter to all the local dealers and tire repair shops in your area.

AUTO UPHOLSTERER

CAREER PROFILE

Duties: Repair or replace damaged upholstery in cars

Alternate Title(s): None

Salary Range: $16,610 to $26,590

Employment Prospects: Excellent

Advancement Prospects: Excellent

Best Geographical Location(s): All locations throughout the country have job possibilities for experienced Auto Upholsterers

Prerequisites:

Education or Training—Most Auto Upholsterers get on-the-job training

Experience—Any previous work in furniture repair or upholstery is helpful

Special Skills and Personality Traits—Patience and attention to detail; willingness to work hard; neatness and dependability

CAREER LADDER

```
┌─────────────────────────┐
│     Self-Employed        │
│    Auto Upholsterer      │
└─────────────────────────┘

┌─────────────────────────┐
│     Auto Upholsterer     │
└─────────────────────────┘

┌─────────────────────────┐
│  Apprentice Auto Upholsterer  │
└─────────────────────────┘
```

Position Description

Auto Upholsterers repair or replace damaged upholstery in vehicles, fitting and repairing upholstery and trim in cars, buses, vans, and trucks. They may work on seat covers, door panels, headliners, floor covers, convertible tops, and other types of upholstery.

To upholster an automobile, Auto Upholsterers begin by measuring, marking, and cutting the material, following patterns or designs. Then, they sew the materials together with heavy-duty sewing machines, and fit the material into place using staples, tacks, and glue.

Upholsterers use many different types of tools in their work. These include hand tools such as shears, knives, screwdrivers, pliers, wrenches, tack hammers, mallets, and measuring tapes, and a variety of power tools including heavy-duty sewing machines, air-powered staplers and wrenches, and electric steaming machines.

Most Upholsterers work in small independently-owned auto upholstery shops; a few work in upholstery franchises.

Salaries

Salaries for this position depend on experience and location, but in general a beginning apprentice Auto Upholsterer can expect to start at about $16,610 to $20,800 annually; an experienced Auto Upholsterer can expect to earn from $21,690 to $26,590 a year.

Employment Prospects

An increase in jobs is expected through the year 2010 as Auto Upholsterers leave the profession for other jobs or retire.

Advancement Prospects

Experienced Auto Upholsterers who have leadership ability may advance to shop supervisor. Others with independence and self-discipline—and sufficient funds—may open independent upholster shops.

Education and Training

Most employers prefer hiring Auto Upholsterers who are high school graduates; they are expected to be able to read, write, and do minor mathematical calculations. High school students should prepare for a career in auto upholstery by taking courses in auto mechanics, mathematics, marketing, and related vocational courses. Most Auto Upholsterers also are given on-the-job training.

Experience, Skills, and Personality Traits

Any previous work in furniture repair or furniture upholstery is good preparatory experience for working with upholstery in cars. Auto Upholsterers need to be flexible and tolerant; they usually work a standard 40-hour week but may be required to work on Saturdays, in noisy and dirty conditions.

Unions and Associations

A few Auto Upholsterers may belong to labor unions such as the International Union, United Automobile, Aerospace and Agricultural Implement Workers of America or the International Brotherhood of Teamsters. They may belong to other associations, such as the National Institute for Automotive Service Excellence, the Automotive Aftermarket Industry Association (AAIA), and the Automotive Service Association.

Tips for Entry

1. Hands-on experience is important; try to improve your skills by working on your own cars, and by taking every relevant course available during high school or vocational school.
2. An internship or summer job at an upholstery shop or upholstery franchise can provide invaluable experience.
3. Check Web sites of local dealers to spot job openings.
4. Upholsterer positions should be advertised in the newspaper classified ad section under "trades: mechanical" or "auto."
5. Send your résumé and a cover letter to all the local upholstery shops and franchises in your area. Because there is always a demand for well-trained Auto Upholsterers, you may get called for an interview even if the job hasn't been advertised in the paper.
6. If you graduated from vocational or postsecondary school, find out if the school has a job placement service and work with them to get a job.

AUTO BODY CUSTOMIZER

CAREER PROFILE

Duties: Install custom equipment and trim that alter the appearance of automobiles

Alternative Title(s): None

Salary Range: $10.49 to $27.10 an hour

Employment Prospects: Good

Advancement Prospects: Good

Best Geographical Location(s): All locations throughout the country have job possibilities for well-trained, experienced Auto Body Customizers

Prerequisites:

Education or Training—A high school diploma is generally required; postsecondary vocational school training programs may be helpful

Experience—Experience in car repairs is helpful

Special Skills and Personality Traits—Patience; artistic ability; attention to detail; good eye-hand coordination

CAREER LADDER

```
┌─────────────────────────────┐
│      Self-Employed          │
│   Auto Body Customizer      │
└─────────────────────────────┘

┌─────────────────────────────┐
│    Auto Body Customizer     │
└─────────────────────────────┘

┌─────────────────────────────┐
│ Auto Body Customizer Apprentice │
└─────────────────────────────┘
```

Position Description

Auto Body Customizers combine skill at bodywork and other mechanics with artistic flair. In fact, some of the most famous customizers are also well known for their artwork. They use paints, wheels, spoilers, seats, body style changes, stereos, and other accessories and alterations to make the ordinary car extraordinary. They might install custom equipment and trim to change a car's appearance to customers' specifications, using both hand and power tools in their work.

Using their broad knowledge of automotive construction and repair techniques, Automotive Body Customizers must develop appropriate methods for each job. In order to do their work, customizers may read specifications to determine desired modifications; cut openings in car bodies to install customized windows; and measure and mark vinyl materials for customized roof installation. They also may cut, bend, and apply decorative trims; paint car bodies in specialized ways; or install window tintings.

Customized body work is challenging and varied. Using their broad knowledge of automotive construction techniques, Auto Body Customizers must develop appropriate

methods for each job. They usually work alone, with only general directions from supervisors, although in some shops, apprentices help experienced customizers.

Customizers face some tough challenges along the way. Clients either know exactly what they want their car to look like (although sometimes this might be unrealistic)—or they aren't sure. Either way, customizers say they spend almost as much time talking to the customer as they do working on the car.

Customizers need a broad range of general knowledge about paint colors and how to best coat different surfaces, as well as an idea of vehicle design and construction.

Customizers work indoors in shops that can be noisy and dirty, although most custom shops are clean and well ventilated. Customizers usually work a standard 40-hour week, although those who are self-employed may work 60 or more hours.

Salaries

Most Auto Body Customizers who work for dealers are paid a set amount for various custom jobs; earnings depend on the amount of work assigned and how fast the customizer can complete it, although employers often offer a guaranteed weekly minimum. Apprentices usually earn about half what an experienced customizer does and at an hourly rate, until they are skilled enough to be paid on an incentive basis. Customizer rates range from a low of $10.49 an hour to a high of $27.10, depending on the worker's experience and the location of the company.

Employment Prospects

Most Auto Body Customizers either work for car dealers or go into business for themselves (about one in eight are self-employed). Employment of Auto Body Customizers is expected to increase about as rapidly as the average for all occupations through the year 2012, according to the U.S. Bureau of Labor Statistics. Opportunities should be best for persons with formal training in car body repair and mechanics.

Advancement Prospects

Auto Body Customizers usually work alone, with only general directions from supervisors. Customizers usually begin as a helper or apprentice to a customizer, eventually learning the trade until they are capable of working on their own projects, moving on to a bigger shop, or going out on their own and starting their own auto custom shop.

Education and Training

Most employers prefer hiring persons who have completed high school. Formal training is desirable in addition to on-the-job training, because advances in technology have changed the structure, components, and materials used in automobile customizing. A fully skilled Auto Body Customizer must have good reading, mathematics, and computer skills to follow instructions and diagrams in print and computer-based technical manuals.

Apprenticeships and trade school programs for customizers are gaining popularity as well. Dozens of schools in North America offer two-year, one-year, or eight-month courses in auto body and mechanical studies. Some customizers also study painting or art.

Because car parts and body materials continue to become more complex and technologically advanced, customizers must continue to gain new skills, read technical manuals, and attend seminars and classes to remain competitive.

Experience, Skills, and Personality Traits

Auto Body Customizers have an artistic and creative interest in form and color as well as a love for cars. In addition, customizers must be patient, with meticulous work standards; pay great attention to detail; be able to work independently; and have good eye-hand coordination. Those who are self-employed must have the discipline to run their own businesses and be able to deal effectively with customers.

Unions and Associations

Some Auto Body Customizers may join a union, such as the International Association of Machinists and Aerospace Workers; the International Union, United Automobile, Aerospace and Agricultural Implement Workers of America; the Sheet Metal Workers' International Association; and the International Brotherhood of Teamsters. Most Auto Body Customizers who are union members work for large car dealers.

Tips for Entry

1. Hands-on experience is important; try to improve your skills by working on your own cars, and by taking every relevant course available during high school or vocational school.
2. An internship or summer job at a dealer, repair shop, or service station can provide invaluable experience.
3. Check Web sites of local dealers to spot job openings.
4. Positions should be advertised in the newspaper classified ad section under "trades: mechanical" or "auto."
5. Send your résumé and a cover letter to all the local dealers in your area. Because there is always a demand for well-trained Auto Body Customizers, you may get called for an interview even if the job hasn't been advertised in the paper.
6. If you graduated from vocational or postsecondary school, find out if the school has a job placement service and work with them to get a job.

RADIATOR REPAIRER

CAREER PROFILE

Duties: Repair and service cooling systems and associated components

Alternate Title(s): None

Salary Range: $33,280 to $57,000+

Employment Prospects: Good

Advancement Prospects: Good

Best Geographical Location(s): All locations throughout the country have job possibilities for experienced radiator repairers

Prerequisites:

Education or Training—A high school education with courses as well in automotive repair

Experience—Experience in car repairs (especially radiator repairs) is helpful

Special Skills and Personality Traits—Attention to detail; mechanical ability; good mathematics and computer skills

Licensure/Certification—Voluntary certification in the heating and air-conditioning test given by the National Institute for Automotive Service Excellence (ASE)

CAREER LADDER

```
┌─────────────────────────────────────┐
│   Self-Employed Automotive Heating,  │
│      Cooling Systems Specialist      │
└─────────────────────────────────────┘

┌─────────────────────────────────────┐
│           Auto Technician            │
└─────────────────────────────────────┘

┌─────────────────────────────────────┐
│          Radiator Repairer           │
└─────────────────────────────────────┘

┌─────────────────────────────────────┐
│     Radiator Repairer Apprentice     │
└─────────────────────────────────────┘
```

Position Description

Radiator Repairers repair and service cooling systems and associated components and carry out welding, soldering, thermal cutting, and thermal heating procedures. They test radiators for obstructions or leaks and make repairs as necessary, modifying and repairing plastic and aluminum tank radiators, pumping water or compressed air through the unit and flushing it with cleaning solvents to remove blockages such as rust or mineral deposits. They may remove and clean the radiator core by inserting a rod or submerging it in a solvent.

Radiator Repairers clean radiators with caustic solutions, locate and solder leaks using a soldering iron or acetylene torch, and install new radiator cores or complete replacement radiators. They also repair heaters and air conditioners, solder leaks in gasoline tanks, and may repair or replace other units in the cooling system, including faulty water pumps, hoses, thermostats, and leaky head gaskets.

Salaries

The salary for Radiator Repairers ranges from $33,280 for entry-level jobs to more than $57,000. Most Radiator Repairers work a standard 40-hour week, although some who own their own repair businesses work longer hours. More and more radiator repair shops have expanded their hours as a convenience to customers. Those repairers who work for firms providing service around the clock may work evenings, nights, and weekends; these repairers usually receive a higher rate of pay for working nontraditional hours.

Employment Prospects

Radiator Repairers primarily work for small specialist radiator repair firms, although a few also find employment with larger car dealers. Repairers with experience rebuilding passenger, commercial, and industrial radiators, including aluminum, metal, copper, and plastic radiators have the best chance of employment.

Advancement Prospects

With additional training, experienced Radiator Repairers with leadership ability may move into positions as automotive technician or shop supervisor. Those who work well with customers may become repair service estimators or service managers. Radiator Repairers who have the ability and funds may go into business for themselves, opening their own radiator repair businesses.

Education and Training

Because new cars can be so complex, most employers require a high school diploma. Courses in automotive repair, electronics, physics, chemistry, English, computers, and mathematics provide a good educational background for a career as a Radiator Repairer. Although it takes five to seven years to become a fully trained automotive technician, automotive Radiator Repairers, who do not need an all-round knowledge of automotive repair, may learn their jobs in considerably less time.

Special Requirements

Radiator Repairers can obtain voluntary certification by Automotive Service Excellence (ASE) in heating and air-conditioning, one of eight tests offered by ASE. For certification in the air-conditioning area, the repairer must have at least two years of experience and pass a written examination. Completion of an automotive mechanic program in high school, vocational or trade school, or community or junior college may be substituted for one year of experience. Radiator Repairers must retake the examination at least every five years to maintain their certification.

Experience, Skills, and Personality Traits

Radiator Repairers should be interested in practical and manual work and be good with their hands and possess mechanical aptitude and good reading, mathematics, and computer skills. Radiator Repairers usually work in clean, well-ventilated repair shops, but because some shops are noisy, the ability to work in noisy environments is important.

Unions and Associations

A few Radiator Repairers may belong to labor unions such as the International Union, United Automobile, Aerospace and Agricultural Implement Workers of America or the International Brotherhood of Teamsters. They may belong to other associations, such as the National Institute for Automotive Service Excellence, the Service Technicians' Society, the International Automotive Technicians' Network, the Mobile Air Conditioning Society Worldwide, the National Automotive Technicians Education Foundation, and the Automotive Service Association.

Tips for Entry

1. Hands-on experience is important; try to improve your skills by working on your own cars, and by taking every relevant course available during high school or vocational school.
2. An internship or summer job at a dealer, radiator repair shop, or service station can provide invaluable experience.
3. Check Web sites of local radiator repair shops or car dealers to spot job openings.
4. Positions should be advertised in the newspaper classified ad section under "trades: mechanical" or "auto."
5. Send your résumé and a cover letter to all the local dealers and radiator repair shops in your area.

AUTOMOTIVE ELECTRICIAN

CAREER PROFILE

Duties: Install, maintain, identify faults, and repair electrical wiring and computer-based equipment in vehicles

Alternate Title(s): Automotive Electrical Fitter, Automotive Electrical Mechanic

Salary Range: $8.49 to $20.41 per hour

Employment Prospects: Good

Advancement Prospects: Good

Best Geographical Location(s): All locations throughout the country have job possibilities for experienced Automotive Electricians

Prerequisites:

   Education or Training—High school diploma required; technical college, community college, or manufacturer-supported training program in auto electronics helpful

   Experience—Electrical, electronics, or mechanical work; computer work and any work involving vehicles; experience as auto technician also helpful

   Special Skills and Personality Traits—A sound electrical background and attention to detail

CAREER LADDER

```
┌─────────────────────────────┐
│   Automotive Electrician    │
│      Project Manager        │
└─────────────────────────────┘

┌─────────────────────────────┐
│   Automotive Electrician    │
└─────────────────────────────┘

┌─────────────────────────────┐
│ Automotive Electrician Assistant │
└─────────────────────────────┘
```

Position Description

Automotive Electricians install, maintain, identify faults in, and repair electrical wiring and computer-based equipment in cars and related equipment such as caravans, trailers, earthmoving equipment, mining equipment, and agricultural equipment. They work with computer-controlled engine management systems and service, identify, and repair faults on electronically-controlled car systems (such as electronic fuel injection, electronic ignition, antilock braking, cruise control, automatic transmission, air bags, and air conditioning).

Automotive Electricians also install electrical equipment such as gauges, lighting, alternators, and starter motors in cars, and install electrically operated accessories such as radios, heating equipment, air conditioners, driving lamps, and antitheft systems.

During the course of their day, they may use meters, test instruments and circuit diagrams to find electrical faults, adjust engine control systems and timing to make sure vehicles are running at peak performance. They may test, recondition, and replace faulty alternators, generators, starter motors, and related items such as voltage regulators and batteries, and repair or replace faulty ignition systems, electrical wiring, fuses, lamps, and switches. They may work on complex electronic systems, such as engine management systems, ABS brakes, airbags, and electronically controlled gearboxes.

Automotive Electricians may use hand tools and specialized electrical tools, instruments, and machines (including drills, grinders, presses, and lathes). They may solder or weld when repairing electrical parts; sell and install electrical parts and accessories; and install, repair, and service air-conditioning systems.

Automotive Electricians may work in specialized automotive electrical workshops, vehicle dealerships, and service stations. They usually work indoors, although some travel in order to work on vehicles. Their work areas need to be clean because the components they work with are sensitive;

however, because they work with vehicles, conditions can be dirty and noisy at times.

Salaries

Pay varies, but Automotive Electricians usually earn between $8.49 and $20.41 per hour. A fully qualified Automotive Electrician typically starts at about $14 per hour. Top-paying states include Louisiana (average $17.39/hour), Kentucky ($17.10), and Missouri ($16.57).

Employment Prospects

Most Automotive Electricians either work for car dealers or go into business for themselves. Employment of Automotive Electricians is expected to grow faster than the average for all occupations through the year 2012, according to the U.S. Bureau of Labor Statistics. Opportunities should be best for persons with formal training in auto electronics.

Advancement Prospects

Experienced Automotive Electricians who have leadership ability may advance to shop supervisor, or they may open their own shop dedicated to auto electrical repairs.

Education and Training

Automotive Electricians should have training in basic engineering, automotive electronics, electrical theory and circuit diagrams, and the basic mechanics of vehicles. Automotive Electricians may also attend training courses on particular vehicles and new equipment.

Special Requirements

Automotive Electricians can obtain voluntary certification by Automotive Service Excellence (ASE) in automobile electrical systems, one of eight tests offered by ASE. For certification in this area, Automotive Electricians must have at least two years of experience and pass a written examination. Completion of an automotive mechanic program in high school, vocational or trade school, or community or junior college may be substituted for one year of experience. Automotive Electricians must retake the examination at least every five years to maintain their certification.

Experience, Skills, and Personality Traits

Useful experience for Automotive Electricians includes electrical or mechanical work, computer work, and any work involving vehicles. Automotive Electricians should be interested in practical and manual work, have normal eyesight and color vision, good hand coordination, technical aptitude and good problem-solving skills, an eye for detail, and be able to approach work in a systematic and thorough way. They also need to have organizational ability, computer skills, and communication skills, and they need to be skilled at working with small, delicate components. Although they usually work alone, they interact with a wide range of people including clients, other Automotive Electricians, and different automotive professionals.

Unions and Associations

A few Automotive Electricians may belong to labor unions such as the International Union, United Automobile, Aerospace and Agricultural Implement Workers of America or the International Brotherhood of Teamsters. They may belong to other associations, such as the National Institute for Automotive Service Excellence, the Institute of Electrical and Electronics Engineers, the Service Technicians' Society, the International Automotive Technicians' Network, the National Automotive Technicians Education Foundation, and the Automotive Service Association.

Tips for Entry

1. Hands-on experience is important; try to improve your skills by working on your own cars, and by taking every relevant course available during high school or vocational school. Courses in electronics may be helpful.
2. An internship or summer job at a dealer, auto electronics repair shop, or service station can provide invaluable experience.
3. Check Web sites of local electronics repair shops or car dealers to spot job openings.
4. Positions should be advertised in the newspaper classified ad section under "trades: mechanical" or "auto."
5. Send your résumé and a cover letter to all the local dealers and repair shops in your area.

REPAIR SHOP FRANCHISE OWNER

CAREER PROFILE

Duties: Run the repair shop franchise; oversee employees; plan and run business

Alternate Title(s): Franchisee

Employment Prospects: Excellent

Advancement Prospects: Good

Best Geographical Location(s): Populated areas near larger cities are typically the best locations for auto-related franchises

Prerequisites:

Education or Training—College education in business and/or a business background is the best training for an auto-related franchise business

Experience—Experience working with cars, plus experience in business or selling

Special Skills and Personality Traits—Willingness to work hard; ability to get along well with people; ability to motivate employees; sales ability

CAREER LADDER

```
┌─────────────────────────────┐
│   Franchise Owner of        │
│   Larger Repair Shop        │
└─────────────────────────────┘

┌─────────────────────────────┐
│   Repair Shop Franchise Owner │
└─────────────────────────────┘

┌─────────────────────────────┐
│   Repair Shop General Manager │
└─────────────────────────────┘
```

Position Description

The Repair Shop Franchise Owner buys a repair franchise (such as MAACO or Midas Muffler) as an already functioning business system. While entrepreneurs must have millions of dollars to set up a profitable business, a franchisee can step into an already established concept, with much less risk of failure. (This is important, since as many as 80 percent of new business start-ups fail each year.)

Franchising gives entrepreneurs who are interested in self-employment a strategic partnership governed by a contract or franchise agreement for a defined period of time. A person who buys a franchise is investing in a proven and refined system with a brand name, a successful operating system, and a history of quality service and success.

The common goal for the franchisor and the franchisee is to dominate a particular market and keep customers coming back. All franchisees of a particular auto-related franchise system share the responsibility of maintaining high standards of quality, consistency, convenience, and other factors that contribute to the success of building a dominant brand, loyal customers, and repeat business for everyone. The ultimate success of the individual franchise owner is based on the proven success of the franchisor.

Typically, the franchise provides a turn-key business opportunity including extensive training in their corporate offices and equipment, supplies, licenses, and advertising support to ensure the greatest potential for success. Most franchises will help the owner find the best site location and help inspect the site. They usually provide specifications for initial and replacement inventory, supplies, equipment, and exterior and interior signs, and provide the owner with promotional and initial advertising for the center's opening.

Salaries

Few financial investments can compete with the potential income and personal growth of an established and reputable franchise. If the franchisor offers an established product or service with a well-recognized brand name and a history of success with company units and existing franchises, and is well financed and motivated, the chance of success is very high. Although franchising is a very tightly regulated industry, it is important that investors ask the right questions, seek the right advice, and consider all the objectives before investing in any franchise opportunity.

Although most franchisees are satisfied, successful businesspeople, some do suffer financial losses. More than nine of 10 franchise owners say they considered their franchise to be somewhat or very successful; two of three say they would not have been successful if they tried to open the same business on their own.

Employment Prospects

Prospects for operating a franchise operation are excellent, for two primary reasons. First, the increasing complexity of automotive technology means comprehensive professional service is replacing the do-it-yourself approach. Second, the number of cars and light trucks on the road is steadily rising; as consumers keep their cars for longer periods, this increases the chance that repairs and servicing will need to be made. For example, the Midas Muffler franchise maintains more than 2,700 franchised and licensed shops throughout the United States. And as traditional service options decline, the market for automotive franchises increases.

Advancement Prospects

Owning and operating a repair shop is considered the peak of this branch of the automotive industry, so opportunities for advancement are limited. Repair Shop Franchise Owners may improve their business by owning and operating additional repair shops in various locations, by increasing the quantity of their business, by securing repeat customers through good service, or by taking on more difficult and expensive repairs. Basically, the repair shop owner may advance with the continued success and growth of the business.

Education and Training

Most franchises provide the owners with copies of the operating manual and related training and operational materials during the initial training program. They often offer specialized marketing/operation systems and provide the best and most complete professional training. Once the repair shop is running, most franchises will provide continuing advisory assistance; allocate funds for advertising and promotion; provide mandatory and suggested specifications, standards, and operating procedures; conduct evaluations and inspections of the center; and provide additional training materials and events.

Experience, Skills, and Personality Traits

Running a business requires a commitment to understanding problems, paying attention to details, and building relationships based on honesty and trust. Prospective Repair Shop Franchise Owners must be dependable, have good people skills, and have the ability and desire to be successful. Franchisees who do well really want to own their own business and be their own boss. The number of women and minority Repair Shop Franchise Owners is dramatically increasing, as is the number of young owners just out of college

Repair Shop Franchise Owners must be able to follow the franchise's established standards and rules, even if the franchise requires decisions the owner might not agree with.

Unions and Associations

Repair Shop Franchise Owners may belong to a range of organizations, including the International Franchise Organization and the American Association of Franchisees and Dealers.

Tips for Entry

1. Visit a Web site dedicated to franchising at www. automotivefranchise.com for more information.
2. Franchises are open particularly to women, who should consider contacting the Franchises for Women staff at (888) 363-3390 (or e-mail them at contactus @franchisesforwomen.com).
3. To find particular franchises for sale, visit the franchise's Web site. For example, Midas Muffler Shops maintain a list of available franchises at www. midasfran.com/opps1.html.

TRANSPORTATION

TAXI DRIVER

CAREER PROFILE

Duties: Take passengers to and from their homes, work-places, and recreational pursuits such as dining, enter-tainment, and shopping, and help out-of-town visitors get around in new surroundings

Alternate Title(s): Cab Driver

Salary Range: $6.37 to $15.51 per hour, plus tips

Employment Prospects: Excellent

Advancement Prospects: Fair

Best Geographical Location(s): Although jobs are avail-able throughout the country, most opportunities occur in large metropolitan areas

Prerequisites:

Education or Training—High school diploma, driver's license, and hack license

Experience—Extensive driving experience in all condi-tions and familiarity with local area

Special Skills and Personality Traits—Pleasant; patient; even-tempered, tolerant; dependable; responsi-ble; self-motivated

CAREER LADDER

```
┌─────────────────────────────┐
│      Taxi Dispatcher        │
│  or Taxi Company Manager    │
└─────────────────────────────┘

┌─────────────────────────────┐
│        Taxi Driver          │
└─────────────────────────────┘

┌─────────────────────────────┐
│        Entry Level          │
└─────────────────────────────┘
```

Position Description

Taxi Drivers help passengers get to and from their homes, jobs, and recreational pursuits such as dining, entertain-ment, and shopping, and help out-of-town visitors get around in new surroundings. Most Taxi Drivers are "lease drivers," paying a daily, weekly, or monthly fee to the com-pany allowing them to lease their car. The fee may also include a charge for maintenance, insurance, and a deposit on the car. Lease drivers may take their cars home with them when they are not on duty.

At the start of a driving shift, Taxi Drivers usually report to a taxicab service or garage where they are assigned a car (usually a large automobile modified for commercial passenger transport). They record their name, work date, and cab ID number on a "trip sheet," check the cab's fuel and oil levels, and make sure the lights, brakes, and windshield wipers are working. Any equipment or part not in good working order is reported to the dispatcher or company mechanic.

Taxi Drivers pick up passengers either by cruising the streets to pick up random passengers, by prearranged pickup, or from pickups at taxi stands established in busy areas such as train stations or hotels. In urban areas, most passengers hail taxis as they drive by. Drivers also pick up passengers waiting at cabstands or in taxi lines at airports, train stations, hotels, and other places where people frequently seek taxis.

Customers also may prearrange a pickup by calling a cab company and giving a location, approximate pick up time, and destination. The cab company dispatcher then relays the information to a driver by two-way radio, cellular tele-phone, or on-board computer. Outside urban areas, most trips are handled this way.

Some drivers transport individuals with special needs, such as the elderly or those with disabilities. These drivers, also known as paratransit drivers, operate specially equipped vehicles designed to accommodate a variety of needs in nonemergency situations. Although special certifi-cation is not necessary, some additional training with the equipment and passenger needs may be required.

Drivers should be familiar with streets in the areas they serve so they can use the most efficient routes to destinations. They should know the locations of frequently requested destinations, such as airports, bus and railroad terminals, convention centers, hotels, and other points of interest. In case of emergency, the driver should also know the location of fire and police stations and hospitals.

Upon reaching the destination, drivers determine the fare. In many cabs, a taximeter measures the fare based on the length of the trip and the amount of time the trip took. Drivers turn the taximeter on when passengers enter the cab and turn it off when they reach the final destination. The fare also may include a surcharge for additional passengers, a fee for handling luggage, or a drop charge (an additional fee added for the use of the cab). In other cases (in such cities as Washington, D.C.), fares are determined by a system of zones through which the taxi passes during a trip. Each zone a cab drives through is an extra fee.

Passengers usually add a tip to the fare, depending on the passengers' satisfaction with the quality and efficiency of the ride and courtesy of the driver.

Drivers issue receipts upon request, and enter onto the trip sheet all information regarding the trip, including the place and time of pick-up and drop-off and the total fee. These logs help check the driver's activity and efficiency.

Taxi Drivers sometimes must handle heavy luggage and packages. Driving for long periods can be tiring and uncomfortable, especially in densely populated urban areas. Drivers must be alert to conditions on the road, especially in heavy and congested traffic or in bad weather. Taxi Drivers also risk robbery because they work alone and often carry large amounts of cash.

Work hours of Taxi Drivers vary; some jobs offer full-time or part-time employment with fluctuating work hours. It is often necessary for drivers to report to work on short notice. Evening and weekend work are common for taxicab services. The work of Taxi Drivers is unstructured; working without supervision, they may break for a meal or a rest whenever their car is free. This occupation is attractive to individuals who need flexible work schedules, such as college and postgraduate students. Similarly, other service workers such as ambulance drivers and police officers often consider moonlighting as Taxi Drivers.

Full-time Taxi Drivers usually work one shift a day, which may last from eight to 12 hours. Part-time drivers may work half a shift each day, or work a full shift once or twice a week. Drivers may work shifts at all times of the day and night, because most taxi companies offer services 24 hours a day. Early morning and late night shifts are common. Drivers work long hours during holidays, weekends, and other special events that support heavier demand for their services. Independent drivers, however, often set their own hours and schedules.

Design improvements in newer cabs have reduced stress and increased the comfort and efficiency of drivers, and often laws require standard amenities such as air-conditioning. Modern taxicabs also may be equipped with sophisticated tracking devices, fare meters, and dispatching equipment. Satellites and tracking systems link many of these state-of-the-art vehicles with company headquarters. In a matter of seconds, dispatchers can deliver directions, traffic advisories, weather reports, and other important communications to drivers anywhere in the transporting area. The satellite link-up also allows dispatchers to track vehicle location, fuel consumption, and engine performance. Drivers can easily communicate with dispatchers to discuss delivery schedules and mechanical problems. For example, automated dispatch systems help dispatchers locate the closest driver to a customer.

When threatened with crime or violence, drivers may have special "trouble lights" to alert authorities of emergencies. Taxi Drivers meet many different types of people; dealing with rude customers and waiting for passengers requires patience. Many municipalities and taxicab companies require Taxi Drivers to wear clean and neat clothes.

Salaries

Earnings of taxi drivers vary a great deal depending on the hours, customers' tips, and other factors. Average hourly earnings of salaried Taxi Drivers, including tips, range from $9.14 to $10.22 an hour. The lowest 10 percent earn less than $6.37, and the highest 10 percent earn more than $15.51 an hour. Most self-employed taxi owner-drivers earn between $20,000 to $32,000 annually, including tips. However, professional drivers with a regular clientele often earn more. Earnings are generally higher in urban areas. Top-paying states are Connecticut (average $13.26/hour), New York ($12.26), and Washington, D.C. ($12.15).

Employment Prospects

Many job openings will occur each year as drivers transfer to other occupations or leave the labor force, although earnings, work hours, and working conditions vary depending on economic and regulatory conditions. Opportunities should be best for people with good driving records and the ability to work flexible schedules.

Employment is expected to grow faster than the average for all occupations through the year 2012, as local and suburban travel increases with population growth. Employment growth will also stem from federal legislation requiring increased services for persons with disabilities. Opportunities should be best in rapidly growing metropolitan areas.

Job opportunities can fluctuate from season to season and from month to month, with extra drivers hired during holiday seasons and peak travel and tourist times. During economic slowdowns, drivers are seldom laid off, but they may have to increase their working hours, and earnings may decline somewhat. In economic upturns, job openings are numerous as drivers leave the occupation for other opportunities.

About one-third of all Taxi Drivers work for local and suburban passenger transportation and taxicab companies. Others work for service-oriented companies such as automotive dealers, automotive rental agencies, hotels, health care facilities, and social services agencies. About 27 percent are self-employed.

Advancement Prospects

Opportunities for advancement are limited; experienced drivers may be given the best routes or shifts. Some drivers advance to dispatcher or manager jobs; others may start their own limousine company. In small and medium-size communities, drivers are sometimes able to buy their taxi, limousine, or other type of automobile and go into business for themselves. These independent owner-drivers require an additional permit allowing them to operate their car as a company.

Some big cities limit the number of operating permits. In these cities, drivers become owner-drivers by buying permits from owner-drivers who leave the business. Although many owner-drivers are successful, some fail to cover expenses and eventually lose their permit and automobile. Good business sense and courses in accounting, business, and business arithmetic can help an owner-driver become successful. Knowledge of mechanics enables owner-drivers to perform routine maintenance and minor repairs to cut expenses.

Education and Training

Taxi Drivers usually must have a high school diploma, a regular driver's license, and a taxi driver's license (or "hack" license). Local governments set license standards and requirements for Taxi Drivers, including minimum qualifications for driving experience and training. Many taxi companies set higher standards than those that are required by law, and typically review applicants' medical, credit, criminal, and driving records.

Local authorities generally require applicants for a hack license to pass a written exam or complete a training program that may include up to 80 hours of classroom instruction. To qualify through either an exam or a training program, applicants must know local geography, driving laws, safe driving practices, taxicab regulations, and have some aptitude for customer service. Many training programs include a test on English proficiency, usually in the form of listening comprehension; applicants who do not pass the English exam must take an English course along with the formal driving program.

In addition, some classroom instruction includes route management, map reading, and service for passengers with disabilities.

Many taxicab companies sponsor applicants and give them a temporary permit that allows them to drive, although they may not yet have finished the training program or passed the test. However, some jurisdictions, such as New York City, have discontinued this practice and now require driver applicants to complete the licensing process before operating a taxi.

Some taxi companies give new drivers on-the-job training, showing drivers how to operate the taximeter and communications equipment, and how to complete paperwork. Other topics covered may include driver safety and popular sightseeing and entertainment destinations.

Many companies have contracts with social service agencies and transportation services to transport elderly and disabled citizens in nonemergency situations. To support these services, new drivers may get special training on how to handle wheelchair lifts and other mechanical devices.

Experience, Skills, and Personality Traits

Taxi Drivers should be pleasant and affable, and able to get along with many different types of people. They must be patient when waiting for passengers or when dealing with rude customers, and be tolerant when driving in heavy and congested traffic. Drivers also must be dependable, since passengers rely on them to be picked up at a prearranged time and taken to the correct destination. Drivers must be responsible and self-motivated because they work with little supervision.

Unions and Associations

Taxicab drivers may belong to the Taxi, Limousine, and Paratransit Association.

Tips for Entry

1. Check newspaper classified ads under "General Help Wanted."
2. Call or send your résumé and a cover letter to all the local taxi companies in your area.
3. Contact your state employment service office for possible job listings.

CHAUFFEUR

CAREER PROFILE

Duties: Operate limousines, vans, and private cars for limousine companies, private businesses, government agencies, and wealthy individuals

Alternate Title(s): Limousine Driver

Salary Range: $13,250 to $50,000, including tips

Employment Prospects: Good

Advancement Prospects: Fair

Best Geographical Location(s): Although Chauffeur jobs are available throughout the country, most opportunities occur in large metropolitan areas

Prerequisites:

Education or Training—High school diploma

Experience—Extensive driving experience in all conditions, and familiarity with local area

Special Skills and Personality Traits—Pleasant; patient; even-tempered; tolerant; dependable; responsible; self-motivated

Licensure/Certification—Driver's license and hack license

CAREER LADDER

```
┌─────────────────────────────┐
│  Limousine Company Owner    │
└─────────────────────────────┘

┌─────────────────────────────┐
│        Chauffeur            │
└─────────────────────────────┘

┌─────────────────────────────┐
│        Entry Level          │
└─────────────────────────────┘
```

Position Description

Chauffeurs operate limousines, vans, and private cars for limousine companies, private businesses, government agencies, and wealthy individuals. This service differs from taxi service in that all trips are prearranged. Many Chauffeurs transport customers in large vans between hotels and airports or bus or train terminals. Others drive luxury automobiles, such as limousines, to business events, entertainment venues, and social events. Still others provide full-time personal transportation for wealthy families and private companies.

At the start of the workday, Chauffeurs ready their automobiles or vans for use. They inspect the vehicle for cleanliness and, when needed, vacuum the interior and wash the exterior body, windows, and mirrors. They check fuel and oil levels and make sure the lights, tires, brakes, and windshield wipers work. Chauffeurs may perform routine maintenance and make minor repairs, such as changing tires or adding oil and other fluids when needed.

Chauffeurs cater to passengers with attentive customer service, helping riders into the car, holding open doors, holding umbrellas when it is raining, and loading packages and luggage into the trunk of the car. They may perform errands for their employers such as delivering packages or picking up clients arriving at airports. Many Chauffeurs offer conveniences and luxuries in their limousines to ensure a pleasurable ride, such as newspapers, magazines, music, drinks, televisions, and telephones.

A growing number of Chauffeurs work as full-service executive assistants, simultaneously acting as driver, secretary, and itinerary planner.

Salaries

Average hourly earnings of Chauffeurs, including tips, range from $9.14 to $10.22 an hour. The lowest 10 percent earn less than $6.37, and the highest 10 percent earn more than $15.51 an hour. Many Chauffeurs who work full time earn from between $24,370 to $50,000, including tips. Earnings are generally higher in urban areas. Top-paying states are Connecticut (average $13.26/hour), New York ($12.26), and Washington, D.C. ($12.15).

Employment Prospects

Persons seeking jobs as Chauffeurs should encounter good opportunities. Many job openings will occur each year as drivers transfer to other occupations or leave the labor force. However, earnings, work hours, and working conditions vary depending on economic conditions. Opportunities should be best for persons with good driving records and the ability to work flexible schedules. Employment of Chauffeurs is expected to grow faster than the average for all occupations through the year 2012, as local and suburban travel increases with population growth. Employment growth will also stem from federal legislation requiring increased services for persons with disabilities. Opportunities should be best in rapidly growing metropolitan areas.

Job opportunities can fluctuate from season to season and from month to month. Extra drivers may be hired during holiday seasons and peak travel and tourist times. During economic slowdowns, drivers are seldom laid off but they may have to increase their working hours, and earnings may decline somewhat. In economic upturns, job openings are numerous as drivers leave the occupation for other opportunities.

Advancement Prospects

Chauffeurs have only limited opportunities for advancement. Experienced Chauffeurs may obtain preferred routes or shifts. Some advance to dispatcher or manager jobs; others may start their own limousine company. In small and medium-size communities, drivers are sometimes able to buy their limousine and go into business for themselves. These independent owner-drivers require an additional permit allowing them to operate their vehicle as a company. Some big cities limit the number of operating permits. In these cities, drivers become owner-drivers by buying permits from owner-drivers who leave the business. Although many owner-drivers are successful, some fail to cover expenses and eventually lose their permit and automobile.

Education and Training

Chauffeurs need a high school diploma and a driver's license; extra courses in accounting, business, and business arithmetic can help an owner-driver become successful. It is common for companies to review applicants' medical, credit, criminal, and driving records. In addition, many companies require a higher minimum age and prefer that drivers be high school graduates.

Some limousine companies give new drivers on-the-job training, showing drivers how to operate the communications equipment and how to complete paperwork. Other topics covered may include driver safety and popular sightseeing and entertainment destinations. Many companies have contracts with social service agencies and transportation services to transport elderly and disabled citizens in nonemergency situations. To support these services, new drivers may get special training on how to handle wheelchair lifts and other mechanical devices. Some Chauffeurs also may take defensive driving courses, or learn counterterrorism driving techniques.

Many Chauffeurs who do not work for private families or companies are called "lease drivers," who pay a daily, weekly, or monthly fee to the company allowing them to lease their vehicle. Leasing also allows the Chauffer access to the limousine company's dispatch system. The fee may also include a charge for vehicle maintenance, insurance, and a deposit on the vehicle.

Special Requirements

Local governments set license standards and requirements for Chauffeurs that include minimum qualifications for driving experience and training, although many limousine companies set higher standards than required by law. Limousine drivers must have a regular automobile driver's license and also must acquire a chauffeur license, commonly called a "hack" license.

Local authorities generally require applicants for a hack license to pass a written exam or complete a training program that may include up to 80 hours of classroom instruction. To qualify through either an exam or a training program, applicants must know local geography, motor vehicle laws, safe driving practices, and display some aptitude for customer service.

In addition, some classroom instruction includes route management, map reading, and service for passengers with disabilities. Many limousine companies sponsor applicants and give them a temporary permit that allows them to drive, although they may not yet have finished the training program or passed the test. However, some jurisdictions, such as New York City, have discontinued this practice and now require driver applicants to complete the licensing process before operating a limousine.

Experience, Skills, and Personality Traits

Chauffeurs should be pleasant and affable, able to get along with many different types of people, and patient when waiting for passengers or when dealing with rude customers. They should be tolerant when driving in heavy and congested traffic, and dependable, since passengers rely on them to be picked up at a prearranged time and taken to the correct destination. Drivers also must be responsible and self-motivated because they work with little supervision. Good business sense and a knowledge of mechanics enables owner-drivers to perform routine maintenance and minor repairs to cut expenses.

Unions and Associations

Chauffeurs are not usually unionized; some Chauffeurs may belong to the National Limousine Association.

Tips for Entry

1. Check newspaper classified ads under "General Help Wanted."
2. Call or send your résumé and a cover letter to all the local limousine companies or private corporations in your area.
3. Contact your state employment service office for possible job listings.

BUS DRIVER

CAREER PROFILE

Duties: Transport people by bus within a metropolitan area or county, between regions of a state, or across the country

Alternate Title(s): Transit Driver, Bus Operator

Salary Range: $17,600 to $47,660

Employment Prospects: Good

Advancement Prospects: Poor

Best Geographical Location(s): Although jobs are available throughout the country, more opportunities occur in large metropolitan areas

Prerequisites:

Education or Training—High school diploma not required but highly desirable

Experience—Bus or truck driving experience is useful

Special Skills and Personality Traits—Courteous; even-tempered; emotionally stable; good customer service skills; good communication skills

Licensure/Certification—Commercial driving license

CAREER LADDER

```
┌─────────────────────────────┐
│   Supervisor or Dispatcher  │
└─────────────────────────────┘

┌─────────────────────────────┐
│         Bus Driver          │
└─────────────────────────────┘

┌─────────────────────────────┐
│         Entry Level         │
└─────────────────────────────┘
```

Position Description

Intercity Bus Drivers transport people between regions of a state or of the country; local transit Bus Drivers transport people within a metropolitan area or county. Drivers pick up and drop off passengers at bus stops and stations, operating the bus safely, especially when traffic is heavier than normal. However, they cannot let light traffic put them ahead of schedule so that they miss passengers.

Local transit and intercity Bus Drivers report to their assigned terminal or garage, where they stock up on tickets or transfers and prepare trip report forms. In some firms, maintenance departments are responsible for keeping vehicles in good condition, but otherwise Bus Drivers may check their vehicle's tires, brakes, windshield wipers, lights, oil, fuel, and water supply, before beginning their routes. Bus Drivers usually verify that the bus has safety equipment, such as fire extinguishers, first aid kits, and emergency reflectors in case of an emergency.

During the course of their shift, Bus Drivers collect fares; answer questions about schedules, routes, and transfer points; and sometimes announce stops. Intercity Bus Drivers may make only a single one-way trip to a distant city or a round trip each day. They may stop at towns a few miles apart or only at large cities hundreds of miles apart. Local transit Bus Drivers may make several trips each day over the same city and suburban streets, stopping as frequently as every few blocks.

Local transit Bus Drivers submit daily trip reports with a record of trips, significant schedule delays, and mechanical problems. Intercity Bus Drivers who drive across state or national boundaries must comply with U.S. Department of Transportation regulations, which include completing vehicle inspection reports and recording distances traveled and the periods they spend driving, performing other duties, and off duty.

Bus Drivers must be alert to prevent accidents, especially in heavy traffic or in bad weather, and to avoid sudden stops or swerves that jar passengers. Driving a bus through heavy traffic while dealing with passengers is more stressful and tiring than physically strenuous. Many Bus Drivers enjoy the opportunity to work without direct supervision, with full responsibility for their bus and passengers.

To improve working conditions and retain Bus Drivers, many bus lines provide them with ergonomically designed seats and controls. Intercity Bus Drivers may work nights, weekends, and holidays and often spend nights away from home, where they stay in hotels at company expense. Senior Bus Drivers with regular routes have regular weekly work schedules, but others do not have regular schedules and must be prepared to report for work on short notice, to drive extra buses on a regular route.

Regular local transit Bus Drivers usually have a five-day work week; Saturdays and Sundays are considered regular workdays. Some Bus Drivers work evenings and after midnight. To accommodate commuters, many work "split shifts," for example, 6 A.M. to 10 A.M. and 3 P.M. to 7 P.M., with time off in between. However, a Bus Driver's hours must be consistent with the Department of Transportation's rules; for example, a Bus Driver may drive for 10 hours and work up to 15 hours (including driving and nondriving duties) before having eight hours off. A Bus Driver may not drive after working 70 hours in the past eight days. Most Bus Drivers are required to document their time in a logbook.

Motorcoach Bus Drivers transport passengers on charter trips and sightseeing tours. Drivers routinely interact with customers and tour guides to make the trip as comfortable and informative as possible. They are directly responsible for keeping to strict schedules, adhering to the guidelines of the tours' itinerary, and the overall success of the trip. These Bus Drivers act as customer service representative, tour guide, program director, and safety guide. Trips frequently last more than one day. The Bus Driver may be away for more than a week if assigned to an extended tour. As with all Bus Drivers who drive across state or national boundaries, motorcoach drivers must comply with Department of Transportation regulations.

Tour and charter Bus Drivers may work any day and all hours of the day, including weekends and holidays. Their hours are dictated by the charter trips booked and the schedule and prearranged itinerary of tours.

Salaries

The average hourly rate for transit and intercity Bus Drivers ranges from $14.29 to $14.98 an hour; the lowest 10 percent earn less than $8.46, and the highest 10 percent earn more than $22.92 an hour. New York has the highest average paid bus drivers ($19.11/hour), followed by California ($17.32) and Washington ($17).

Most intercity and local transit Bus Drivers receive paid health and life insurance, sick leave, and free bus rides on any of the regular routes of their line or system. Drivers who work full time also get as much as four weeks of vacation a year. Most local transit Bus Drivers are also covered by dental insurance and pension plans. In a number of states, local transit Bus Drivers employed by local governments are covered by a statewide public employee pension system.

Employment Prospects

There should be good opportunities for Bus Driver jobs, since many employers have recently had trouble finding qualified candidates to fill vacancies left by departing employees. Opportunities should be best for individuals with good driving records who are willing to start on a part-time or irregular schedule. However, higher-paying intercity and public transit Bus Driver positions may be competitive.

Employment is expected to increase about as fast as average for all occupations through the year 2012, primarily because of local environmental concerns and as bus ridership increases due to population growth. Thousands of additional job openings are expected to occur each year because of the need to replace workers who take jobs in other occupations, retire, or leave the occupation for other reasons. There may be competition for positions with more regular hours and steady driving routes.

Competition from airplanes, trains, and cars will temper growth in the intercity bus industry, but like cars, buses have many more possible travel destinations than airplanes or trains.

Full-time Bus Drivers are rarely laid off during recessions, although employers might cut hours of part-time local transit and intercity Bus Drivers if fewer people ride the bus, because fewer extra buses would be needed. Seasonal layoffs are common. Many intercity Bus Drivers with little seniority, for example, are furloughed during the winter when regular business falls off.

Advancement Prospects

Opportunities for promotion are generally limited. However, experienced Bus Drivers may become supervisors or dispatchers, assigning buses to drivers, checking whether drivers are on schedule, rerouting buses to avoid blocked streets or other problems, and dispatching extra vehicles and service crews to scenes of accidents and breakdowns. In transit agencies with rail systems, Bus Drivers may become train operators or station attendants. A few Bus Drivers become managers. Promotion in publicly owned bus systems is often by competitive civil service examination. Some motorcoach drivers purchase their own equipment and go into business for themselves.

Education and Training

Many employers prefer high school graduates and require a written test of ability to follow complex bus schedules. However, a diploma is not an absolute requirement; most Bus Drivers learn the trade on the job. Many intercity and public transit bus companies prefer applicants who are at least 24 years of age; some require several years of bus or truck driving experience.

Most intercity bus companies and local transit systems give driver trainees two to eight weeks of classroom and behind-the-wheel instruction. In the classroom, trainees learn work rules, safety regulations, driving regulations, and safe driving practices. They also learn to read schedules, determine fares, keep records, and deal courteously with passengers.

During training, Bus Drivers practice driving on set courses, negotiating turns and zigzag maneuvers, backing up, and driving in narrow lanes. Then they drive in light traffic and, eventually, on congested highways and city streets. They also make trial runs without passengers to improve their driving skills and learn the routes.

Local transit trainees memorize and drive each of the runs operating out of their assigned garage. New Bus Drivers begin with a "break-in" period. They make regularly scheduled trips with passengers, accompanied by an experienced driver who gives helpful tips, answers questions, and evaluates the new driver's performance. New intercity and local transit Bus Drivers are usually placed on an "extra" list to drive charter runs, extra buses on regular runs, and special runs (for example, during morning and evening rush hours and to sports events). They also substitute for regular drivers who are ill or on vacation. New Bus Drivers remain on the extra list, and may work only part time, perhaps for several years, until they have enough seniority to receive a regular run.

Senior Bus Drivers may bid for runs they prefer, such as those with more work hours, lighter traffic, weekends off, or, in the case of intercity Bus Drivers, higher earnings or fewer workdays per week.

Special Requirements

Federal regulations require that Bus Drivers who operate vehicles designed to transport 16 or more passengers must hold a state Commercial Driver's License (CDL). To qualify for a CDL, applicants must pass a written test on rules and regulations and then demonstrate they can operate a bus safely. A national databank permanently records all driving violations incurred by people who hold commercial licenses, and a state may not issue a commercial driver's license to a driver who already has a license suspended or revoked in another state. A driver with a CDL must accompany trainees until they get their own CDL. (Information on how to apply for a commercial Driver's license may be obtained from the state motor vehicle administration.)

While many states allow those who are 18 years or older to drive buses within state borders, the Department of Transportation establishes minimum qualifications for Bus Drivers who drive across state lines. Federal laws require these Drivers to be at least 21 years old and pass a physical examination once every two years. The main physical requirements include good hearing, 20/40 vision with or without glasses or corrective lenses, and a 70-degree field of vision in each eye. Drivers must not be color-blind, and they must

be able to hear a forced whisper in one ear at five feet, with or without a hearing aid. Drivers also must have normal use of arms and legs and normal blood pressure, and they may not use any controlled substances unless prescribed by a doctor. People with epilepsy or diabetes controlled by insulin are not permitted to be interstate Bus Drivers.

Federal regulations also require employers to test their Bus Drivers for alcohol and drug use as a condition of employment, and require periodic random tests while on duty. In addition, a Bus Driver must not have been convicted of a felony involving the use of a motor vehicle; a crime involving drugs; driving under the influence of drugs or alcohol; or hit-and-run driving incident that resulted in injury or death. All Bus Drivers must be able to read and speak English well enough to read road signs, prepare reports, and communicate with law enforcement officers and the public. In addition, Bus Drivers must take a written examination on driving safety.

Some states also require Bus Drivers to attend classes at a driver's school.

Experience, Skills, and Personality Traits

Because Bus Drivers deal with passengers, they must be courteous, with an even temperament and emotional stability, because driving in heavy, fast-moving, or stop-and-go traffic and dealing with passengers can be stressful. Drivers must have strong customer service skills, including communication skills and the ability to coordinate and manage large groups of people.

Unions and Associations

Most intercity and many local transit Bus Drivers are members of the Amalgamated Transit Union. Local transit Bus Drivers in New York and several other large cities belong to the Transport Workers Union of America; some Bus Drivers belong to the United Transportation Union and the International Brotherhood of Teamsters. Bus Drivers also may belong to the American Bus Association.

Tips for Entry

1. Check newspaper classified ads under "General Help Wanted."
2. Call or send your résumé and a cover letter to all the local bus companies in your area. Check out the yellow pages under Bus Lines, Bus Tours, or Charter Buses.
3. Contact your state employment service office for possible job listings.
4. Check America's Job Bank on the Internet at www.ajb.dni.us.

SCHOOL BUS DRIVER

CAREER PROFILE

Duties: Drive students over the same route each day, picking up children in the morning and dropping them off in the afternoon

Alternate Title(s): None

Salary Range: $12,890 to $34,440

Employment Prospects: Good

Advancement Prospects: Poor

Best Geographical Location(s): Jobs are available throughout the country, but more opportunities occur in suburban and rural areas where school districts need buses to transport students

Prerequisites:

Education or Training—Between one and four weeks of driving instruction including training in state/local laws, regulations, and policies

Experience—Experience with children or driving large vehicles helpful

Special Skills and Personality Traits—Patience; tolerance; courteous; understanding; with an even temperament and emotional stability; ability to manage large groups of children

Licensure/Certification—Commercial driver's license (CDL) from the state

CAREER LADDER

```
┌─────────────────────────────┐
│    School Bus Supervisor    │
│    or Company Manager       │
└─────────────────────────────┘

┌─────────────────────────────┐
│      School Bus Driver      │
└─────────────────────────────┘

┌─────────────────────────────┐
│         Entry Level         │
└─────────────────────────────┘
```

Position Description

School Bus Drivers usually drive the same routes each day, picking up students in the morning and dropping them off in the afternoon. Some School Bus Drivers also transport students and teachers on field trips or to sporting events. In addition to driving, some School Bus Drivers work part time in the school system as janitors, mechanics, or classroom assistants.

School Bus Drivers must be alert to prevent accidents, especially in heavy traffic or in bad weather, and to avoid sudden stops or swerves that jar passengers. School Bus Drivers must exercise particular caution when children are getting on or off the bus, and must maintain order on their bus and enforce school safety standards by allowing only students to board. In addition, they must know and enforce rules regarding student conduct used throughout the school system.

School Bus Drivers do not always have to report to an assigned terminal or garage. School Bus Drivers often have the choice of taking their bus home or parking it in a convenient area.

School Bus Drivers do not collect fares; instead, they prepare weekly reports on the number of students, trips or runs, work hours, miles, and the amount of fuel consumption. Their supervisors set time schedules and routes for the day or week.

Driving a bus through heavy traffic while dealing with passengers is more stressful and fatiguing than physically strenuous. Many drivers enjoy the opportunity to work without direct supervision, with full responsibility for their bus and passengers. To improve working conditions and retain drivers, many bus lines provide ergonomically designed seats and controls.

School Bus Drivers work only when school is in session, often working 20 hours a week or less driving one or two routes in the morning and afternoon. School Bus Drivers taking field or athletic trips or who also have midday kindergarten routes may work more hours a week. As more students with a variety of physical and behavioral disabilities attend mainstream schools, School Bus Drivers must learn how to accommodate their special needs.

Salaries

Average hourly earnings of School Bus Drivers range from $10.86 to $11.05 an hour. The lowest 10 percent earn less than $6.20, and the highest 10 percent earn more than $16.56 an hour. In addition, School Bus Drivers receive sick leave, and many are covered by health and life insurance. Because they generally do not work when school is closed, they do not get vacation. In a number of states, School Bus Drivers employed by local governments are covered by a statewide public employee pension system. Many school systems also extend benefits to drivers who supplement their driving by working in the school system. School bus drivers average the highest pay in Washington, D.C. ($14.62/hour), followed by Washington ($14.29) and Nevada ($14.13).

Employment Prospects

School bus driving jobs are usually easy to get because most are part-time positions with high turnover and minimal training requirements. The number of School Bus Drivers is expected to rise because of increasing school enrollment. In addition, more School Bus Drivers will be needed as the population rises in suburbia (where students generally ride school buses), and drops in the inner cities (where school bus transportation is not provided for most pupils).

Advancement Prospects

Opportunities for promotion are generally limited, but experienced School Drivers may become supervisors, dispatchers, or school bus company managers.

Education and Training

Qualifications for School Bus Drivers are established at the state and federal level.

Many people who want to become School Bus Drivers have never driven any vehicle larger than a car. They receive between one and four weeks of driving instruction plus classroom training on state and local laws, regulations, and policies of operating school buses; safe driving practices; driver-pupil relations; first aid; special needs of students with disabilities and emotional trouble; and emergency evacuation procedures. School Bus Drivers also must know school system rules for discipline, and know the guidelines for conduct for bus drivers and the students they transport.

During training, School Bus Drivers practice driving on set courses, practicing turns and zigzag maneuvers, backing up, and driving in narrow lanes. Then they drive in light traffic and, eventually, on congested highways and city streets. They also make trial runs, without students, to improve their driving skills and learn the routes.

Special Requirements

School Bus Drivers must obtain a commercial driver's license (CDL) from the state in which they live. To qualify for a commercial driver's license, applicants must pass a written test on rules and regulations and then demonstrate they can operate a bus safely. A national data bank permanently records all driving violations incurred by people who hold commercial licenses. A state may not issue a commercial driver's license to a driver who already has a license suspended or revoked in another state. A driver with a CDL must accompany trainees until they get their own commercial license.

Experience, Skills, and Personality Traits

School Bus Drivers should like children and be tolerant, courteous, and understanding. They need an even temperament and emotional stability because driving in heavy, fast-moving, or stop-and-go traffic and dealing with children can be stressful. Drivers must have strong communication skills and the ability to manage large groups of children.

Unions and Associations

Some School Bus Drivers belong to the United Transportation Union and the International Brotherhood of Teamsters.

Tips for Entry

1. Check newspaper classified ads under "General Help Wanted."
2. Call or send your résumé and a cover letter to all the local school bus companies that lease or provide buses to school districts.
3. Contact your local school district to see if vacancies are posted.
4. Contact your state employment service office for possible job listings.

HEAVY TRUCK DRIVER

CAREER PROFILE

Duties: Drive trucks with a capacity of at least 26,000 Gross Vehicle Weight (GVW), transporting cars, livestock, and other materials in liquid, loose, or packaged form

Alternate Title(s): Tractor-Trailer Driver

Salary Range: $20,850 to $49,520

Employment Prospects: Excellent

Advancement Prospects: Fair

Best Geographical Location(s): Large metropolitan areas along major interstate roadways where major trucking, retail, and wholesale companies have distribution centers

Prerequisites:

Education or Training—High school diploma and commercial driving license

Experience—Driving experience in the armed forces an asset

Special Skills and Personality Traits—Good people skills; self-confidence; initiative; tact; neat appearance; responsibility; independence

Licensure/Certification—Driver's license and commercial driver's license, plus certain state/federal requirements

CAREER LADDER

```
┌─────────────────────────────────┐
│  Dispatcher or Trucking Owner   │
└─────────────────────────────────┘

┌─────────────────────────────────┐
│       Heavy Truck Driver        │
└─────────────────────────────────┘

┌─────────────────────────────────┐
│      Truck Driver's Helper      │
└─────────────────────────────────┘
```

Position Description

Trucks are useful for pickup and delivery of goods because no other form of transportation can deliver goods from doorstep to doorstep. Even if goods travel in part by ship, train, or airplane, trucks carry nearly all goods at some point in their journey from producer to consumer. Heavy Truck Drivers drive trucks or vans with a capacity of at least 26,000 Gross Vehicle Weight (GVW), transporting cars, livestock, and other materials in liquid, loose, or packaged form from city to city. Some companies use two drivers on very long runs (one drives while the other sleeps in a berth behind the cab). "Sleeper" runs may last for days or weeks, usually stopping only for fuel, food, loading, and unloading.

Some Heavy Truck Drivers who have regular runs transport freight to the same city on a regular basis. Others perform unscheduled runs because shippers request varying service to different cities every day. Dispatchers tell these drivers when to report for work and where to haul the freight. Modern trucking companies use automated routing equipment to track goods during shipment.

Before leaving the terminal, Heavy Truck Drivers check the fuel level and oil in their trucks and ensure that brakes, windshield wipers, and lights are working and that a fire extinguisher, flares, and other safety equipment are aboard. Drivers make sure their cargo is secure and adjust their mirrors so that both sides of the truck are visible from the driver's seat, and report to the dispatcher equipment that is broken, missing, or loaded improperly.

After Heavy Truck Drivers reach their destination or complete their operating shift, the U.S. Department of Transportation requires that they complete reports detailing the trip, the condition of the truck, and any accidents. In addition, federal regulations require drivers to take random alcohol and drug tests while on duty.

Long-distance Heavy Truck Drivers spend most of their working time behind the wheel, but they may load or unload their cargo after arriving at the final destination, especially with specialty cargo (they may be the only ones at the destination familiar with procedures or certified to handle the materials). For example, auto-transport drivers drive and position cars on the trailers and head ramps at the manufacturing plant and remove them at the dealerships.

The length of deliveries varies according to the type of merchandise and its final destination. Local Heavy Truck Drivers may provide daily service for a specific route, while other drivers make intercity and interstate deliveries that take longer and may vary from job to job. The driver's responsibilities and assignments change according to the time spent on the road, the type of payloads transported, and vehicle size.

Heavy Truck Drivers also may be considered truck brokers who act as go-betweens for shippers and receivers. In most cases, truck brokers have their own trucks but may hire other truckers to take cargo on the return trip to their home base.

The Heavy Truck Driver's responsibilities depend on the kind of load to be delivered. For example, if the product needs to be cold, the driver needs to check the refrigeration equipment. If livestock is delivered, the driver needs to know how to feed and water the animals. Hazardous materials requires knowledge of how to handle the products according to regulations. The driver also must know how to operate special equipment on the truck for loading and unloading the product.

Truck driving has become less physically demanding because most trucks now have more comfortable seats, better ventilation, and better-designed cabs. Still, driving for long hours, unloading cargo, and making deliveries can be tiring. Some self-employed long-distance Heavy Truck Drivers who own and operate their trucks spend most of the year away from home.

Many of the newer trucks are equipped with refrigerators, televisions, and bunks, and satellites and global positioning systems link trucks with company headquarters. Trouble-shooting information, directions, weather reports, and other important communications can be delivered to the truck anywhere in the country within seconds, and drivers can easily communicate with dispatchers to discuss delivery schedules and mechanical problems. The satellite linkup also allows the dispatcher to track the truck's location, fuel consumption, and engine performance.

Many Heavy Truck Drivers must also use computerized inventory tracking equipment so that the producer, warehouse, and customer know the product's location at all times. For example, voice recognition software has replaced bar code readers in some freezer and refrigerator trucks, reducing error rates and improving function in cold conditions.

The U.S. Department of Transportation governs work hours and other working conditions of Heavy Truck Drivers engaged in interstate commerce. A long-distance driver cannot work more than 60 hours in any seven-day period. Federal regulations also require that truckers rest eight hours for every 10 hours of driving. Many drivers, particularly on long runs, work close to the maximum time permitted because they typically are compensated according to the number of miles or hours they drive.

Salaries

Average hourly earnings of tractor-trailer and Heavy Truck Drivers range between $16.01 and $16.51 an hour; the lowest 10 percent earn less than $10.02, and the highest 10 percent earn more than $23.81 an hour. As a general rule, local Heavy Truck Drivers receive an hourly wage and extra pay for working overtime, usually after 40 hours. Employers pay long-distance drivers primarily by the mile. Their rate per mile can vary from employer to employer, and may depend on the type of cargo. Typically, earnings increase with mileage driven, seniority, and the size and type of truck driven. Most self-employed Heavy Truck Drivers specialize in long-distance hauling. After deducting their living expenses and the costs associated with operating their trucks, they usually earn from $20,000 to $25,000 a year. Heavy truckers on average earn the most in Alaska ($19.42/hour), followed by Massachusetts ($18.55) and Connecticut ($18.48).

Employment Prospects

The high cost of insurance makes it difficult to get a job as a Heavy Truck Driver if you are under the age of 25. Most drivers work in cities along major interstate roadways where major trucking, retail, and wholesale companies have distribution centers. Trucking companies hired about 28 percent of all Heavy Truck Drivers in the United States. Fewer than one out of 10 Heavy Truck Drivers are self-employed; of these, many are owner-operators who either serve a variety of businesses independently or lease their services and trucks to a trucking company.

Opportunities should be good for people interested in truck driving. Although growth in demand for Heavy Truck Drivers will create thousands of openings, many jobs also will occur as experienced drivers transfer to other fields of work, retire, or leave the labor force for other reasons.

Earnings, weekly work hours, number of nights spent on the road, and quality of equipment vary; competition is higher for jobs with the most attractive earnings and working conditions.

Employment of Heavy Truck Drivers is expected to increase about as fast as the average for all occupations through the year 2012, as the economy grows and the amount of freight carried by truck increases, according to the Bureau of Labor Statistics. The increased use of rail, air, and ship transportation requires Heavy Truck Drivers to pick up and deliver shipments. Growth in the number of long-distance drivers will remain strong because these drivers transport perishable and time-sensitive goods more efficiently than do alternative modes of transportation, such as railroads.

Still, job opportunities may vary from year to year because the strength of the economy dictates the amount of freight moved by trucks. Companies tend to hire more drivers when the economy is strong and deliveries are in high demand. Consequently, when the economy slows, employers hire fewer drivers, or even lay off drivers. Independent owner-operators are particularly vulnerable to slowdowns. Industries least likely to be affected by economic fluctuation tend to be the most stable places for employment.

Advancement Prospects

Advancement generally is limited to moving into runs that provide better money, schedules, or working conditions. Working for companies that also employ long-distance drivers is the best way to advance to these positions. In some cases, a person may start as a truck driver's helper, driving part of the day and helping to load and unload freight. Senior helpers then receive promotion when driving vacancies occur.

Although most new Heavy Truck Drivers are assigned immediately to regular driving jobs, some start as extra drivers, substituting for regular drivers who are ill or on vacation. They receive a regular assignment when an opening occurs.

A delivery truck driver may advance to driving heavy or special types of trucks, or transfer to long-distance truck driving. A few Heavy Truck Drivers may move into jobs for dispatcher, manager, or traffic work. Others may become driver trainers or supervisors of warehouses, terminals and docks.

Some long-distance Heavy Truck Drivers buy a truck and go into business for themselves. Although many of these owner-operators are successful, some fail to cover expenses and eventually go out of business. Owner-operators should have good business sense as well as truck driving experience; courses in accounting, business, and business math are helpful. Being able to fix their own trucks enables owner-operators to save money on routine maintenance and minor repairs.

Education and Training

A truck driver training course is a good way to prepare for truck driving jobs and obtain a commercial driver's license.

High school courses in driver training and automotive mechanics also may be helpful. Classes in automobile mechanics and driver training, especially school bus driver instruction given by many school districts, improve chances of getting hired as a trucker. However, public high schools do not usually train Heavy Truck Drivers because it is very expensive to have heavy trucks for students to practice with.

Many private and public vocational/technical schools offer tractor-trailer driver training programs where students learn to maneuver large trucks on crowded streets and in highway traffic. They also learn to inspect trucks and freight for compliance with all laws. Some programs provide only a limited amount of actual driving experience, and completion of a program does not guarantee a job. A list of private schools certified to train Heavy Truck Drivers may be obtained from the Truck Driver Institute of America.

Anyone interested in attending a driving school should check with local trucking companies to make sure the school's training is acceptable. Some states require prospective drivers to complete a training course in basic truck driving before being issued their commercial driver's license (CDL). In Maine, for example, prospective applicants must complete an eight-week course at a school certified by the Professional Truck Drivers Institute (PTDI). PTDI-certified schools provide training that meets Federal Highway Administration guidelines for training tractor-trailer drivers.

Training given to new drivers by employers is usually informal, and may consist of only a few hours of instruction from an experienced driver, sometimes on the new employee's own time. New drivers may also ride with and observe experienced drivers before assignment of their own runs. Drivers receive additional training to drive special types of trucks or handle hazardous materials. Some companies give one or two days of classroom instruction covering general duties, the operation and loading of a truck, company policies, and the preparation of delivery forms and company records.

Special Requirements

All Heavy Truck Drivers must have a driver's license issued by the state in which they live, and most employers require a clean driving record. Drivers of trucks designed to carry at least 26,000 pounds (including most tractor-trailers, as well as bigger straight trucks) must have a commercial driver's license from the state in which they live.

All Heavy Truck Drivers who operate trucks transporting hazardous materials must obtain a commercial driver's license (CDL), regardless of truck size. (Certain groups don't need to have a CDL, including farmers, emergency medical technicians, firefighters, some military drivers, and snow and ice removers).

To qualify for a commercial driver's license, applicants must pass a written test on rules and regulations, and then demonstrate that they can operate a commercial truck safely. A national databank permanently records all driving violations incurred by persons who hold commercial licenses. A state will check these records and deny a commercial driver's license to a driver who already has a license suspended or revoked in another state. Licensed drivers must accompany trainees until the trainees get their own CDL.

While many states allow those who are at least 18 years old to drive trucks within state borders, the U.S. Department of Transportation establishes minimum qualifications for Heavy Truck Drivers who drive over state lines: they must be at least 21 years old and pass a physical examination once every two years, with good hearing, at least 20/40 vision with glasses or corrective lenses, and a 70-degree field of vision in each eye. Drivers cannot be color-blind, and they must be able to hear a forced whisper in one ear at not less than five feet. Drivers must have normal use of arms and legs and normal blood pressure, and they cannot use any controlled substances unless prescribed by a doctor. Anyone with epilepsy or diabetes controlled by insulin cannot be an interstate Heavy Truck Driver.

Federal regulations also require employers to test their drivers for alcohol and drug use as a condition of employment, and require periodic random tests of the drivers while they are on duty. In addition, a driver must not have been convicted of a felony involving the use of a motor vehicle; a crime using drugs; driving under the influence of drugs or alcohol; or a hit-and-run driving incident that resulted in injury or death.

All drivers must be able to read and speak English well enough to read road signs, prepare reports, and communicate with law enforcement officers and the public. Also, drivers must take a written examination on the Motor Carrier Safety Regulations of the U.S. Department of Transportation.

Many trucking operations have even higher standards than those listed above, requiring Heavy Truck Drivers be at least 22 years old, be able to lift heavy objects, and have driven trucks for three to five years. Companies have an economic incentive to hire good drivers, because they can increase fuel economy with their driving skills and decrease liability costs for the company.

There are no formal apprenticeship programs for Heavy Truck Drivers, but one is being proposed by the American Trucking Association and the Truck Driver Institute of America. If adopted, it will create a new Licensed Apprentice Driver classification, which would team the apprentice driver with a commercial licensed driver for on-the-job training. Some trucking firms have formal on-the-job training programs.

Experience, Skills, and Personality Traits

Drivers must get along well with people because they often deal directly with customers. Employers seek drivers who speak well and have self-confidence, initiative, tact, and a neat appearance. Employers also look for responsible, self-motivated individuals able to work with little supervision.

Unions and Associations

Many Heavy Truck Drivers are members of the International Brotherhood of Teamsters. Some drivers employed by companies outside the trucking industry are members of unions representing the plant workers of the companies for which they work.

Tips for Entry

1. The best way to get started as a Heavy Truck Driver is to apply directly to companies for work as a driver-helper, warehouse worker, or dock loader.
2. Contact your state employment service office for possible job listings.
3. Check America's Job Bank on the Internet at www.ajb.dni.us.
4. Contact the International Brotherhood of Teamsters.

DELIVERY SERVICE TRUCK DRIVER

CAREER PROFILE

Duties: Drive trucks or vans smaller than three tons to deliver or pick up merchandise and packages within a specific area

Alternate Title(s): Light Truck Driver or Service Truck Driver

Salary Range: $7.10 to $20.79 per hour ($14,770 to $43,250 annually)

Employment Prospects: Good

Advancement Prospects: Fair

Best Geographical Location(s): Although jobs are available throughout the country, more opportunities occur in large metropolitan areas

Prerequisites:

    Education or Training—High school diploma preferred

    Experience—Truck driving experience helpful

    Special Skills and Personality Traits—Self-confidence; responsibility; self-motivation; a good appearance

    Licensure/Certification—A driver's license is required; some states may require a commercial driver's license

CAREER LADDER

```
┌─────────────────────────────────┐
│   Delivery Service Truck Driver  │
│         in larger area           │
└─────────────────────────────────┘

┌─────────────────────────────────┐
│   Delivery Service Truck Driver  │
└─────────────────────────────────┘

┌─────────────────────────────────┐
│ Delivery Service Truck Driver Helper │
└─────────────────────────────────┘
```

Position Description

Delivery Service Truck Drivers drive trucks or vans smaller than three tons to deliver or pick up merchandise and packages within a specific area. This may include short "turn-arounds" to deliver a shipment to a nearby city, pick up another loaded truck or van, and drive it back to their home base the same day. They may deliver anything from parcels, household goods, medications, magazines, medical supplies, and bread, to oxygen tanks, meat and poultry, groceries, seeds, plumbing supplies, and auto parts.

Delivery Service Truck Drivers work for many different kinds of businesses, including grocery stores, take-out restaurants, flower shops, drugstores, bakeries, dairies, newspaper companies, dry cleaning establishments, and vending machine companies, and may work for municipal governments as well.

Drivers may use delivery tracking or location software to track the whereabouts of the merchandise or packages. At the start of work, Delivery Service Truck Drivers get a delivery schedule from the dispatcher, and material handlers load the trucks and arrange items in order of delivery.

Delivery Service Truck Drivers usually load or unload the merchandise at the customer's place of business, and they may use a helper if there are many deliveries to make during the day, or if the load requires heavy moving.

Customers must sign receipts for goods and pay drivers the balance due on the merchandise if there is a cash-on-delivery arrangement. At the end of the day, drivers turn in receipts, money, records of deliveries made, and any reports on mechanical problems with their trucks.

Most Delivery Service Truck Drivers are in regular contact with their offices; some have computers in their delivery vehicles that provide directions and information throughout the day. There may or may not be a fixed route, but drivers are usually responsible for planning the route as efficiently as possible.

Truck driving can be physically demanding. Delivery Service Truck Drivers must be able to unload and load goods; therefore, they must be able to lift and carry heavy items, and they must drive in difficult conditions such as bad weather, heavy traffic, and sometimes on mountain roads. Although trucks are being made with more comfortable seats and better ventilation systems, they may not have air-conditioning. Physical endurance is needed for long work shifts.

Salaries

Wages can be different due to experience, where the work is, and company size. Average hourly earnings of Delivery Service Truck Drivers is $11.58 an hour. The lowest 10 percent earn $7.10 and the highest 10 percent earn more than $20.79 an hour. Beginning pay goes from $5 to $17 per hour. Nationally, half of all people employed in this group earn $24,090 each year.

Delivery Service Truck Drivers work 48 hours a week or more, eight- to 10-hour days, and five or six days a week. Most start work very early in the morning to make deliveries to chain grocery stores, produce markets, or bakeries. Some drivers get health and life insurance, disability, and retirement pensions. Some drivers must use their own vehicles on the job.

Employment Prospects

The outlook for Delivery Service Truck Drivers is good. Although the turnover among beginning drivers is high, there are frequent job openings due to retirements and career changes. The need for local deliveries has grown as a result of the constant development of shopping centers, homes, and malls. Because of this growth, Delivery Service Truck Drivers are needed to make more deliveries from central warehouses in order to meet customer demand.

Advancement Prospects

Chances for promotion for Delivery Service Truck Drivers are somewhat limited, but some drivers become trainers, supervisors of warehouses, terminals and docks, or company branch managers. Some may undergo the special training to become a heavy truck driver.

Education and Training

High school students can take classes in shop and auto mechanics to prepare themselves for the job. Completion of a program at an accredited truck driving school can provide the training needed to job applicants; those with no experience have a better chance of finding a job if they have completed a program at an accredited truck driving school. Community colleges and vocational schools also give needed training.

To boost their chance of success, independent contractors may take courses in small business management at a community college or a university with adult continuing education programs, or take a course given by the federal Small Business Administration Agency.

Special Requirements

All Delivery Service Truck Drivers must have a valid driver's license. Some states may require a commercial driver's license. Some employers require drivers to be 25 years old in order to avoid paying high insurance premiums. Drivers who handle money or other valuables may need to be bonded. Some delivery drivers specialize in carrying dangerous goods, or very heavy items. In some cases drivers may need a special driver's license to transport certain goods.

Experience, Skills, and Personality Traits

Companies prefer high school graduates with a good driving record. Good hearing and eyesight and the ability to lift and carry are required to do the job. Employers prefer applicants who are self-confident, responsible, self-motivated, and have a good appearance. Map-reading skills and a good sense of direction are also helpful.

Unions and Associations

Delivery Service Truck Drivers may belong to a number of professional associations or unions, such as America's Independent Truckers Association, American Trucking Associations, or the International Brotherhood of Teamsters.

Tips for Entry

1. Contact your state employment service office for possible job listings.
2. Contact local trucking companies or wholesale distribution centers to see if there are any job openings.
3. Contact retail stores, government agencies, and Job Service offices.
4. Check out the newspaper classified ads under "delivery," "drivers," or "trucking."
5. Check America's Job Bank on the Internet at www.ajb.dni.us.

ROUTE DRIVER

CAREER PROFILE

Duties: Deliver and sell their firm's products over established routes or within an established territory

Alternate Title(s): Truck Driver/Sales Worker

Salary Range: $6.02 to $19.63 per hour

Employment Prospects: Good

Advancement Prospects: Fair

Best Geographical Location(s): Although jobs are available throughout the country, more opportunities occur in large metropolitan areas

Prerequisites:

Education or Training—High school diploma

Experience—Truck driving experience helpful

Special Skills and Personality Traits—Self-confident; responsible; self-motivated; neat appearance

Licensure/Certification—A driver's license is required; in some states a commercial driver's license may be required

CAREER LADDER

```
┌─────────────────────────────┐
│   Route Driver in Bigger Area│
│      or Franchise Owner      │
└─────────────────────────────┘

┌─────────────────────────────┐
│        Route Driver          │
└─────────────────────────────┘

┌─────────────────────────────┐
│        Entry Level           │
└─────────────────────────────┘
```

Position Description

Route Drivers have sales and customer service responsibilities in addition to their truck delivery role. Their primary responsibility is to deliver and sell their firm's products over established routes or within an established territory. They sell goods such as food products (including restaurant takeout items) or pick up and deliver items such as laundry and dry cleaning.

Their response to customer complaints and requests can make the difference between a large order and a lost customer. Route Drivers may also take orders and collect payments.

The duties of Route Drivers vary according to their industry, the policies of their particular company, and the emphasis placed on their sales responsibility. Most have wholesale routes that deliver to businesses and stores rather than to homes. For example, wholesale bakery driver/sales workers deliver and arrange bread, cakes, rolls, and other baked goods on display racks in grocery stores. They estimate the amount and variety of baked goods to stock by paying close attention to the items that sell well and to those remaining on the shelves. They may recommend changes in a store's order or encourage the manager to stock new bakery products.

Route Drivers who work for laundries that rent linens, towels, work clothes, and other items visit businesses regularly to replace soiled laundry. From time to time, they solicit new orders from businesses along their route. Other companies (such as diaper delivery services) visit private homes on prearranged routes.

After completing their route, driver/sales workers order items for the next delivery based on product sales trends, weather, and customer requests.

Salaries

Average hourly earnings of Route Drivers (including commission) range from $9.79 to $11.38 an hour. The lowest 10 percent earn less than $6.02, and the highest 10 percent earn more than $19.63 an hour. Most Route Drivers work more than 40 hours a week, eight- to 10-hour days, five or six days a week. Top-paying states are New Jersey (average $15.36/hour), New Hampshire ($14.39), and Massachusetts ($14.34).

Employment Prospects

The outlook for Route Drivers is good. Although the turnover among beginning drivers is high, there are frequent job openings due to retirements and career changes. The need for Route Drivers has grown as a result of the constant development of shopping centers, homes, and malls.

Advancement Prospects

Chances for promotion for Route Drivers are somewhat limited, but some drivers become trainers, supervisors of warehouses, terminals and docks, or company branch managers. Some may undergo the special training to become a truck driver. Others buy their own franchise and maintain their own delivery routes.

Education and Training

High school students can take classes in shop and auto mechanics to prepare themselves for the job of Route Driver. Completion of a program at an accredited truck driving school can provide the training needed for job applicants; those with no experience have a better chance of finding a job if they have completed a program at an accredited truck driving school. Community colleges and vocational schools also give needed training.

To boost their chance of success, route franchise owners may take courses in small business management at a community college or a university with adult continuing education programs, or take a course given by the federal Small Business Administration Agency.

Experience, Skills, and Personality Traits

Companies usually prefer high school graduates with a good driving record. Good hearing and eyesight and the ability to lift and carry are required to do the job. Employers prefer applicants who are self-confident, responsible, self-motivated, and have a good appearance. Map-reading skills and a good sense of direction are also helpful.

Special Requirements

All Route Drivers must have a valid driver's license. In some states a commercial driver's license is required. Some employers require drivers to be 25 years old in order to avoid paying high insurance premiums. Drivers who handle money or other valuables may need to be bonded. Some Route Drivers specialize in carrying dangerous goods or very heavy items. In some cases Route Drivers may need a special driver's license to transport certain goods.

Tips for Entry

1. Contact your state employment service office for possible job listings.
2. Check America's Job Bank on the Internet at www.ajb.dni.us.
3. Contact local trucking companies or wholesale distribution centers to see if there are any job openings.
4. Contact retail stores, government agencies, and Job Service offices.
5. Check out the newspaper classified ads under "delivery," "drivers," or "trucking."

AMBULANCE DRIVER

CAREER PROFILE

Duties: Drive ambulances to move patients who are sick, injured, or recovering

Alternate Title(s): None

Salary Range: $6.33 to $13.73 an hour ($13,160 to $28,550 annually)

Employment Prospects: Very good

Advancement Prospects: Good

Best Geographical Location(s): Although jobs are available throughout the country, most opportunities occur in large metropolitan areas

Prerequisites:

Education or Training—High school diploma

Experience—Extensive driving experience in all conditions and familiarity with local area

Special Skills and Personality Traits—Even-tempered; tolerant; dependable; responsible; able to handle stress; willingness to serve others; motivated

Licensure/Certification—Driver's license; some states require certification as an emergency medical technician

CAREER LADDER

```
┌─────────────────────────────────────┐
│   Emergency Medical Technician       │
│   or Ambulance Dispatcher            │
└─────────────────────────────────────┘

┌─────────────────────────────────────┐
│          Ambulance Driver            │
└─────────────────────────────────────┘

┌─────────────────────────────────────┐
│            Entry Level               │
└─────────────────────────────────────┘
```

Position Description

Ambulance Drivers may work for ambulance companies, fire companies, hospitals, or local government agencies, moving patients who are sick, injured, or recovering to hospitals, back home, or other recovery facilities. They must drive quickly but carefully in order to avoid sudden movements that might be harmful to patients.

When they arrive at the scene, some Ambulance Drivers help emergency medical technicians put patients on stretchers and into ambulances. If necessary, they administer first aid.

Ambulance Drivers may pass on important information about an accident or an emergency to police or hospital staff.

Ambulance Drivers are also required to take care of the ambulance, making sure it is clean and maintaining the inventory of supplies.

Ambulance Drivers should be familiar with streets in the areas they serve so they can use the most efficient route to destinations. They should know the locations of hospitals and nursing homes and other emergency facilities. Drivers periodically take classes to keep their driving and first aid skills up-to-date.

Driving critically ill patients can be extremely stressful, especially in densely populated urban areas. Drivers must be alert to conditions on the road, especially in heavy and congested traffic or in bad weather. Evening and weekend work are common (sometimes in 24-hour shifts); drivers may work full time or part time.

It is important for Ambulance Drivers to be exact in their work, since errors could have serious effects on patients' health. There is also a high level of social interaction in this job; Ambulance Drivers work with emergency medical technicians (EMTs), hospital workers, and dispatchers.

They often are exposed to diseases and infections, with some possibility of moderate injury from this exposure. Working both indoors and outdoors, occasionally they are exposed to contaminants.

Salaries

Salaries may range between $9.14 and $9.73 an hour. The lowest 10 percent earn less than $6.33 an hour; the highest to 10 percent earn more than $13.73 an hour. Top-paying states for Ambulance Drivers are Rhode Island (average $13.43/hour), Colorado ($12.02), and California ($11.39).

Employment Prospects

Nationally, the number of jobs for Ambulance Drivers is expected to increase faster than average through the year 2012, according to the Bureau of Labor Statistics. Much of the demand for Ambulance Drivers will be due to a growing and aging population. As the population grows, the number of health care emergencies will increase; in addition, older people are more likely than younger ones to need emergency medical care. Ambulance Drivers will also be needed to transport elderly residents of long-term care facilities to and from hospitals.

Job openings occur as Ambulance Drivers transfer to other occupations. Opportunities should be best for people with good driving records, the ability to work flexible schedules, and training in emergency medical technology. Opportunities should be most abundant in rapidly growing metropolitan areas.

Advancement Prospects

Experienced Ambulance Drivers may become emergency medical technicians after taking extra training, which can improve their employability. Some drivers advance to dispatcher.

Education and Training

Ambulance Drivers must have a high school diploma and a good driving record. Helpful high school classes include first aid, health, and driver's education.

Drivers usually learn their skills through on-the-job training. Depending on the duties, training can in some cases be less than three months. Certification as an EMT is recommended.

Special Requirements

Some states require Ambulance Drivers to be certified as EMTs.

Experience, Skills, and Personality Traits

Ambulance Drivers should be pleasant and be able to get along with many different types of people, including those who may be argumentative or combative. They must be tolerant when driving in heavy and congested traffic. Drivers also must be dependable, responsible, and motivated, since their work involves life-and-death decisions for their patients.

Unions and Associations

Ambulance Drivers may belong to a number of related professional groups such as the National Association of Emergency Medical Technicians or state EMT associations.

Tips for Entry

1. Check newspaper classified ads under "General Help Wanted."
2. Call or send your résumé and a cover letter to all the local hospitals, fire companies, and ambulance companies in your area.
3. Contact your state employment service office for possible job listings.
4. Check America's Job Bank on the Internet at www.ajb.dni.us.

TOW TRUCK DRIVER

CAREER PROFILE

Duties: Drive and operate a truck to tow vehicles that have broken down, been damaged, or illegally parked

Alternate Title(s): Vehicle Recovery Operator

Salary Range: $10 to $15 per hour

Employment Prospects: Excellent

Advancement Prospects: Good

Best Geographical Location(s): Large metropolitan areas or towns along major interstate roadways are best, but any location that is not excessively rural should have plenty of opportunities

Prerequisites:

Education or Training—High school diploma helpful

Experience—Experience in car mechanics and crane lifting helpful

Special Skills and Personality Traits—Good people skills; mechanical skills; responsible; independent; physical strength

Licensure/Certification—Driver's license and tow truck certification or license, plus certain state/federal requirements

CAREER LADDER

```
┌─────────────────────────────────┐
│    Owner of Towing Company      │
└─────────────────────────────────┘

┌─────────────────────────────────┐
│        Tow Truck Driver         │
└─────────────────────────────────┘

┌─────────────────────────────────┐
│          Entry Level            │
└─────────────────────────────────┘
```

Position Description

More than 85 percent of all tows in the United States involve passenger cars and light trucks, most of which are towed by small, family-owned towing businesses. In the past 15 years, towing and recovery equipment has dramatically changed and has become much more sophisticated. Today's tower must be well trained to use many types of tools and equipment, including: hydraulics, electric winches, dollies, wheel lifts, car carriers (roll backs), air cushions, rotators. Tow Truck Drivers drive their trucks to accidents, breakdowns, illegally parked vehicles, or vehicles in need of assistance. At the scene, a Tow Truck Driver opens a locked vehicle and releases the parking brake, then attaches the vehicle to the tow truck or winches the vehicle onto the truck. They may tow vehicles to the shop, to a vehicle dismantler, or to the customer's home. In some cases, the Tow Truck Driver may need to jump-start a vehicle.

Alternatively, some Tow Truck Drivers tow away confiscated, stolen, impounded, or abandoned vehicles for the police department, taking them to the towing company yard (or the police department) for impounding.

Tow Truck Drivers use different methods for freeing trapped vehicles and securing them for towing. They must make sure that the car is correctly placed and secure it by using ropes and/or chains to avoid damage to the car or tow truck. Once the car is loaded, they must drive defensively and be able to handle hazardous road conditions.

Once the job is completed, the Tow Truck Driver must collect payments and issue receipt. Their work does not end merely with towing the car, however. They also must keep records of vehicles that have been towed and details of their trips. They also must maintain and clean the tow truck.

Tow truck operators often work in shifts, at night or on weekends. In some states, there may be rules for how long they are permitted to work during one shift or in one week.

Being a Tow Truck Driver may mean early starts and days away from family and friends.

There is usually a lot of overtime, and Tow Truck Drivers can accumulate a lot of hours in a week, especially during the two busiest times of the year: summer and winter. In summer there are more calls from travelers and tourists, and in winter many calls come in for battery boosts, fender-bender accidents, and pulling people out of ditches. They must work in all weather and traffic conditions, and may also have to work in dangerous places, for example, the vehicle they are towing has fallen down a bank or into a river.

Salaries

Pay rates vary across the country, but in general pay rates range from about $10 to $12 per hour to more than $15 per hour for more experienced Tow Truck Drivers. Typically, companies pay both an hourly wage and extra pay for working overtime, usually after 40 hours (or on holidays).

Employment Prospects

The outlook for Tow Truck Drivers is good, and the number of people employed in this occupation is expected to increase moderately through 2008. A major factor influencing the demand for Tow Truck Drivers is the increasing popularity of four-wheel-drive vehicles, which cannot be towed in the traditional way (they require a special roll-back truck that lifts the car completely off the road). Because of this, more people are using the services of towing and vehicle recovery businesses rather than attempting to tow vehicles themselves. Turnover among Tow Truck Drivers is low to moderate.

Advancement Prospects

Tow Truck Drivers usually begin by driving company-owned vehicles, and later move on and advance by either working for a larger firm, driving their own truck, or opening their own towing company. Many tow truck operators are self-employed. Owner-drivers usually must obtain their own tow truck work.

Education and Training

The towing environment is becoming more and more technically driven; towers will have to become adept at the use of computers and computer technology in the management of business and in the delivery of towing and recovery services.

There are no specific educational requirements to become a Tow Truck Driver, but a high school diploma is helpful, as are training in auto mechanics, the ability to work irregular hours, and good standard English. Training is done on the job. New Tow Truck Drivers usually work with an experienced person until they are able to work on their own. In some jobs, Tow Truck Drivers may require a police clearance.

Tow truck operators need to know how to operate a tow truck, how to tow vehicles safely, different types of vehicles and their locking mechanisms, which vehicles can be towed and which need to be winched onto the tow truck to avoid transmission damage, and how to use radio equipment. They also should be familiar with street names and routes in their local area.

Tow Truck Drivers who tow or recover heavy vehicles and trucks need to know how to safely tow vehicles carrying hazardous substances. Useful experience for Tow Truck Drivers include working with vehicles, working as a truck driver's assistant, and working with cranes or forklifts. Customer service experience is also helpful.

Special Requirements

The towing and recovery industry is highly regulated at the federal, state, and local levels of government. Tow Truck Drivers can be certified by the National Driver Certification Program; many states require certification and/or licensure. New regulations mandating drug and alcohol testing for drivers in the trucking industry also covers Tow Truck Drivers.

Experience, Skills, and Personality Traits

A Tow Truck Driver should have good map-reading skills, good driving skills, and basic mechanical skills, so they can fix minor mechanical problems on the spot. They must enjoy practical work and be able to work at all hours of the day or night.

They must have good customer service skills (especially sensitivity and an understanding nature), be calm, helpful, diplomatic, and good at dealing with customers who may be stressed or angry when their vehicles break down or are towed away. Tow truck operators usually work alone, but they may work in teams on difficult jobs, interacting with the public, police, ambulance drivers, firefighters, vehicle dismantlers, and parking wardens. They also should be respectful of other people's property and have good communication, record-keeping, and problem-solving skills.

Tow Truck Drivers also must have a safe driving record and meet age limits the employer may set. They should be physically fit, as the job involves stretching, leaning, bending, lifting, and climbing, especially in difficult salvage situations. They also need to have an eye for detail so they can identify any damage already done to the vehicle before they tow it. Honesty is important, and they must be efficient and able to work quickly, as they may have to tow a vehicle that is blocking traffic.

Unions and Associations

Tow Truck Drivers may belong to the International Brotherhood of Teamsters or a number of professional associations, including state tow driver groups and the Towing and Recovery Association of America.

Tips for Entry

1. Contact your state towing association, or the Towing and Recovery Association of America (www.towinfo.com/members/affiliates/traa/traa.html) for information on jobs.
2. Apply directly to companies for work as a Tow Truck Driver's helper or assistant.
3. Contact your state employment service office for possible job listings.
4. Check America's Job Bank on the Internet at www.ajb.dni.us.

SALES

NEW CAR SALESPERSON

CAREER PROFILE

Duties: Sell new cars and arrange financing

Alternate Title(s): Car Sales Associate; Car Salesman

Salary Range: Average $18.25 an hour

Employment Prospects: Good

Advancement Prospects: Good

Best Geographical Location(s): All locations throughout the country have job possibilities for well-trained, experienced New Car Salespeople

Prerequisites:

Education or Training—High school diploma

Experience—Any type of sales experience helpful

Special Skills and Personality Traits—Outgoing personality; good communication skills; ability to sell

CAREER LADDER

```
┌─────────────────────────────┐
│       Sales Manager         │
└─────────────────────────────┘


┌─────────────────────────────┐
│    New Car Salesperson      │
└─────────────────────────────┘


┌─────────────────────────────┐
│        Entry Level          │
└─────────────────────────────┘
```

Position Description

Car salespeople represent the dealership as well as the car manufacturer, and they must understand the cars they sell, in addition to details on finance, insurance, state and federal laws, warranties, and the automobile industry in general. Like many high-technology fields demanding extensive product knowledge, car salespeople are specialized. In many dealerships there are separate sales forces for new vehicles; used vehicles; trucks; recreational vehicles; fleet sales; and rental and leasing operations. How well a salesperson can sell cars and services determines the success of the dealership.

New Car Salespeople usually are the first to greet customers and determine their interests by asking a series of questions, explaining and demonstrating a car's features in the showroom and on the road. Working closely with supervisors and their customers, they negotiate the final terms and price of the sale.

The new car sales department in a full-service dealership accounts for more than half of all dealership sales, making it the cornerstone and lifeblood of the dealership. Although profit margins on new vehicle sales are quite small in comparison with those of other departments, these sales spawn additional revenue for more profitable departments of the dealership. By putting new vehicles on the road, dealerships can count on aftermarket additions, new repair and service customers, and future used vehicle trade-ins.

Sales of new cars, trucks, and vans depend on changing consumer tastes, popularity of the manufacturers' vehicle models, and the intensity of competition with other dealers. The business cycle greatly affects automobile sales—when the economy of the nation is declining, car buyers may postpone purchases of new vehicles and, conversely, when the economy is growing and consumers feel more financially secure, vehicle sales increase.

Car and truck leasing is included in the new vehicle sales department. Leasing services have grown in recent years to accommodate changing consumer purchasing habits. As vehicles have become more costly, growing numbers of consumers are unable or reluctant to make the long-term investment entailed in the purchase of a new car or truck. Leasing provides an alternative to high initial investment costs while typically yielding lower monthly payments.

Employees in motor vehicle dealerships work longer hours than do those in most other industries. About 86 percent of motor vehicle dealership employees worked full time in 2000; nearly 42 percent worked more than 40 hours a week. To satisfy customer service needs, many dealers provide evening and weekend service. The five-day, 40-hour week usually is the exception, rather than the rule, in this industry. Most automobile salespersons and administrative workers spend their time in dealer showrooms; individual offices are a rarity. Multiple users share limited office space that may be cramped and sparsely equipped. The competitive nature of selling is stressful to automotive salespersons, as they try to meet company sales quotas and personal earnings goals. Compared with that for all occupations in general, the proportion of workers who transfer from automotive sales jobs to other occupations is relatively high.

Workers in motor vehicle dealerships tend to be somewhat older than those in other retail trade industries. The median age of workers in dealerships was 38.7, with 26 percent between the ages of 35 and 44. Since 1950, the trend in this industry has been toward consolidation. Franchised dealers have decreased in number, while their sales volume has increased. Larger dealerships can offer more services, typically at lower costs to the dealership and the customer. More than 75 percent of motor vehicle dealerships employ at least 10 workers, compared with about 32 percent for retail trade establishments in general. Dealerships with 10 or more workers employ about 98 percent of the workers in the industry, whereas such establishments account for fewer than 85 percent of all retail trade employment. On average, motor vehicle dealers employ nearly 24 employees per establishment, compared with an average of 16 employees in all retail businesses.

Salaries

Most automotive sales workers are paid on a commission-only basis. Commission systems vary, but dealers often guarantee new salespersons a modest salary for the first few months until they learn how to sell cars. Many dealers also pay experienced, commissioned sales workers a modest weekly or monthly salary to compensate for the unstable nature of sales. Dealerships (especially larger companies) also pay bonuses with special incentive programs for exceeding sales quotas. With increasing customer service requirements, some dealerships and manufacturers have adopted a noncommissioned sales force paid entirely by salary. The hourly wage for New Car Salespeople averages $18.25.

Employment Prospects

Jobs in car dealerships are projected to increase 13 percent over the 2000–2012 period, compared with projected growth of about 16 percent for all industries combined, according to the Bureau of Labor Statistics. Growth in the automobile industry strongly reflects consumer confidence and purchasing habits. The structure of dealerships, the strength of the nation's economy, and trends in consumer preferences all influence the employment outlook. Through 2012, population growth is expected to increase demand for cars; consequently, the number of available jobs in car dealerships should also

increase. Growth of the labor force and in the number of families in which both spouses need cars to commute to work will contribute to rising employment. As people earn more money, many individuals will be able to buy more than one car, which also should increase sales. On the other hand, the tendency for people to keep their cars for many more years than in the past may have a dampening effect on car sales.

The trend toward dealership consolidation should have little effect on the industry because of continued demand for cars and related services. Dealerships will always need well-qualified salespeople to help sell cars.

Opportunities for sales positions will depend largely on the state of the economy, which will continue to play a dominant role in car sales. There tends to be a high turnover of sales jobs in the car business, which will ensure job openings for sales workers in car dealerships. In addition, as consumers' expectations and demands continue to increase, dealerships will seek more highly educated salespersons.

Advancement Prospects

Although a college degree is not necessarily a requirement for car sales, people with a college degree and previous sales experience should have the best opportunities. Successful New Car Salespeople can move into sales manager positions

Education and Training

To keep the sales staff up to date on the latest product developments and sales techniques, dealers and manufacturers conduct regular training sessions and encourage salespeople to take advantage of a wide variety of outside sales and business courses. The majority of positions do not require postsecondary education—more than half of those employed have not received any formal education past high school. In today's competitive job market, however, nearly all dealers demand a high school diploma.

Sales workers require strong communication skills to deal with the public because they represent the dealership. Most new sales workers receive extensive on-the-job training, beginning with mentoring from sales managers and experienced sales workers. In large dealerships, beginners receive several days of classroom training to learn the models for a sale, methods for approaching prospective customers, negotiation techniques, and ways to close sales. Some manufacturers furnish training manuals and other informational materials for sales workers. Managers continually guide and train sales workers, both on the job and at periodic sales meetings.

Experience, Skills, and Personality Traits

New Car Salespeople are organized self-starters who can stick to a tough daily routine and prospect for new customers by telephone, mail, and personal contacts. Most important, the sales staff should be excellent communicators who truly enjoy working with people. Automotive salespersons must be tactful, well-groomed, and able to express themselves well. Their success in sales depends upon their ability to win the respect and trust of prospective customers.

Tips for Entry

1. To find out exactly how to qualify for a specific sales job, contact local dealerships and ask the dealer or manager in charge.

2. Check newspaper classified ads under "Help Wanted: sales" or "Help Wanted: auto."

3. Visit your school's career counseling office for help in identifying companies where you would like to work.

4. Use your contacts. The easiest way to network is to ask someone you already know for the name of someone else. When you call, say, "So-and-so suggested I call you."

USED CAR SALESPERSON

CAREER PROFILE

Duties: Sell used cars and arrange financing

Alternate Title(s): Car Sales Associate; Car Salesman

Salary Range: $18.25 per hour

Employment Prospects: Good

Advancement Prospects: Good

Best Geographical Location(s): All locations throughout the country have job possibilities for well-trained, experienced Used Car Salespeople

Prerequisites:

Education or Training—High school diploma

Experience—Previous sales experience of any kind helpful

Special Skills and Personality Traits—Organizational skills; excellent communication skills; tactful; well-groomed; self-confidence; outgoing personality

CAREER LADDER

```
┌─────────────────────────────┐
│   Used Car Sales Manager    │
└─────────────────────────────┘

┌─────────────────────────────┐
│    Used Car Salesperson     │
└─────────────────────────────┘

┌─────────────────────────────┐
│        Entry Level          │
└─────────────────────────────┘
```

Position Description

A salesperson's success in selling used cars and automotive services determines the success of a full-service dealership or stand-alone used car dealer. The used vehicle sales department of a full-service dealership sells trade-ins and former rental and leased cars, trucks, and vans. Stand-alone used car dealers also sell these types of used cars, ranging from small one location stores to nationwide superstores. Each one takes advantage of the increased demand for used cars and the relatively large profits on sales of these used cars, trucks, and vans. Many larger used car dealers contract out warranty and other service-related work to other dealers or satellite service facilities. Growth in leasing agreements and rental companies will continue to provide quality cars to these dealers.

Because new car prices continue to increase faster than used car prices, used cars have become more popular. Moreover, innovative technology has increased the longevity of new cars, resulting in higher-quality used cars. In recent years, the sale of used cars has become a major source of profits for many dealers as margins for new cars decreased. In fact, some luxury car manufacturers promote "certified pre-owned" cars to customers who may be unable to afford new cars. In economic downturns, the demand for used cars often increases as sales of new cars decline.

The modern consumer is an educated buyer, regularly checking out the Internet before entering the dealership to research and compare car prices, features, and options. This means that the Used Car Salesperson must be very familiar with the cars in order to be most effective.

The Used Car Salesperson is usually the first to greet customers and determine their interests through a series of questions. Salespersons then explain and demonstrate the car's features in the showroom and on the road. Working closely with supervisors and their customers, the Used Car Salesperson negotiates the final terms and price of the sale.

To satisfy customer service needs, many dealers provide evening and weekend service. As a result, Used Car Salespeople in car dealerships work long hours; in fact, about 86 percent work more than 40 hours a week, according to the Bureau of Labor Statistics. The five-day, 40-hour week usually is the exception, rather than the rule, in this industry.

Most Used Car Salespersons spend their time in dealer showrooms; individual offices are a rarity. Multiple users share limited office space that may be cramped and sparsely equipped.

The competitive nature of selling, with its company sales quotas and personal earnings goals, can be stressful, which is probably one reason why so many workers transfer from used car sales jobs to other occupations.

Salaries

Most Used Car Salespersons are paid on a commission-only basis. Although commission systems vary, dealers often guarantee new salespersons a modest salary for the first few months until they learn how to sell cars. Many dealers also pay experienced, commissioned sales workers a modest weekly or monthly salary to compensate for the unstable nature of sales. Dealerships (especially larger ones) also pay bonuses and have special incentive programs for exceeding sales quotas.

However, as customer service requirements mount, some dealerships and manufacturers have adopted a noncommissioned sales force paid entirely by salary. In this case, according to the Bureau of Labor Statistics, the hourly wage for Used Car Salespeople averages $18.25 an hour.

Employment Prospects

Because of consolidation, the number of car dealerships continues to decline while remaining dealerships increase in size. As a result, opportunities for sales positions depend on the health of the nation's economy, which continues to play an important role in car sales.

Despite the volatile nature of the business, the continual high turnover of sales jobs means there will be many job openings for sales workers in car dealerships. In addition, as consumers' expectations and demands continue to increase, dealerships will seek more highly educated salespersons.

However, if alternative sales techniques and unique compensation systems become more common, the greater income stability may mean slower turnover of sales jobs.

Advancement Prospects

With hard work and a successful track record, Used Car Salespeople can advance to sales manager in the same size or larger dealer. Chances are better if the individual has had supervisory experience in the past.

Education and Training

Most positions do not require postsecondary education; more than half of those employed have not received any formal education past high school. In today's competitive job market, however, nearly all dealers demand a high school diploma.

Sales workers need strong communication skills to deal with the public because they represent the dealership. Most new sales workers receive extensive on-the-job training, beginning with mentoring from sales managers and experienced sales workers. In large dealerships, beginners receive several days of classroom training to learn the models for a sale, methods for approaching prospective customers, negotiation techniques, and ways to close sales. Some manufacturers furnish training manuals and other informational materials for sales workers. Managers continually guide and train sales workers, both on the job and at periodic sales meetings.

Experience, Skills, and Personality Traits

Salespeople are organized self-starters who can stick to a tough daily routine and prospect for new customers by telephone, mail, and personal contacts. Most important, the sales staff should be excellent communicators who truly enjoy working with people. Used Car Salespersons must be tactful, well-groomed, and able to express themselves well. Their success in sales depends upon their ability to win the respect and trust of prospective customers.

Unions and Associations

Car salespersons may belong to a number of auto-related organizations such as the National Auto Dealers Association.

Tips for Entry

1. To find out exactly how to qualify for a specific dealership job, contact local used car dealerships and ask the dealer or manager in charge.
2. Mail a résumé to top companies where you would like to work.
3. Visit your school's career counseling office for help in identifying companies where you would like to work.
4. Use your contacts. The easiest way to network is to ask someone you already know for the name of someone else. When you call, say, "So-and-so suggested I call you."
5. Check out the classified ads under "Help Wanted: Automotive" or "Help Wanted: Manufacturing."

DETAILER

Duties: Prepare new and used cars for display in the show-room or sales lot and for delivery to customers

Alternate Title(s): Vehicle Cleaner

Salary Range: $12,660 to $28,080

Employment Prospects: Good

Advancement Prospects: Fair

Best Geographical Location(s): All locations throughout the country have job possibilities for well-trained, experienced Detailers

Prerequisites:

Education or Training—High school diploma

Experience—Experience with cars helpful

Special Skills and Personality Traits—Attention to detail; good communication skills

```
┌─────────────────────────────┐
│      Car Painter            │
│  or Automotive Technician   │
└─────────────────────────────┘

┌─────────────────────────────┐
│         Detailer            │
└─────────────────────────────┘

┌─────────────────────────────┐
│        Entry Level          │
└─────────────────────────────┘
```

Position Description

Detailers prepare new and used cars for display in the show-room or parking lot and for delivery to customers. They may wash and wax vehicles by hand and perform simple services such as changing a tire or battery. Detailers operate cleaning equipment, such as pressure washers, and make sure that all cleaning equipment is working properly, reporting any problems to a supervisor. Detailers mix cleaning solutions according to formulas and make sure enough cleaning supplies are on hand.

Detailers start by inspecting the car, assessing how dirty it is and whether there is any damage that needs to be repaired. Detailers use scrapers, brushes, soaps, water, or steam to wash the outside of cars. Sometimes they disassemble parts in order to clean them thoroughly, soaking some parts in cleaning solutions. When these parts are clean, Detailers put them back together. To clean the inside of vehicles, Detailers first sweep or vacuum loose dirt, removing more difficult stains on carpet or upholstery with steam.

Some cars may need to be polished. Detailers apply wax and remove it by hand or with a buffing machine. They also may apply paint to restore the car's color or condition.

Detailers also may perform minor maintenance, such as checking tire pressure or adding water to the radiator, replacing windshield wiper blades, or changing tires. On new cars, Detailers remove protective coatings and plastic coverings, and may pick up or deliver cars to customers. They are usually responsible for keeping their work area neat.

Whether they work full or part time, Detailers may need to work evenings or weekends as companies try to attract consumers by offering attractive hours. They usually work outdoors, but sometimes work inside car washes or mechanic shops. They are sometimes exposed to contaminants, such as abrasive cleansers, and are sometimes exposed to hazardous equipment, such as power washers. However, the likelihood of injury is very slight.

Salaries

The average hourly rate for a Detailer ranges between $8.27 and $9.15 an hour, according to the Bureau of Labor Statistics. Half of all Detailers earn between $17,190 and $19,030 each year. The lowest paid detailers earn less than $6.08 an hour; the highest 10 percent earn more than $13.50 an hour. Top-paying states are Michigan (average $11.17/hour), Massachusetts ($10.79), and Colorado ($10.54).

Employment Prospects

Most Detailers work at car washes, car dealers, and car rental agencies. The number of jobs for Detailers is expected to grow as fast as average through the year 2010, according to the Bureau of Labor Statistics. Jobs are expected to be created as industries that use Detailers expand. As long as the economy remains strong, many people will spend money on having their cars washed and cleaned.

Growth in the occupation may be somewhat slowed as more employers hire temporary workers. In addition, some employers are adding car cleaning tasks to the jobs of other workers rather than hiring Detailers.

Job turnover is high in this occupation because of the low wages and high physical demands; many job openings occur as Detailers move on to find better-paying jobs.

Advancement Prospects

Detailers who demonstrate strong work skills may become supervisors. With additional training, they may become vehicle painters or automotive technicians.

Education and Training

Detailers do not need formal education past high school, but a GED or high school diploma is generally required. In today's competitive job market, nearly all dealers demand a high school diploma. Helpful high school classes include physical education and auto maintenance. Some employers require applicants to pass a drug test.

In general, experience is not required for entry-level Detailers; many cleaners receive training on the job. Some experience or training may be required for performing tasks such as painting and making minor repairs. Employers also may require a valid driver's license.

Experience, Skills, and Personality Traits

Employers look for people who are reliable and hardworking and who are at least 16 years old, and who can physically perform the job. Because this job requires long periods of standing and much physical activity, people interested in becoming Detailers should be in good physical condition.

Unions and Associations

Detailers do not usually belong to unions or associations.

Tips for Entry

1. Contact local car dealerships or car rental shops and inquire about job openings. To find out exactly how to qualify for a Detailer job, contact local dealerships and ask the manager.
2 Check newspaper classified ads under "Help Wanted: automotive."
3. Use your contacts. The easiest way to network is to ask someone you already know who works in the detailing business for the name of someone else. When you call, say, "So-and-so suggested I call you."

GENERAL MANAGER

CAREER PROFILE

Duties: Direct all of the dealership's operations

Alternate Title(s): None

Salary Range: Average $42.84 per hour

Employment Prospects: Good

Advancement Prospects: Good

Best Geographical Location(s): All locations throughout the country have job possibilities for well-trained, experienced General Managers at auto dealerships

Prerequisites:

Education or Training—Four-year college degree in business administration or marketing

Experience—Experience in sales, service, or administration

Special Skills and Personality Traits—Excellent business management skills; ability to manage others; sales experience; experience in all dealership departments

CAREER LADDER

```
┌─────────────────────────────────┐
│     Dealer or Franchise Owner    │
└─────────────────────────────────┘

┌─────────────────────────────────┐
│          General Manager         │
└─────────────────────────────────┘

┌─────────────────────────────────┐
│          Sales Manager           │
│      or Marketing Manager        │
└─────────────────────────────────┘
```

Position Description

General Managers are in charge of all of the car dealership's operations—dealership performance and profitability ultimately are their responsibility. Because of this, they need extensive business and management skills, usually acquired through experience as a manager of one or more of the dealership departments. General Managers sometimes have an ownership interest in the dealership.

Although many dealerships have been in the hands of a family for generations, many General Managers come up through the ranks, starting at the bottom of the dealership ladder and progressing upward through hard work, talent, and ambition.

A General Manager oversees the sales force and sets policy; he or she plans, directs, organizes, and controls the daily operation of the dealership, while also planning for the future. The General Manager also recruits, trains and motivates a management team that helps meet company objectives. He or she has final responsibility for hiring and firing employees.

The General Manager establishes short- and long-range plans to operate the dealership efficiently and coordinates finances for adequate funding. A General Manager also develops promotions, ad campaigns, and an operating budget for the company. Periodic management meetings with department managers are also part of the job. Finally, the General Manager attends meetings and conferences as necessary.

Salaries

The salary for a General Manager of a dealership depends on the location of the dealership, whether the dealership focuses on new or used cars (new car dealerships pay higher salaries, in general), and the experience and training of the manager. Typically, the average hourly rate for a General Manager is about $42.84, plus significant bonuses and special incentive programs.

Employment Prospects

Jobs in car dealerships are projected to increase 13 percent over the 2000–2012 period, compared with projected growth of about 16 percent for all industries combined, according to the U.S. Bureau of Labor Statistics. Opportunities as General Manager will be best for persons who have a college degree and considerable industry experience.

However, consolidation of dealerships will slow the growth of managerial jobs, and competition for General Manager positions will remain relatively keen. Growth in the automobile industry strongly reflects consumer confidence and purchasing habits. The structure of dealerships, the strength of the nation's economy, and trends in consumer preferences all influence the employment outlook for the auto industry. Over the 2000–2012 period, population growth will increase demand for cars and jobs in dealerships. Growth of the labor force and in the number of families in which both spouses need vehicles to commute to work will contribute to increased car sales and employment. As personal incomes continue to grow, more people will be able to afford the luxury of owning several cars, which also should increase sales. However, as more people keep their cars for many more years than in the past, car sales may slump.

The trend toward dealership consolidation should not affect the industry very much because consumers will continue to buy cars and need repair services.

Advancement Prospects

After gaining experience in sales, service, or administration, sales workers can advance to management positions in dealerships. Dealers hire General Managers who have a four-year college degree in business administration and marketing. General Managers who want to advance typically look for jobs in larger dealerships, or buy out a dealership.

Education and Training

General Managers must have a four-year college degree (preferably with a business or marketing major). In addition, some car manufacturers offer management training classes and seminars. Additional management or business classes can help General Managers advance.

Experience, Skills, and Personality Traits

A General Manager must have excellent business management skills, the ability to manage and motivate employees, sophisticated sales and marketing experience, and experience in all dealership departments.

Unions and Associations

General Managers typically may belong to a wide range of auto- or business-related associations, including the National Automobile Dealers Association, the Institute for Automotive Service Excellence, the Automotive Warehouse Distributors Association, Automotive Training Managers Council, Automotive Service Association, Automotive Industry Planning Council, Automotive Industry Action Group, and the International Automobile Dealers Association.

Tips for Entry

1. Send your résumé and a cover letter to dealerships where you are interested in working.
2. Look for these positions in the classified sections (or display ads) of the newspaper under "sales" or "professional."
3. Check auto dealership Web sites.
4. Join trade associations such as the National Automobile Dealers Association; these groups may offer joblines and can provide information to help you search for training programs and jobs in the field.
5. Look for jobs online; try www.monster.com or www.hotjobs.com.
6. Take seminars and workshops in promotion, marketing, management techniques, sales, publicity, and public relations to give you an edge over other applicants.

SALES MANAGER

CAREER PROFILE

Duties: Hire, train, and supervise the dealership's sales force and help negotiate all transactions between sales workers and customers

Alternate Title(s): None

Salary Range: $19.03 to $55.59 per hour

Employment Prospects: Fair

Advancement Prospects: Fair

Best Geographical Location(s): All locations throughout the country have job possibilities for well-trained, experienced Sales Managers

Prerequisites:

Education or Training—Four-year college degree in business administration or marketing

Experience—Experience in sales, service, or administration

Special Skills and Personality Traits—Good communication skills; personable; ability to supervise and manage staff; willingness to motivate others and work hard

CAREER LADDER

```
┌─────────────────────────────┐
│   General Sales Manager     │
└─────────────────────────────┘

┌─────────────────────────────┐
│     Car Sales Manager       │
└─────────────────────────────┘

┌─────────────────────────────┐
│     Car Sales Associate     │
└─────────────────────────────┘
```

Position Description

New car and used car Sales Managers plan, organize, and coordinate the activities of their staffs, ensuring that the dealership meets sales quotas. Sales Managers hire, train, and supervise the dealership's sales force. They are the lead negotiators in all transactions between car sales associates and customers. Most are promoted to their positions after a successful career selling cars in the dealership. Sales Managers review market analyses to determine consumer needs, estimate volume potential for various car models, and develop sales campaigns to accomplish dealership goals. They coordinate the market research, marketing strategy, sales, advertising, promotion, pricing, product development, and public relations activities for the dealership.

They also direct the dealership's sales program, setting goals and establishing training programs for the sales associates. Sales Managers advise sales associates on how to improve their performance.

Sales Managers maintain contact with distributors, and analyze sales statistics gathered by their staffs to determine sales potential and inventory requirements and monitor customer preferences.

Salaries

Sales Managers can earn high salaries, as well as incentive and executive benefits, (often including the use of a car)—but at the same time the job requires very long hours, including evenings, holidays, and weekends. Pay ranges from $19.03 to $55.59 an hour. Average pay for Sales Managers is $51.18 an hour. Top-paying states are New York (average $60.87/hour), Connecticut ($54.54), and New Jersey ($54.05).

Employment Prospects

Motor vehicle dealerships are expected to decline in number but increase in size, as consolidation continues in the industry. This will slow the growth of managerial jobs, and competition for Sales Manager positions will remain relatively keen, according to the U.S. Bureau of Labor

Statistics. College graduates with related experience, a high level of creativity, strong communication skills, and considerable industry experience should have the best job opportunities. Those who have new media and interactive marketing skills will be particularly sought after.

Advancement Prospects

Most Sales Managers start their careers as car sales associates, and need years of experience in sales, service, or administration to advance to management positions in dealerships. Most Sales Manager positions are filled by promoting experienced staff or related professional or technical personnel.

In small dealerships, the number of positions is limited, and advancement to a management position usually comes slowly. In larger dealerships, promotion may occur more quickly. Well-trained, experienced, successful Sales Managers often are chosen for advancement to the highest ranks in their own, or other, dealerships.

Although experience, ability, and leadership are emphasized for promotion, advancement can be accelerated by participation in management-training programs conducted by many large dealerships. Many also provide their employees with continuing-education opportunities, either in-house or at local colleges and universities, and encourage employee participation in seminars and conferences, often provided by professional societies. In collaboration with colleges and universities, numerous marketing and related associations sponsor national or local management-training programs. Some car manufacturers also offer management-training classes and seminars. Courses may include sales-management evaluation, direct sales, interactive marketing, promotion, market research, organizational communication, and data-processing-systems management. Many firms pay all or part of the cost for those who successfully complete courses.

Education and Training

Courses in management and internships while a person is still in school are highly recommended. More and more dealers prefer to hire Sales Managers with a four-year college degree in business administration and marketing, especially in larger, more competitive, and more efficient dealerships. A bachelor's degree in sociology, psychology, literature, journalism, or philosophy, among other subjects, is acceptable.

Some dealers prefer a bachelor's or master's degree in business administration with an emphasis on marketing. Courses in business law, economics, accounting, finance, mathematics, and statistics are helpful. Familiarity with word processing and database applications also is important for many positions. Computer skills are vital because interactive marketing, product promotion, and advertising on the Internet are getting more and more common.

Experience, Skills, and Personality Traits

Persons interested in becoming Sales Managers should be mature, creative, highly motivated, resistant to stress, flexible, and decisive. The ability to communicate persuasively, both orally and in writing, with other managers, staff, and the public is vital. Sales Managers also need tact, good judgment, and exceptional ability to establish and maintain effective personal relationships with supervisory and professional staff members.

The ability to communicate in a foreign language (especially Spanish) may open up job opportunities in many rapidly growing areas around the country and in cities with large Spanish-speaking populations.

Unions and Associations

Some Sales Managers may belong to a variety of general business groups, such as Sales and Marketing Executives International, the American International Automobile Dealers Association, Automotive Warehouse Distributors Association, or the National Automotive Dealers Association.

Tips for Entry

1. To find out exactly how to qualify for a job as Sales Manager, contact local dealerships and ask the dealer or manager in charge.
2. Search the Internet for Sales Manager positions.
3. For information about careers and certification in sales and marketing management, contact: Sales and Marketing Executives International, 5500 Interstate North Parkway, No. 545, Atlanta, Georgia 30328-4662 (Web site: http://www.smei.org).

MARKETING MANAGER

Duties: Develops marketing plans for the dealership, handles day-to-day marketing functions; plans and implements special events and oversees public relations campaigns

Alternate Title(s): Marketing Director

Salary Range: $20.34 to $55.39 an hour

Employment Prospects: Fair

Advancement Prospects: Good

Best Geographical Location(s): Jobs can be found throughout the country

Prerequisites:

Education or Training—Four-year college degree in business administration or marketing preferred

Experience—Experience in dealership marketing, sales, service, or administration

Special Skills and Personality Traits—Creativity; good written, oral, and computer skills; pleasant personality

```
General Manager
```

```
Marketing Manager
```

```
Assistant Marketing Manager
```

Position Description

Auto dealership Marketing Managers develop marketing plans for the dealership, handle day-to-day marketing functions; plan and implement special events and oversee public relations campaigns. Marketing Managers develop the dealership's detailed marketing strategy. With the help of subordinates, they determine the demand for cars and services offered by the dealership and its competitors, and identify potential markets for their cars.

Marketing Managers also may develop pricing strategy with an eye toward maximizing the dealership's profits while ensuring that customers are satisfied. In collaboration with sales department and other managers, they monitor car-buying trends and work with advertising and promotion managers to attract potential customers.

Marketing Managers in motor vehicle dealerships work longer hours than do those in most other industries. Long hours, including evenings and weekends, are common, since many dealers provide evening and weekend service to satisfy consumers. Working under pressure is unavoidable when schedules change and problems arise, but deadlines and goals must still be met.

Salaries

Salary for a Marketing Manager at an auto dealership depends in part on the location and size of the dealership and the experience of the manager, but averages $40.01 an hour. Salaries range from $20.34 to more than $55.39 an hour. Top-paying states are New York (average $55.92/hour), New Jersey (54.18), and Minnesota (53.87).

Employment Prospects

Marketing Manager jobs are highly coveted and will be sought by other managers or highly experienced professional and technical personnel, which means there is usually keen competition for these positions. College graduates with related experience, a high level of creativity, and strong communication skills should have the best job opportunities. Those who have new media and interactive marketing skills will be particularly sought after.

Employment of Marketing Managers is expected to increase faster than the average for all occupations through 2012, according to the U.S. Bureau of Labor Statistics. Increasingly intense domestic and global competition in the automotive industry should require greater marketing, promotional, and public relations efforts. At the same time, the number of auto dealerships is expected to decline as consolidation continues in the industry.

Advancement Prospects

Because of the importance and high visibility of their jobs, Marketing Managers often are prime candidates for advancement to the highest ranks. Well-trained, experienced, successful managers may be promoted to higher positions in their own or other dealerships. Some become top executives. Managers with extensive experience and sufficient capital may open their own businesses.

Marketing Managers are usually promoted from within the dealership or hired from among applicants who have worked in other dealerships in some marketing capacity. Most marketing management positions are filled by promoting experienced staff or related professional or technical personnel. For example, many Marketing Managers in auto dealerships are former car salesmen. In small dealerships, where the number of positions is limited, advancement to a management position usually comes slowly. In large dealerships, promotion may occur more quickly.

Although experience, ability, and leadership are important in order to be promoted, employees can be promoted more quickly by participating in management training programs conducted by many large dealerships. Companies also provide their employees with continuing education opportunities, either in-house or at local colleges and universities, and encourage employee participation in seminars and conferences, often provided by professional societies.

In collaboration with colleges and universities, numerous marketing and related associations sponsor national or local management training programs. Courses include brand and product management, international marketing, sales management evaluation, telemarketing and direct sales, interactive marketing, promotion, marketing communication, market research, organizational communication, and data processing systems procedures and management. Some dealerships pay all or part of the cost for those who successfully complete courses.

Education and Training

A four-year college degree with a business or public relations/communication major is usually required for Market-ing Manager positions; some employers prefer a bachelor's or master's degree in business administration with an emphasis on marketing. Courses in business law, economics, accounting, finance, mathematics, and statistics are helpful. Courses in management while one is in school are highly recommended. Familiarity with word processing and database applications also is important. Computer skills are vital because interactive marketing, product promotion, and advertising on the Internet are increasingly common.

Experience, Skills, and Personality Traits

Marketing Managers should be mature, creative, highly motivated, flexible, decisive, and able to handle stress. The ability to communicate persuasively, both orally and in writing, with other managers, staff, and the public is vital. Marketing Managers also need tact, good judgment, and exceptional ability to establish and maintain effective personal relationships with supervisory staff and employees.

The ability to communicate in a foreign language (especially Spanish) may open up employment opportunities in many rapidly growing niche markets around the country, especially in large cities and in areas with large Spanish-speaking populations.

Unions and Associations

Marketing Managers may belong to a number of trade associations that can provide support and career guidance, including the American Marketing Association, the Marketing Research Association, the Public Relations Society of America, the National Automobile Dealers Association, the Automotive Training Managers Council, Automotive Industry Planning Council, or the International Automobile Dealers Association.

Tips for Entry

1. Check the classified section of the newspaper under "marketing," "professional," "business," or "corporate marketing."
2. Send your résumé and cover letter to dealerships for which you're interested in working.
3. Join trade associations, such as the American Marketing Association or the National Automobile Dealers Association; jobs may be listed in their trade journals.
4. Look for jobs online, at Web sites such as www.monster.com or www.hotjobs.com.

FINANCE/INSURANCE MANAGER

CAREER PROFILE

Duties: Establishes relationships with financing and insurance companies and sells those products to vehicle purchasers

Alternate Title(s): None

Salary Range: $29.96 an hour

Employment Prospects: Fair

Advancement Prospects: Fair

Best Geographical Location(s): All locations throughout the country have positions

Prerequisites:

Education or Training—Bachelor's degree helpful, preferably with a business major

Experience—Sales, finance, and dealership experience helpful

Special Skills and Personality Traits—Attention to detail; good communication, mathematics, and computer skills

CAREER LADDER

```
┌─────────────────────────────────────┐
│  Sales Manager or General Manager    │
└─────────────────────────────────────┘

┌─────────────────────────────────────┐
│      Finance/Insurance Manager       │
└─────────────────────────────────────┘

┌─────────────────────────────────────┐
│      Finance Assistant Manager       │
└─────────────────────────────────────┘
```

Position Description

A Finance/Insurance Manager at a car dealership establishes relationships with financing and insurance companies and sells those products to car purchasers. Typically, they work in the aftermarket sales department, which sells additional services and merchandise after a car salesperson has closed a deal.

Finance/Insurance Managers oversee the selling of service contracts and insurance to new and used vehicle buyers and arrange financing for their purchase.

Representatives offer extended warranties and additional services, such as undercoat sealant and environmental paint protection packages, to increase the revenue generated for each vehicle sold. After the buyer has negotiated a price for a car, the salesperson escorts the buyer to the Finance Manager's office to sign the final sale or lease contract. The Finance Manager arranges financing, if required, and tries to get the buyer to purchase additional service contracts, insurance, sealants, or paint protection

Salaries

Salary for a Finance/Insurance Manager at an auto dealership depends on the location and size of the dealership, and the experience and training of the manager, but salaries typically average $29.96 an hour.

Employment Prospects

As dealers continue to gobble up smaller dealers, there will be fewer, but larger auto dealerships, which will slow the growth of managerial jobs. As a result, competition for Finance/Insurance Manager positions will remain relatively stiff, according to the U.S. Bureau of Labor Statistics. College graduates with financial experience, good communication skills, and excellent business skills should have the best job opportunities.

Advancement Prospects

Experienced Finance/Insurance Managers are often promoted to higher positions in their own dealerships, or hired from among applicants who have worked in other dealerships in some financial capacity.

Experience, ability, and leadership are important characteristics of those Finance/Insurance Managers who want to be promoted, but employees can be promoted more quickly by participating in management training programs conducted by large dealers. Dealerships also provide their employees with continuing education opportunities and encourage employee participation in finance or insurance seminars and conferences.

Education and Training

Financial/Insurance Managers must have a four-year college degree (preferably as a business major); completion of extra management or financial training classes and seminars is desirable

Experience, Skills, and Personality Traits

Finance/Insurance Managers should be mature, motivated, discreet, and decisive, and have superior computer and mathematical skills, tact, and good judgment. The ability to communicate persuasively, both orally and in writing, with other managers and the public, is important. Several years of experience in the finance department of an auto dealership is also helpful.

Unions and Associations

Finance/Insurance Managers typically may belong to a wide range of auto- or business-related associations, including the National Automobile Dealers Association, the Automotive Training Managers Council, Automotive Industry Planning Council, or the International Automobile Dealers Association.

Tips for Entry

1. Check the classified section of the newspaper under "finance," "professional," "business," or "corporate finance."
2. Send your résumé and a cover letter to dealerships for which you're interested in working.
3. Join trade associations, such as the National Automobile Dealers Association; jobs may be listed in their trade journals.
4. Look for jobs online, at Web sites such as www.monster.com or www.hotjobs.com.

AUTOMOTIVE FRANCHISE TOOL DEALER

CAREER PROFILE

Duties: Sell name brand (franchise) tools and equipment directly to shop owners, managers, and service technicians

Alternate Title(s): None

Salary Range: $35,000 to $80,000+

Employment Prospects: Good

Advancement Prospects: Fair

Best Geographical Location(s): Anywhere throughout the United States may have opportunities for Automotive Franchise Tool Dealers

Prerequisites:

Education or Training—A high school diploma required; formal training in auto repair and/or business subjects helpful

Experience—Auto technician experience vital; selling experience helpful

Special Skills and Personality Traits—Discipline; independence; good math and business skills; good sales ability; ability to work well with people

CAREER LADDER

```
┌─────────────────────────────────────┐
│ Automotive Tool Sales Field Manager  │
└─────────────────────────────────────┘

┌─────────────────────────────────────┐
│  Automotive Franchise Tool Dealer    │
└─────────────────────────────────────┘

┌─────────────────────────────────────┐
│          Auto Technician             │
└─────────────────────────────────────┘
```

Position Description

Automotive Franchise Tool Dealers sell tools and equipment directly to shop owners, managers, and service technicians who work in car dealerships, body shops, independent repair shops, marinas, airports—wherever cars, trucks, boats, and other vehicles are repaired and maintained. Because almost all technicians buy and own their own tools, tool dealers provide a valuable and necessary service.

There are several large, well-respected tool franchises in the United States, including Snap-On Tools, MAC tools, and Matco. A tool franchise is already a functioning business system. While entrepreneurs must have many thousands (or millions) of dollars to set up a profitable business, a franchisee can step into an already established concept, with much less risk of failure. This is important, since as many as 80 percent of new business start-ups fail each year.

Dealers keep their customers informed about new products and service ideas, handle warranty repair and replacement when necessary, and provide affordable programs for technicians to expand and develop their tools and capabilities. This development is very important to auto technicians, since their tools and equipment define the amount and type of work they can do. In order to become a better technician and make more money, they must buy tools to do the jobs they want to do.

Automotive Franchise Tool Dealers usually own their businesses, which must include a walk-in van and an inventory of tools for sale. They usually visit each customer once a week, selling tools or collecting money from previous sales.

This means they must build personal relationships with their customers, learning about their goals, aspirations, and needs, and working with them to build their tool inventories.

Salaries

Although the success rate for franchise-owned business is generally better than for many independent businesses, there is no guarantee of success. Often an Automotive Franchise Tool Dealer's profit margin is a reflection of the ability to properly run a franchise. Salaries may range from a beginning annual net income of $35,000 to more than $80,000 for experienced Automotive Franchise Tool Dealers.

Employment Prospects

Motor vehicle dealerships are expected to decline in number but increase in size, so consolidation should not hurt the hardworking Automotive Franchise Tool Dealer. College graduates with sales experience, engaging personality, and considerable mechanic experience should have the best chance of a successful career in selling tools on a franchise basis.

Advancement Prospects

Once a tool dealer obtains a franchise to sell tools, the only way to advance is to enlarge the business or the territory. Alternatively, the tool dealer may choose to leave the business and move into a field manager position for the national franchise.

Education and Training

The best Automotive Franchise Tool Dealers are former automotive technicians who understand the kinds of tools they are selling. The franchise company (such as Snap-on Tools or MAC) usually provides classroom and in-the-field training. In addition, tool dealers can usually turn to an experienced field manager, who often serves as coach and business consultant.

Experience, Skills, and Personality Traits

Running a business and selling tools to professionals requires a commitment to understanding problems, paying attention to details, and building relationships based on honesty and trust. Prospective Automotive Franchise Tool Dealers must be dependable, good with people, and have the ability and desire to be successful. If you are the type of person who desires to own your own business and be your own boss, then there may be a place for you in franchising. The varied opportunities available in franchising are drawing people from every walk of life, as corporate and professional people are buying franchises every day. The numbers of women and minority franchise owners is dramatically increasing, as is the number of young owners recently out of college. Investors at all levels are finding that few financial investments can compete with the potential income and personal growth of an established and reputable franchise.

However, franchising is not for everyone; some people do not adjust well to a franchisor setting. Franchisors have established standards and rules, sometimes making decisions with which the tool dealer might not agree. Before you invest in a tool franchise, you should investigate the business and make sure you understand the franchise model.

Unions and Associations

Automotive Franchise Tool Dealers may wish to join the American Association of Franchisees, the National Institute for Automotive Service Excellence, or the Dealers International Franchise Association.

Tips for Entry

1. Visit a Web site dedicated to franchising at www.automotivefranchise.com for more information.
2. Franchises are open particularly to women, who should consider contacting the Franchises For Women staff at (888) 363-3390 or contactus@franchisesforwomen.com.
3. To find out exactly how to go about buying a tool dealer franchise, contact local dealerships and ask for names of tool salesmen who visit the dealership.
4. Visit your school's career counseling office for help in identifying franchises with whom you'd like to work.
5. Use your contacts. The easiest way to network is to ask an Automotive Franchise Tool Dealer you already know for the name of someone else, or for a regional manager. When you call, say, "So-and-so suggested I call you."

RACING

RACE CAR DRIVER

CAREER PROFILE

Duties: Drive cars in competitive racing events

Alternate Title(s): Auto Racer

Salary Range: $17,100 to $577,500+

Employment Prospects: Fair

Advancement Prospects: Fair

Best Geographical Location(s): All locations throughout the country with race tracks have job possibilities for experienced Race Car Drivers, although southern areas of the country may have more tracks (NASCAR in North Carolina, for example). Certain types of racing may be predominant in different parts of the country, such as dirt tracks in the Midwest.

Prerequisites:

Education or Training—High school diploma recommended; vocational auto mechanics courses highly desirable; driving school training highly desirable

Experience—Experience as an auto mechanic highly desirable

Special Skills and Personality Traits—Good concentration; attention to detail; physical strength; quick reactions

Licensure/Certification—Each race sanctioning body requires provisional, regional, and/or national competition license

CAREER LADDER

> **Professional Race Car Driver for one of the premier series run by NASCAR, IRL, SCCA, etc.**

> **Professional Race Car Driver**

> **Amateur Race Car Driver**

Position Description

Race Car Drivers drive in competitive racing events, trying to finish a race as quickly as possible without damaging the car. Today there are many kinds of auto races and many kinds of special racing cars, including drag racing, NASCAR racing (racetracks in the United States), formula racing, Grand Prix racing (primarily in Europe), short track, road racing, and off-road racing. Races using other vehicles are also popular, including go-karts, tractors, trucks, motorcycles, and boats. Most drivers specialize in one kind of racing.

Race Car Drivers usually begin by driving the car over the track before the race to familiarize himself or herself with the course, and then participate in qualifying and elimination races to qualify the car for the race. The Race Car Driver drives the car in the race, analyzing the speed and position of other cars to determine when and where to maneuver the car into a favorable position to win while keeping track of instruments on the dashboard to ensure that the car is operating efficiently. At the same time, the Race Car Driver watches for warning signs (such as flags or lights) that indicate an incident on the course, while in some instances maintaining radio contact with pit crew. Afterward, the Race Car Driver may help maintain the car, advising about handling and further developments to improve performance.

The winner is not always the fastest driver; instead, it may be the person who can drive very fast and, by acquired experience, complete the race with smart moves at the right time.

Salaries

Salaries for this job ranges wildly from a low of $17,100 to $18,900 for beginning drivers to a high of between $19,800 to $577,500 and up (for the sport's elite). As in any sport, very few ever qualify for the highest echelon teams, where multimillion-dollar fortunes can be made.

Employment Prospects

The sport of auto racing is extremely competitive and requires dedication, training, excellent driving skills, and a great deal of money. While very few Race Car Drivers will ever break into the highest levels of the sport, winning national recognition and seven-figure salaries, there is plenty of opportunity at the local level for young, enthusiastic racers to participate in the sport and earn a moderate living. Employment of automobile racers is expected to increase about as rapidly as the average for all occupations through the year 2010. Many Race Car Drivers are self-employed or work for a large sponsoring agency.

Advancement Prospects

There are many more amateur Race Car Drivers than professionals. Professionals usually begin racing as amateurs and work their way up. Many drivers begin by building or buying their own race cars as a hobby, and then joining a race-sanctioning organization (such as NASCAR) that typically runs a series of racing events on a local, regional, or national level.

Education and Training

There is no minimum educational requirement for this job, but it is recommended that Race Car Drivers graduate from high school. High school students interested in this field should consider taking vocational courses in auto mechanics, because the best drivers are usually also good mechanics who understand the inner workings of the vehicle. An engineering degree could also be considered a plus.

In addition, there are a host of specialized professional driving schools in the United States and Canada, including many schools run by auto clubs and professional racing organizations that offer training for potential Race Car Drivers. In general, auto racers need some type of specialized training in order to obtain a provisional competition license.

Many race teams offer apprenticeship intern programs. For example, NASCAR offers a program in which an apprentice candidate works for a minimum of three teams; each team assigns the apprentice different tasks during their stay. This way the candidate learns different aspects of the job without being confused by each team doing the same things differently. Candidates also will learn different jobs to help determine interest and abilities. In many cases, these programs may lead to a full-time position with one of the teams or serve as a recommendation to teams looking for employees.

Experience, Skills, and Personality Traits

Successful Race Car Drivers must be hard workers with a lot of physical strength to control a race car at high speeds. They also must be willing to travel to attend different race sites. Flexibility is also important, since the hours of races and preparation for races varies a great deal. When drivers are not racing, they are usually working on the car, seeking sponsors, or testing equipment. Race Car Drivers also need a high tolerance for speed and danger.

Special Requirements

Each race sanctioning body (such as NASCAR) has their own requirements for a special "competition license" in order to compete on their racetracks. The beginning race car license is a "provisional" competition license; these may be followed by a regional or national competition license. While requirements may differ slightly from one sanctioning body to another, in general Race Car Drivers are expected to demonstrate knowledge of theory and driving ability, pass a written test, have some training experience, and pass a physical exam.

Unions and Associations

Depending on the type of car racing a Race Car Driver is interested in, there are a number of sanctioning bodies to which he or she could belong. These include NASCAR, national Hot Rod Association (NHRA), AHRA (drag racing), SCCA, IRL (Indy Racing League), USAC, ARCA (stockcars), or IMSA.

Tips for Entry

1. Join a race-sanctioning organization (such as NASCAR), as listed above (see Appendix I for contact information).
2. Get experience in mechanical aspects of the type of car you want to race.
3. Try to get any type of job at all (or even volunteer for free) on a race team to get experience.
4. Compete on a grassroots level (such as at your local racetrack) or at a race driving school for the experience, and to determine if this is a good career choice for you before you spend a great deal of your own money.
5. Visit the Web site at www.racejobs.com to check on job availability in professional auto racing.
6. Consider signing up with a race car employment agency to get started in auto racing (such as Pro Motorsports Employment).
7. Check out apprenticeship intern programs offered by different race-sanctioning organizations (such as NASCAR).
8. Visit www.jobsinsports.com to find potential jobs or internships in the auto racing field.

RACE CAR TEAM MECHANIC

CAREER PROFILE

Duties: Build, diagnose, and repair race cars; perform preventive care

Alternate Title(s): Race Mechanic

Salary Range: $14,000 to $100,000

Employment Prospects: Fair

Advancement Prospects: Fair

Best Geographical Location(s): Any area that has significant motorsport activity, such as Charlotte, N.C., for NASCAR-related races or Indianapolis for IRL

Prerequisites:

Education or Training—High school or postsecondary vocational school automotive service technician training program; specialized race mechanic training; engineering degree

Experience—Experience in car repairs

Special Skills and Personality Traits—Superior diagnostic skills; attention to detail; mechanical ability; mathematics and computer skills; ability to work under pressure; flexibility; willingness to work long hours

Licensure/Certification—Voluntary certification in one or more of the eight tests given by the National Institute for Automotive Service Excellence (ASE)

CAREER LADDER

```
┌─────────────────────────────────┐
│   Crew Chief or Team Manager    │
└─────────────────────────────────┘

┌─────────────────────────────────┐
│     Race Car Team Mechanic      │
└─────────────────────────────────┘

┌─────────────────────────────────┐
│       Technician Trainee        │
└─────────────────────────────────┘
```

Position Description

The Race Car Team Mechanic is responsible for inspecting, maintaining, and building components of race cars and repairing race cars for a racing team. The ability to diagnose the source of a problem quickly and accurately requires good reasoning ability and a thorough knowledge of cars. Race Car Team Mechanics are high-tech problem solvers who must understand a race car's complex components, working with electronic diagnostic equipment and computer-based technical reference materials. The increasing sophistication of automotive technology today means that Race Car Team Mechanics must use computerized shop equipment while maintaining their skill with traditional hand tools. Mechanics must keep abreast of modern repair techniques for all the advanced components and systems and Race Car Team Mechanics are often at the cutting edge of new technologies.

To locate a problem, Race Car Team Mechanics first test components and systems, and then isolate those that could not logically be the cause of the problem. Mechanics may have to test-drive the car or use onboard and handheld diagnostic computers and other testing devices to identify the source of the problem, or rely on a driver's observations to diagnose problems. They can also make adjustments with precise calculations downloaded from large computerized databases. Mechanics are also responsible for routine service, assessing and lubricating engines and other major components, and repairing or replacing worn parts before they cause problems that could damage critical components of the race car.

While teams provide large diagnostic equipment, mechanics are expected to provide their own tools; many experienced workers have invested thousands of dollars in their own equipment.

Salaries

Average hourly earnings of Race Car Team Mechanics range between $10 and $19 an hour. The lowest 10 percent may earn less than $8, and the highest 10 percent earn more than $24 an hour. Beginning Race Car Team Mechanics earn an average of $25,018, and the most experienced master technicians can earn more than $70,000 a year.

Employment Prospects

Because working for race car teams is highly desirable, jobs as Race Car Team Mechanics are limited and extremely competitive. Job opportunities are expected to be fair for those who complete auto training programs in high school, vocational and technical schools, community colleges, or race car mechanic schools.

Advancement Prospects

Beginners usually start as trainee mechanics or mechanics' helpers and gradually acquire and practice their skills by working with experienced Race Car Team Mechanics. It usually takes two to five years of experience to become a fully trained Race Car Team Mechanic who can quickly perform the more difficult types of routine service and repairs. Experienced Race Car Team Mechanics with leadership ability may advance to team supervisory positions.

Education and Training

Because of the complexity of race cars, teams require a high school diploma plus postsecondary training. Courses in automotive repair, electronics, physics, chemistry, English, computers, and mathematics provide a good educational background. While some Race Car Team Mechanics still learn the trade by serving as an apprentice, today's sophisticated technology almost requires a formal training program in high school or postsecondary vocational school. Many high schools, community colleges, and public and private vocational and technical schools offer automotive service technician training programs.

Although high school programs are helpful, their quality is uneven. The better programs, such as the Automotive Youth Education Service (AYES), provide students with a technician's certification and high school diploma. While others try to equip graduates with enough skills to get a job as a mechanic's helper or trainee mechanic, some schools offer just an introduction to automotive technology and service that would be helpful only to consumers and hobbyists.

Traditional postsecondary programs usually offer combined classroom instruction and hands-on practice. Some trade and technical school programs provide concentrated training for six months to a year, depending on how many hours the student attends each week. Community college programs awarding an associate degree or certificate normally spread the training over two years, and supplement the automotive training with instruction in English, basic mathematics, computers, and other subjects. Some students earn repair certificates and opt to leave the program to begin their careers before graduation. More recently, some programs have added classes in stress management to help mechanics learn to deal with the high-stress environment of the racetrack.

A growing number of programs at colleges and specialty schools (especially in the South) are developing educational and practical training programs. The University of North Carolina Charlotte, for instance, has a highly regarded motorsports and automotive engineering program within its Lee College of Engineering. The program's students enter various competitions while studying automotive theory and applications. North Carolina A & T University in Greensboro has a motorsports program that allows students to participate in various competitions as they learn. The Bobby Isaac Motorsports Program at Catawba Valley Community College's East Campus in Hickory, North Carolina, prepares students for entry-level jobs as team mechanics or metal fabricators in motorsports.

The NASCAR Technical Institute, an official educational partner of the stock car-sanctioning body, offers instruction on the basics of engine construction, body and aero applications, chassis applications, body fabrication, chassis fabrication, and dyno testing for performance and durability. The first of its kind in the country, "NASCAR Tech" combines automotive and NASCAR technology programs.

Many car manufacturers and their dealers sponsor two-year associate degree programs at postsecondary schools. The Accrediting Commission of Career Schools and Colleges of Technology (ACCSCT) currently certifies a number of automotive and diesel technology schools. Race Car Team Mechanic schools also offer specialized training.

Education continues on the job; teams send mechanics to manufacturer training centers to learn to repair new models or receive special training in repair of components, such as electronic fuel injection or engine management systems.

Special Requirements

Voluntary certification by the National Institute of Automotive Service Excellence (ASE) is the standard credential for automotive technicians and also may be helpful for Race Car Team Mechanics, although certification is not required.

Certification is available in eight different service areas, including electrical systems, engine repair, brake systems, suspension, heating, and air-conditioning. To be certified in a specific area, mechanics must have at least two years of experience and pass a written examination. Completion of an automotive training program in high school, vocational or trade school, or community or junior college may be substituted for one year of experience. In some cases, graduates of ASE-certified programs achieve certification in up to three specialties.

For certification as a master automotive technician, mechanics must be certified in all eight areas. Mechanics must retake each examination at least every five years to maintain their certification.

Experience, Skills, and Personality Traits

Race Car Team Mechanics should have mechanical aptitude, strong analytical abilities, and an understanding of how cars work, in addition to good reading, mathematics, and computer skills. Persistence and attention to detail is important, as is the ability to withstand significant stress and be a team player.

Mechanics usually work indoors in clean, well-ventilated, well-lit repair shops, but some shops are drafty and noisy, so a high tolerance to noisy, dirty environments is important. Although mechanics can fix some problems with simple adjustments, they often work with dirty and greasy parts or in awkward positions, lifting heavy parts and tools. Minor cuts, burns, and bruises are common, but mechanics usually avoid serious accidents if the shop is kept clean and orderly and safety practices are observed. Work also may take place at race venues under varying conditions. Race Car Team Mechanics can expect to work more than 40 hours a week, especially before and during races.

Unions and Associations

Race Car Team Mechanics may belong to associations such as the Service Technicians Society or the National Institute for Automotive Service Excellence.

Tips for Entry

1. Try to obtain skills by working on your own cars and by taking every relevant course available during high school, followed by training at a Race Car Team Mechanic school.
2. An internship or summer job with a race car team (even volunteering for free) can provide invaluable experience.
3. Check Web sites of racing associations or teams to spot job openings; consider joining a race sanctioning organization (such as NASCAR or SCCA).
4. Check classifieds at Service Technicians Society jobsite: http://www.sts.sae.org/misc/classified.htm.
5. Positions should be advertised in the newspaper classified ad section or specialty racing publication under "trades: mechanical" or "auto."
6. Send your résumé and a cover letter to all the grassroots teams in your state.
7. If you graduated from vocational or Race Car Team Mechanic school, find out if the school has a job placement service and work with them to land a position.

MOTORSPORTS PUBLIC RELATIONS SPECIALIST

CAREER PROFILE

Duties: Serve as advocate for racetrack, motor racing team, car-related business, or nonprofit motorsports associations; create favorable attitudes among various organizations, special interest groups, and the public through effective communication

Alternate Title(s): None

Salary Range: $24,240 to $75,100

Employment Prospects: Excellent

Advancement Prospects: Excellent

Best Geographical Location(s): All parts of the country may hire PR specialists for motorsports, but the South has more racing-related jobs in general

Prerequisites:

Education or Training—College degree in communications, PR, English, or journalism

Experience—Motorsports or car-related experience helpful; racing school experience desirable

Special Skills and Personality Traits—Excellent writing skills; ability to communicate well in public

Licensure/Certification—Accreditation is available from the Public Relations Society of America and the International Association of Business communicators

CAREER LADDER

```
┌─────────────────────────────┐
│     Motorsports Public      │
│    Relations Director       │
└─────────────────────────────┘

┌─────────────────────────────┐
│     Motorsports Public      │
│    Relations Specialist     │
└─────────────────────────────┘

┌─────────────────────────────┐
│     Motorsports Public      │
│    Relations Assistant      │
└─────────────────────────────┘
```

Position Description

Motorsports Public Relations Specialists may serve as advocates for racetracks, motor racing teams, car-related businesses, and nonprofit auto-related associations, as well as build and maintain positive relationships with the public. People who handle publicity for a racing-related individual or team, or who direct public relations for an auto racing organization, may contact people, plan, research, and prepare material for distribution. They also may handle advertising or sales promotion work to support marketing.

As managers recognize the growing importance of good public relations to the success of their organizations, they increasingly rely on Motorsports Public Relations Specialists for advice on the strategy and policy of such programs.

Public relations specialists handle organizational functions such as media, community, and consumer relations.

However, public relations is not only "telling the organization's story"; it is also important that the specialist understand the attitudes and concerns of consumers, employees, and various other groups.

To improve communications, Motorsports Public Relations Specialists establish and maintain cooperative relationships with representatives of community, consumer, employee, and public interest groups, as well as with representatives from print and broadcast journalism.

Informing the general public about an organization's policies, activities, and accomplishments is an important part of a Motorsports Public Relations Specialist's job. The work also involves helping managers understand public attitudes and concerns of the many groups and organizations with which they must deal.

Public relations specialists prepare press releases and contact people in the media who might print or broadcast their material. In fact, many radio or television special reports, newspaper stories, and magazine articles start out as a press release from a PR specialist.

Motorsports Public Relations Specialists also arrange and conduct programs to keep up contact between organization representatives and the public. For example, they might set up speaking engagements and prepare speeches for racing officials. They might represent their employers in community projects; make film, slide, or other visual presentations at meetings and school assemblies; and plan conventions. In addition, they are responsible for preparing annual reports and writing proposals for various projects.

Some Motorsports Public Relations Specialists work a standard 35- to 40-hour week, but unpaid overtime is common in this field. Occasionally, they must be at the job or on call around the clock, especially if there is an emergency, crisis, or important race. Public relations offices are busy places; work schedules can be irregular and frequently interrupted. Schedules often have to be rearranged so that workers can meet deadlines, deliver speeches, attend meetings and community activities, or travel.

Typically, Motorsports Public Relations Specialists are concentrated in large southern cities, where press services and other communications facilities are readily available and many auto racing-related businesses and trade associations have their headquarters.

Salaries

Average annual earnings for Motorsports Public Relations Specialists are $41,710; the lowest 10 percent earn less than $24,240, and the top 10 percent earn more than $75,100.

Employment Prospects

Although employment is projected to increase much faster than the average, keen competition is expected for entry-level jobs. Opportunities should be best for college graduates who combine a degree in public relations or other communications-related fields with a motorsports public relations internship and related work experience in the automotive or auto racing field.

Keen competition will likely continue for public relations jobs as there will probably be more qualified applicants than job openings. Many people are attracted to this profession due to the high-profile nature of the work and the relative ease of entry.

The need for good public relations in an increasingly competitive business environment should spur demand for Motorsports Public Relations Specialists in organizations of all sizes. In addition to employment growth, job opportunities should result from the need to replace PR specialists who take other jobs.

Advancement Prospects

A Motorsports Public Relations Specialist may be hired as a research assistant or account assistant and be promoted to account executive, account supervisor, vice president, and, eventually, senior vice president. Promotion to supervisory jobs may come as specialists show that they can handle more demanding assignments.

A portfolio of published automotive articles, television or radio programs, slide presentations, and other work can help in getting a better position in a larger, more prestigious organization related to racing. Ultimately, public relations specialists can move into positions as director of public relations at corporations, racing teams, racetracks, and other automotive organizations.

Some experienced Motorsports Public Relations Specialists start their own consulting firms.

Education and Training

There are no defined standards for entry into a racing public relations career. A college degree in English, journalism, public relations, or communications, combined with PR experience (usually gained through an internship) is considered excellent preparation for automotive public relations work. In fact, internships are becoming vital to obtaining employment.

Some racing teams, racetracks, and racing organizations seek college graduates who have worked in electronic or print journalism; others look for applicants with demonstrated communication skills and training or experience in a field related to racing—engineering, sales, or repairs, for example. Many colleges and universities offer bachelor's and postsecondary degrees in public relations, usually in a journalism or communications department. In addition, many other colleges offer at least one course in this field. A common public relations sequence includes courses in public relations principles and techniques; public relations management and administration, including organizational development; writing, emphasizing news releases, proposals, annual reports, scripts, speeches, and related items; visual communications, including desktop publishing and computer graphics; and research, emphasizing social science research and survey design and implementation. Courses in advertising, journalism, business administration, finance, psychology, sociology, and creative writing also are helpful. In addition, many colleges help students gain part-time internships in public relations that provide valuable experience and training.

Some auto racing organizations, particularly those with a large public relations staff, have formal training programs for new employees. In smaller organizations, new employees work under the guidance of experienced staff members.

Special Requirements

The Public Relations Society of America accredits public relations specialists who have at least five years of experience in the field and have passed a comprehensive six-hour examination (five hours written, one hour oral).

The International Association of Business Communicators (IABC) also has an accreditation program for public relations specialists. Those who meet all the requirements of the program earn the "Accredited Business Communicator" designation. Candidates must have at least five years of experience in a communication field and pass a written and oral examination, and submit a portfolio of work samples demonstrating involvement in a range of communication projects and a thorough understanding of communication planning. Employers may consider professional recognition through accreditation a sign of competence in this field, which could be especially helpful in a competitive job market.

Experience, Skills, and Personality Traits

Creativity, initiative, good judgment, and the ability to express thoughts clearly and simply are essential in landing a job as a Motorsports Public Relation Specialist. Decision making, problem solving, and research skills also are important. People who choose motorsports public relations as a career need an outgoing personality, self-confidence, an understanding of human psychology, an enthusiasm for motivating people, and an interest in auto racing. They should be competitive, yet flexible, and able to function as part of a team.

Unions and Associations

Membership in local chapters of the Public Relations Student Society of America (affiliated with the Public Relations Society of America) or the International Association of Business Communicators provides an opportunity for students to exchange views with public relations specialists and to make professional contacts that may help them find a job in the motorsports public relations field.

Tips for Entry

1. Before graduation, writing about motorsports for a school publication or television or radio station provides valuable experience and material for a portfolio.
2. Check job listings on the Web site of the Public Relations Society of America, Inc. (www.prsa.org).
3. Send your résumé and a cover letter to all the racing teams and local racetracks in your area.
4. Try to find an internship in motorsports public relations.
5. Check PR positions advertised in automotive trade journals or specialized help wanted sections.
6. Check employment Web sites such as www.monster.com or www.hotjobs.com.
7. Check job listings on racing company Web sites or race team Web sites.

RACING SCHOOL INSTRUCTOR

CAREER PROFILE

Duties: Teach safe motorsports techniques to students of an auto racing school

Alternate Title(s): None

Salary Range: $35,000 to $80,000+

Employment Prospects: Fair

Advancement Prospects: Fair

Best Geographical Location(s): More than 70 racing schools are located throughout the United States and Canada

Prerequisites:

Education or Training—High school graduate or higher; vocational training helpful

Experience—Professional motorsports experience as a successful race car driver essential

Special Skills and Personality Traits—Patience; attention to detail; ability to communicate well with students; ability to withstand stress; successful driving career

CAREER LADDER

```
┌─────────────────────────────┐
│   Racing School Manager     │
└─────────────────────────────┘

┌─────────────────────────────┐
│  Racing School Instructor   │
└─────────────────────────────┘

┌─────────────────────────────┐
│      Race Car Driver        │
└─────────────────────────────┘
```

Position Description

A Racing School Instructor teaches students how to drive a race car safely and successfully, identifying specific bad driving habits that keep a student from achieving a personal best. Instructors may spend part of their time in the classroom, discussing hand and seating positions, driving dynamics, heel and toe downshifting, and so on. For more advanced drivers, this means shaving precious seconds from pit stops and hairpin turns.

Instructors may perform "follow the leader" exercises, driving the correct racing line around the course so students can learn where on the track they should be driving.

Often instructors ride with students, offering advice to improve skills. If the instructor cannot ride along with the racers, they rely on advanced software in the cars to automatically identify trouble spots. For example, at each Skip Barber school in the United States (there are 20), one special racer is designated the "computer car," equipped with a state-of-the-art software package that collects video footage of the driver in the cockpit and specific information such as how much pressure the driver applies to the brake pedal and how many G forces are created during turns. Instructors and students study the results to determine how a student can improve. Some schools use video equipment positioned at various points around a track as well.

Salaries

Salaries depend on a Racing School Instructor's experience and background, but typically range from $35,000 to more than $80,000.

Employment Prospects

Employment prospects for Racing School Instructors are fair. Competition is incredibly stiff for a relatively small number of positions throughout the country. For example, recently at one driving school, 400 résumés were received, and 30 drivers were interviewed for the instructor position; none were hired.

Advancement Prospects

There are few direct advancement opportunities for Racing School Instructors. They can improve their status by gaining experience and demonstrating success with their students.

Some may move on to become racing school managers. Others may leave to start new racing schools. Racing School Instructors advance primarily through continued accomplishment and success with their students.

Education and Training

A high school diploma is generally required, and a successful professional career as a race car driver is also expected. Additional training in the automotive field, including auto technician experience or fabrication, is highly desirable.

Experience, Skills, and Personality Traits

The ability to remain calm under pressure, patience, attention to detail, ability to concentrate, and considerable skills in communication are all helpful for the highly stressful job of Racing School Instructor.

Unions and Associations

Depending on the type of car racing a Racing School Instructor specializes in, there are a number of sanctioning bodies to which he or she could belong. These include NASCAR, National Hot Rod Association (NHRA), AHRA (drag racing), SCCA, IRL (Indy Racing League), USAC, ARCA (stockcars), or IMSA.

Tips for Entry

1. Visit www.racingjobs.com to see the latest listings for racing-related jobs or to post your résumé online.
2. Send your résumé and a cover letter to every racing school in the United States and Canada where you would like to work.

OTHER AUTOMOTIVE CAREERS

MOTORCYCLE MECHANIC

CAREER PROFILE

Duties: Repair and overhaul motorcycles, motor scooters, mopeds, dirt bikes, and all-terrain vehicles

Alternate Title(s): Motorcycle Technician

Salary Range: $17,250 to $44,360+

Employment Prospects: Fair

Advancement Prospects: Fair

Best Geographical Location(s): All locations throughout the country have job possibilities for well-trained, experienced Motorcycle Mechanics

Prerequisites:

Education or Training—High school or postsecondary vocational school automotive service technician training program

Experience—Experience in motorcycle repairs

Special Skills and Personality Traits—Good diagnostic skills; attention to detail; mechanical ability; mathematics and computer skills

CAREER LADDER

```
┌─────────────────────────────────────┐
│   Shop Supervisor or Shop Owner      │
└─────────────────────────────────────┘

┌─────────────────────────────────────┐
│         Motorcycle Mechanic          │
└─────────────────────────────────────┘

┌─────────────────────────────────────┐
│     Motorcycle Mechanic Trainee      │
└─────────────────────────────────────┘
```

Position Description

Motorcycle Mechanics repair and overhaul motorcycles, motor scooters, mopeds, dirt bikes, and all-terrain vehicles. Besides working on engines, they may work on transmissions, brakes, and ignition systems, and make minor body repairs. Mechanics usually specialize in the service and repair of one type of equipment, although they may work on closely related products. They may service only a few makes and models of motorcycles because usually the dealers service only the products they sell.

Small engines require periodic service to minimize the chance of breakdowns and to keep them operating at peak performance. During routine equipment maintenance, Motorcycle Mechanics follow a checklist including the inspection and cleaning of brakes, electrical systems, fuel injection systems, plugs, carburetors, and other parts. Following inspection, mechanics usually repair or adjust parts that do not work properly, or replace unfixable parts.

Routine maintenance is normally a major part of the Motorcycle Mechanic's work. When equipment breakdowns occur, mechanics use various techniques to diagnose the source and extent of the problem. This may involve use of voltmeters, ammeters, ohmmeters, and electronic analyzers as well as pressure, compression, and vacuum testers. The mark of a skilled mechanic is the ability to diagnose mechanical, fuel, and electrical problems, and to make repairs quickly. Quick and accurate diagnosis requires problem-solving ability and a thorough knowledge of the equipment's operation.

In larger repair shops, Motorcycle Mechanics may use special computerized diagnostic testing equipment as a preliminary tool in analyzing equipment. These computers provide a systematic performance report of various components to compare them to normal ratings. After pinpointing the problem, the mechanic makes the needed adjustments, repairs, or replacements.

Some jobs require minor adjustments or the replacement of a single item. In contrast, a complete engine overhaul requires a number of hours to disassemble the engine and replace worn internal parts. Some skilled mechanics use highly specialized components and the latest computerized equipment to customize and tune motorcycles for racing.

Motorcycle Mechanics usually work in repair shops that are well lighted and ventilated, but they can be noisy when engines are being tested.

The most important work possessions of mechanics are their hand tools; mechanics usually provide their own, and many experienced mechanics have invested thousands of dollars in them. Employers typically furnish expensive power tools, computerized engine analyzers, and other diagnostic equipment. Computerized engine analyzers, compression gauges, ammeters and voltmeters, and other testing devices help mechanics locate faulty parts and tune engines, and hoists may be used to lift heavy motorcycles.

Salaries

Average annual earnings of Motorcycle Mechanics is $27,630; the lowest 10 percent earn less than $17,250, and the highest 10 percent earn more than $44,360. Motorcycle Mechanics who work in small shops do not often receive many benefits, but those hired by larger outfits can expect paid vacations, sick leave, and health insurance. Some employers also pay for work-related training and provide uniforms. Top-paying states include Colorado (average $17.11/hour), Hawaii ($17.03), and Massachusetts ($16.70).

Employment Prospects

Employment for Motorcycle Mechanics is expected to grow slowly, according to the Bureau of Labor Statistics, but those with formal mechanic training should enjoy good job prospects. Motorcycle Mechanics held about 15,000 jobs in 2002, according to the bureau. About one-third worked for retail motorcycle dealers, and most of the rest were hired by independent repair shops or equipment rental companies. About one in four were self-employed.

Most job openings are expected to occur as experienced small engine mechanics leave to transfer to other occupations, retire, or stop working for other reasons. Job prospects should be especially favorable for those who complete mechanic training programs.

As the economy improves through 2012, government experts believe that consumers should accumulate more money with which to buy motorcycles, which will require more mechanics to keep the increasing amount of equipment in operation. In addition, routine service will always be a significant source of work for mechanics. While advancements in technology will lengthen the interval between checkups, the need for qualified mechanics to perform this service will increase.

Employment of Motorcycle Mechanics should increase slowly as the popularity of motorcycles continues to grow. Experts believe that motorcycles should continue to be popular with young adults between the ages of 18 and 24, an age group that historically has had the greatest proportion of motorcycle enthusiasts. Motorcycles also are increasingly popular with those over age 40. Traditionally, this group has the most disposable income to spend on recreational equipment such as motorcycles.

During the winter months in the northern United States, Motorcycle Mechanics may work fewer than 40 hours a week because the amount of repair and service work declines when motorcycles are not being used. Many mechanics work only during the busy spring and summer seasons and may service other types of equipment in the winter. On the other hand, Motorcycle Mechanics may work considerably more than 40 hours a week when demand is strong.

Advancement Prospects

The skills used as a small engine mechanic generally can be transferred to other occupations such as automobile, diesel, or heavy vehicle and mobile equipment mechanics. Experienced Motorcycle Mechanics with leadership ability may become shop supervisors or service managers. Mechanics with sales ability may become sales representatives or open their own repair shops.

Education and Training

Due to the increasing complexity of motorcycles, most employers prefer to hire Motorcycle Mechanics who graduate from formal training programs for small engine mechanics. Because the number of these specialized postsecondary programs is limited, most mechanics learn their skills on the job or while working in related occupations. For trainee jobs, employers hire persons with mechanical aptitude who understand the fundamentals of small two- and four-stroke engines.

Many trainees develop an interest in mechanics and acquire some basic skills by working on cars and motorcycles as a hobby. Others may be introduced to mechanics through vocational automotive training in high school, or one of many postsecondary institutions.

Trainees learn routine service tasks under the guidance of experienced mechanics by replacing ignition points and spark plugs or by taking apart, assembling, and testing new equipment. As trainees gain experience and proficiency, they progress to more difficult tasks such as advanced computerized diagnosis and engine overhauls.

Up to three years of on-the-job training may be necessary before a novice worker becomes competent in all aspects of the repair of motorcycle engines. Employers often send mechanics and trainees to special training courses conducted by motorcycle manufacturers or distributors. These courses, which can last as long as two weeks, upgrade the worker's skills and provide information on repairing new models. They are usually a prerequisite for any mechanic who performs warranty work for manufacturers or insurance companies.

Most employers prefer to hire high school graduates for trainee mechanic positions, but will accept applicants with less education if they possess adequate reading, writing, and arithmetic skills. Many equipment dealers employ students part time and during the summer to help assemble new equipment and perform minor repairs. Helpful high school courses include small engine repair, automobile mechanics, science, and business arithmetic. Knowledge of basic electronics is essential for small engine mechanics, since electronics control engine performance, instrument displays, and a variety of other functions.

Experience, Skills, and Personality Traits

Motorcycle Mechanics should have mechanical aptitude, strong analytical abilities, and an understanding of how motorcycles work, in addition to good reading, mathematics, and computer skills. Persistence and attention to detail is important. To recognize and fix potential problems, mechanics should be familiar with the basic principles of electronics. Although mechanics usually work indoors in clean, well-ventilated, well-lit repair shops, some shops are drafty and noisy, so a high tolerance to noisy, dirty environments is important.

Although Motorcycle Mechanics can fix some problems with simple adjustments, they often work with dirty and greasy parts or in awkward positions, lifting heavy parts and tools. Minor cuts, burns, and bruises are common, but mechanics usually avoid serious accidents when the shop is kept clean and orderly and safety practices are observed.

Unions and Associations

Motorcycle Mechanics may belong to the International Association of Machinists and Aerospace Workers; the International Union, United Automobile, Aerospace and Agricultural Implement Workers of America; the Sheet Metal Workers' International Association; and the International Brotherhood of Teamsters. Mechanics can also join several professional associations, such as the American Motorcycle Institute or the Motorcycle Mechanics Institute.

Tips for Entry

1. Try to obtain skills by working on your own motorcycle or engines and by taking every relevant course available during high school or vocational school.
2. An internship or summer job at a dealer or repair shop can provide invaluable experience.
3. Check Web sites of local dealers and repair shops to spot job openings.
4. Positions should be advertised in the newspaper classified ad section under "Trades: Mechanical."
5. Send your résumé and a cover letter to all the local dealers and repair shops in your area. Because there is always a demand for well-trained mechanics, you may get called for an interview even if the job hasn't been advertised in the paper.
6. If you graduated from vocational or postsecondary school, find out if the school has a job placement service and work with them to land a position.

MOTORBOAT MECHANIC

Duties: Repair and adjust the electrical and mechanical equipment of inboard and outboard boat engines

Alternate Title(s): Marine Equipment Mechanic

Salary Range: $18,740 to $44,380+

Employment Prospects: Fair

Advancement Prospects: Fair

Best Geographical Location(s): All locations throughout the country have job possibilities for well-trained, experienced Motorboat Mechanics, but areas along the eastern or western seaboard, or near large bodies of water, have the most opportunities

Prerequisites:

Education or Training—High school or postsecondary vocational school training program

Experience—Experience in motorboat repairs

Special Skills and Personality Traits—Good diagnostic skills; attention to detail; mechanical ability; mathematics and computer skills

```
┌─────────────────────────────┐
│     Shop Supervisor         │
│   or Marine Shop Owner       │
└─────────────────────────────┘

┌─────────────────────────────┐
│     Motorboat Mechanic       │
└─────────────────────────────┘

┌─────────────────────────────┐
│  Motorboat Mechanic Trainee  │
└─────────────────────────────┘
```

Position Description

Motorboat Mechanics repair and adjust the electrical and mechanical equipment of inboard and outboard boat engines. Most small boats have portable outboard engines that are removed and brought into the repair shop. Larger craft, such as cabin cruisers and commercial fishing boats, are powered by diesel or gasoline inboard or inboard-outboard engines, which are removed only for major overhauls. Most of these repairs are performed at the docks or marinas. Motorboat Mechanics may also work on propellers, steering mechanisms, marine plumbing, and other boat equipment.

Motorboat engines require periodic service to minimize the chance of breakdowns and to keep them operating at peak performance. During routine equipment maintenance, Motorboat Mechanics follow a checklist including the inspection and cleaning of electrical systems, fuel systems, and other parts. Following inspection, mechanics usually repair or adjust parts that do not work properly, or replace unfixable parts. Routine maintenance is normally a major part of the mechanic's work.

Motorboat Mechanics use a variety of techniques to diagnose the source and extent of breakdown problems. The mark of a skilled mechanic is the ability to diagnose mechanical, fuel, and electrical problems, and to make repairs quickly, which requires problem-solving ability and a thorough knowledge of the boat's operation.

In larger marine repair shops, mechanics may use special computerized diagnostic testing equipment as a preliminary tool in analyzing equipment. These computers provide a systematic performance report of various components to compare them to normal ratings. After pinpointing the problem, the mechanic makes the needed adjustments, repairs, or replacements. Some jobs require minor adjustments or the replacement of a single item, but a complete engine overhaul requires a number of hours to disassemble the engine and replace worn parts. Some skilled Motorboat Mechanics use highly specialized components and the latest computerized equipment to customize and tune motorboats for racing.

To recognize and fix potential problems, mechanics should be familiar with the basic principles of electronics.

The most important work possessions of mechanics are their hand tools, including wrenches, pliers, and screwdrivers, power tools, and computerized engine analyzers, compression gauges, ammeters and voltmeters, and other testing devices to locate faulty parts and tune engines. Mechanics usually provide their own tools and many experienced mechanics have invested thousands of dollars in them. Employers typically furnish expensive power tools, computerized engine analyzers, and other diagnostic equipment.

Mechanics usually work in repair shops that are well lighted and ventilated but are sometimes noisy when testing engines. In addition, Motorboat Mechanics may work outdoors at docks or marinas, as well as in all weather conditions when making repairs aboard boats. They may work in cramped or awkward positions to reach a boat's engine.

Salaries

The average salary for a Motorboat Mechanic ranges between $29,170 and $30,420. The lowest 10 percent earn less than $18,740, and the highest 10 percent earn more than $44,380.

Motorboat Mechanics tend to receive few benefits in small shops, but those who work in larger shops often receive paid vacations, sick leave, and health insurance. Some employers also pay for work-related training and provide uniforms. Top-paying states are Hawaii (average $20.16/hour), Massachusetts ($17.82), and Connecticut ($17.77).

Employment Prospects

Motorboat Mechanics held about 22,000 jobs in 2002, according to the Bureau of Labor Statistics; about one-third worked for retail marine dealers. Most of the rest were employed by independent repair shops, marinas, and boat yards; about one in four were self-employed. Employment of Motorboat Mechanics is expected to grow about as fast as the average for all occupations through the year 2012.

Most job openings are expected to occur as experienced small engine mechanics transfer to other occupations, retire, or stop working for other reasons. Job prospects should be especially favorable for those who complete Motorboat Mechanic training programs.

Growth of personal disposable income over the 2000–2012 period should provide consumers with more discretionary dollars to buy motorboats, which will require more mechanics to keep the growing amount of equipment in operation. In addition, routine service will always be a significant source of work for mechanics. While advancements in technology will lengthen the interval between checkups, the need for qualified mechanics to perform this service will increase.

Motorboats are increasingly popular with consumers over age 40; this group is responsible for the largest segment of marine craft purchases, since traditionally they have more disposable income to spend on recreational equipment. Over the next decade, more people will be entering the 40 and over age group; these potential buyers will help expand the market for motorboats, while helping to maintain the demand for qualified mechanics.

During the winter months in the northern United States, Motorboat Mechanics may work fewer than 40 hours a week because the amount of repair and service work declines when motorboats are not in use. Many Motorboat Mechanics work only during the busy spring and summer seasons, and they may service other types of equipment or work reduced hours in the winter. In addition, many mechanics schedule time-consuming engine overhauls and work on motorboats during winter downtime. Mechanics may work considerably more than 40 hours a week when demand is strong.

Advancement Prospects

The skills needed as a marine mechanic generally transfer to other occupations such as automobile, diesel, or heavy vehicle and mobile equipment mechanics. Experienced mechanics with leadership ability may advance to shop supervisor or service manager jobs. Mechanics with sales ability sometimes become sales representatives or open their own marine repair shops.

Education and Training

Due to the increasing complexity of motorboats, most employers prefer to hire mechanics who graduate from formal training programs for small engine mechanics. Because the number of these specialized postsecondary programs is limited, most mechanics learn their skills on the job or while working in related occupations. For trainee jobs, employers hire persons with mechanical aptitude who are knowledgeable about the fundamentals of small two- and four-stroke engines. Many trainees develop an interest in mechanics and acquire some basic skills through working on motorboats as a hobby. Others may be introduced to mechanics through vocational automotive training in high school, or one of many postsecondary institutions.

Trainees learn routine service tasks under the guidance of experienced mechanics by replacing ignition points and spark plugs or by taking apart, assembling, and testing new equipment. As trainees gain experience and proficiency, they progress to more difficult tasks such as advanced computerized diagnosis and engine overhauls. Up to three years of on-the-job training may be necessary before a novice worker becomes competent in all aspects of the repair of motorboat engines.

Employers often send mechanics and trainees to special training courses conducted by motorboat equipment manufacturers or distributors. These courses upgrade the worker's skills and provide information on repairing new models, and they are usually a prerequisite for any mechanic who performs warranty work for manufacturers or insurance companies.

Most employers prefer to hire high school graduates for trainee mechanic positions, but will accept applicants with less education if they possess adequate reading, writing, and arithmetic skills. Many equipment dealers hire students part time and during the summer to help assemble new equipment and perform minor repairs. Helpful high school courses include small engine repair, automobile mechanics, science, and business arithmetic. Knowledge of basic electronics is essential for small engine mechanics. Electronic components control engine performance, instrument displays, and a variety of other functions of motorboats.

Experience, Skills, and Personality Traits

Motorboat Mechanics should have mechanical aptitude, strong analytical abilities, and an understanding of how boats work, in addition to good reading, mathematics, and computer skills. Persistence and attention to detail is important. Service technicians usually work indoors in clean, well-ventilated, well-lit repair shops, but some shops are drafty and noisy, so a high tolerance to noisy, dirty environments is important. In addition, Motorboat Mechanics may work outdoors at docks or marinas, as well as in all weather conditions when making repairs aboard boats. They may work in cramped or awkward positions to reach a boat's engine.

Although Motorboat Mechanics can fix some problems with simple adjustments, they often work with dirty and greasy parts or in awkward positions, lifting heavy parts and tools. Minor cuts, burns, and bruises are common, but mechanics usually avoid serious accidents when the shop is kept clean and orderly and safety practices are observed.

Unions and Associations

Motorboat Mechanics can belong to the International Association of Machinists and Aerospace Workers; the International Union, United Automobile, Aerospace and Agricultural Implement Workers of America; the Sheet Metal Workers' International Association; and the International Brotherhood of Teamsters. Motorboat Mechanics also may choose to belong to professional organizations such as the American Marine Institute, the American Watercraft Institute, or the Marine Mechanics Institute.

Tips for Entry

1. Try to obtain skills by working on your motorboat or by taking every relevant course available during high school or vocational school.
2. An internship or summer job at a dealer or repair shop can provide invaluable experience.
3. Check Web sites of local dealers, marinas, and repair shops to spot job openings.
4. Positions should be advertised in the newspaper classified ad section under "Trades: Mechanical."
5. Send your résumé and a cover letter to all the local dealers, marinas, and repair shops in your area. Because there is always a demand for well-trained mechanics, you may get called for an interview even if the job hasn't been advertised in the paper.
6. If you graduated from vocational or postsecondary school, find out if the school has a job placement service and work with them to land a position.

OUTDOOR POWER EQUIPMENT MECHANIC

CAREER PROFILE

Duties: Service and repair outdoor power equipment such as lawn mowers, garden tractors, edge trimmers, chain saws, portable generators, go-karts, snowblowers, and snowmobiles

Alternate Title(s): None

Salary Range: $15,290 to $37,910+

Employment Prospects: Fair

Advancement Prospects: Fair

Best Geographical Location(s): All locations throughout the country have job possibilities for well-trained, experienced Outdoor Power Equipment Mechanics

Prerequisites:

    Education or Training—High school or postsecondary vocational school small engine technician training program

    Experience—Experience in small engine repairs

    Special Skills and Personality Traits—Good diagnostic skills; attention to detail; mechanical ability; mathematics and computer skills

CAREER LADDER

```
┌─────────────────────────────────┐
│        Shop Supervisor          │
└─────────────────────────────────┘

┌─────────────────────────────────┐
│ Outdoor Power Equipment Mechanic │
└─────────────────────────────────┘

┌─────────────────────────────────┐
│     Outdoor Power Equipment      │
│     Technician Assistant         │
└─────────────────────────────────┘
```

Position Description

Outdoor power equipment and other small engine mechanics service and repair outdoor power equipment such as lawnmowers, garden tractors, edge trimmers, chain saws, portable generators and go-carts. In addition, small engine mechanics in northern parts of the country may work on snowblowers and snowmobiles, but demand for this type of repair is seasonal. Outdoor power equipment requires periodic service to minimize the chance of breakdowns and to keep them operating at peak performance. During routine equipment maintenance, mechanics follow a checklist including the inspection and cleaning of brakes, electrical systems, fuel injection systems, plugs, carburetors, blades, and other parts. Following inspection, mechanics usually repair or adjust parts that do not work properly, or replace unfixable parts.

Routine maintenance is normally a major part of the mechanic's work. When equipment breakdowns occur, mechanics use various techniques to diagnose the source and extent of the problem. The mark of a skilled mechanic is the ability to diagnose mechanical, fuel, and electrical problems, and to make repairs in a minimal amount of time. Quick and accurate diagnosis requires problem-solving ability and a thorough knowledge of the equipment's operation.

After pinpointing the problem, the mechanic makes the needed adjustments, repairs, or replacements. Some jobs require minor adjustments or the replacement of a single item, such as a carburetor or fuel pump. In contrast, a complete engine overhaul requires a number of hours to disassemble the engine and replace worn valves, pistons, bearings, and other internal parts.

Electronic components control engine performance, instrument displays, and a variety of other functions of outdoor power equipment. To recognize and fix potential problems, mechanics should be familiar with the basic principles of electronics.

The most important work possessions of mechanics are their hand tools. Outdoor Power Equipment Mechanics use common hand tools such as wrenches, pliers, and screwdrivers, or power tools, such as drills and grinders. Computerized engine analyzers, compression gauges, ammeters and voltmeters, and other testing devices help mechanics locate faulty parts and tune engines. Mechanics usually provide their own tools, and many experienced mechanics have invested thousands of dollars in them. Employers typically furnish expensive power tools, computerized engine analyzers, and other diagnostic equipment, but mechanics accumulate hand tools with experience.

Mechanics often refer to service manuals for detailed directions and specifications while performing repairs. They usually work in repair shops that are well lit and ventilated, but are sometimes noisy when testing engines.

Salaries

Average annual salaries for Outdoor Power Equipment Mechanics range between $24,820 and $25,920. The lowest 10 percent earn less than $15,290, and the highest 10 percent earn more than $37,910.

Small engine mechanics tend to receive few benefits in small shops, but those employed in larger shops often receive paid vacations, sick leave, and health insurance. Some employers also pay for work-related training and provide uniforms. Top-paying states include Vermont (average $12.36/hour), Montana ($11.87), and Maine ($12.20).

Employment Prospects

Outdoor power equipment and other small engine mechanics held about 30,000 jobs in 2002; about half worked for retail hardware and garden stores or retail dealers of miscellaneous vehicles. Most of the rest were employed by independent repair shops, equipment rental companies, wholesale distributors, and landscaping services. About 15 percent were self-employed.

Employment of small engine mechanics is expected to grow about as fast the average for all occupations through the year 2012. Most job openings are expected to be replacement jobs because many experienced small engine mechanics leave each year to transfer to other occupations, retire, or stop working for other reasons. Job prospects should be especially favorable for persons who complete mechanic training programs.

Growth of personal disposable income over the 2000–2012 period should provide consumers with more discretionary dollars to buy garden power equipment, which will require more mechanics to keep the growing amount of equipment in operation. In addition, routine service will always be a significant source of work for mechanics. While advancements in technology will lengthen the interval between checkups, the need for qualified mechanics to perform this service will increase.

Construction of new single-family houses will result in an increase in lawn and garden equipment in operation, increasing the need for mechanics. However, equipment growth will be slowed by trends toward smaller lawns and contracting out their maintenance to lawn service firms. Growth also will be tempered by the tendency of many consumers to dispose of and replace relatively inexpensive items rather than have them repaired.

During the winter months in the northern United States, Outdoor Power Equipment Mechanics may work fewer than 40 hours a week because the amount of repair and service work declines when lawnmowers and other types of outdoor equipment are not in use. Many of these mechanics work only during the busy spring and summer seasons, although others schedule time-consuming engine overhauls and work on snowmobiles and snowblowers during winter downtime. Mechanics may work considerably more than 40 hours a week when demand is strong.

Advancement Prospects

The skills used as a small engine mechanic generally transfer to other occupations such as automobile, diesel, or heavy vehicle and mobile equipment mechanics. Experienced mechanics with leadership ability may advance to shop supervisor or service manager jobs. Mechanics with sales ability sometimes become sales representatives or open their own repair shops.

Education and Training

Most employers prefer to hire Outdoor Power Equipment Mechanics who graduate from formal training programs for small engine mechanics. Because the number of these specialized postsecondary programs is limited, most mechanics learn their skills on the job or while working in related occupations. For trainee jobs, employers hire persons with mechanical aptitude who are knowledgeable about small engine fundamentals.

Many trainees develop an interest in mechanics and acquire some basic skills through working on outdoor power equipment as a hobby. Others may be introduced to mechanics through vocational automotive training in high school or postsecondary institution.

Trainees learn routine service tasks under the guidance of experienced mechanics by replacing ignition points and spark plugs or by taking apart, assembling, and testing new equipment. As trainees gain experience and proficiency, they progress to more difficult tasks such as engine overhauls.

Employers often send mechanics and trainees to special training courses conducted by outdoor power equipment manufacturers or distributors. These courses, which can last as long as two weeks, upgrade the worker's skills and provide information on repairing new models. They are usually a prerequisite for any mechanic who performs warranty work for manufacturers.

Most employers prefer to hire high school graduates for trainee mechanic positions, but will accept applicants with less education if they possess adequate reading, writing, and arithmetic skills. Many equipment dealers employ students part time and during the summer to help assemble new equipment and perform minor repairs. Helpful high school courses include small engine repair, automobile mechanics, science, and business arithmetic. Knowledge of basic electronics is essential for small engine mechanics.

Experience, Skills, and Personality Traits

Small engine mechanics should have mechanical aptitude, strong analytical abilities, and an understanding of how outdoor power equipment works, in addition to good reading, mathematics, and computer skills. Persistence and attention to detail is important. Service mechanics usually work indoors in clean, well-ventilated, well-lit repair shops, but some shops are drafty and noisy, so a high tolerance to noisy, dirty environments is important. Although mechanics can fix some problems with simple adjustments, they often work with dirty and greasy parts or in awkward positions, lifting heavy parts and tools. Minor cuts, burns, and bruises are common, but mechanics usually avoid serious accidents when the shop is kept clean and orderly and safety practices are observed.

Unions and Associations

Outdoor Power Equipment Mechanics may belong to the International Association of Machinists and Aerospace Workers; the International Union, United Automobile, Aerospace and Agricultural Implement Workers of America; the Sheet Metal Workers' International Association; and the International Brotherhood of Teamsters.

Tips for Entry

1. Try to obtain skills by working on small engines and power equipment, and by taking every relevant course available during high school or vocational school.
2. An internship or summer job at a dealer, hardware store, or repair shop can provide invaluable experience.
3. Check Web sites of local dealers and repair shops to spot job openings.
4. Positions should be advertised in the newspaper classified ad section.
5. Send your résumé and a cover letter to all the local dealers, hardware stores, and repair shops in your area. Because there is always a demand for well-trained mechanics, you may get called for an interview even if the job has not been advertised in the paper.
6. If you graduated from vocational or postsecondary school, find out if the school has a job placement service and work with them to land a position.

AUTO DAMAGE APPRAISER

CAREER PROFILE

Duties: Appraises car damage to determine cost of repair for insurance claim settlement; tries to secure agreement with car repair shop on costs

Alternate Title(s): None

Salary Range: $27,410 to $60,470+

Employment Prospects: Good

Advancement Prospects: Good

Best Geographical Location(s): All parts of the country have good opportunities for Auto Damage Appraisers

Prerequisites:

Education or Training—Four year college degree or equivalent experience and industry coursework preferred

Experience—Auto body work and computer experience desirable

Special Skills and Personality Traits—Minimum of three years' experience in damage appraisals, experience with collision damage estimating, and estimating software experience

Licensure/Certification—Four states require auto damage appraisers to be licensed

CAREER LADDER

```
┌─────────────────────────────────┐
│   Auto Damage Claims Manager    │
│    or Appraisal Firm Owner      │
└─────────────────────────────────┘

┌─────────────────────────────────┐
│     Auto Damage Appraiser       │
└─────────────────────────────────┘

┌─────────────────────────────────┐
│  Auto Damage Appraiser Trainee  │
└─────────────────────────────────┘
```

Position Description

An Auto Damage Appraiser appraises car or other vehicle damage to determine how much the repair will cost for insurance claim settlement. The appraiser also tries to reach an agreement with the car repair shop on the cost of the repairs. The appraiser is an unbiased automotive specialist who can assess car damage and establish a fair cost of repair instead of relying on body shop estimates or estimates prepared by unqualified personnel. The appraiser prepares insurance forms to indicate repair cost or cost estimates and recommendations, and estimates of parts and labor to repair damage, using standard automotive labor and parts-cost manuals and knowledge of automotive repair. The appraiser reviews repair-cost estimates with the car repair shop and examines the damaged car to determine the extent of structural, body, mechanical, electrical, or interior damage.

Auto Damage Appraisers usually are hired by insurance companies and independent adjusting firms to inspect car damage after an accident and to provide repair cost estimates. Auto Damage Appraisers are valued by insurance companies because they can provide an unbiased judgment of repair costs. Otherwise, the companies would have to rely on auto mechanic estimates, which might be unreasonably high.

Many Auto Damage Appraisers are equipped with laptop computers, from which they can download the necessary forms and files from insurance company databases. Many appraisers also use digital cameras, which allow photographs of the damage to be sent to the company via the Internet or satellite. New software programs can give estimates of damage based on the information input directly into the computer, which allows for faster and more efficient processing of claims.

The Auto Damage Appraiser examines the damaged vehicle to determine the extent of structural, body, mechanical, electrical, or interior damage. Next, the appraiser estimates the cost of labor and parts to repair or replace each damaged item, using standard car labor and parts cost manuals and knowledge of car repair. If repairs are not possible, the appraiser determines the salvage value on a total-loss vehicle. As part of this job, the appraiser evaluates whether it is more practical to repair the car or declare the car a loss and pay its market value before the accident.

The Auto Damage Appraiser prepares insurance forms to indicate repair-cost estimates and recommendations, and reviews repair-cost estimates with the car repair shop to reach an agreement on the cost of repairs. Occasionally, the appraiser arranges to have the damage appraised by another appraiser to resolve a disagreement with a repair shop on repair costs.

Auto Damage Appraisers assess car damage and make unbiased repair decisions based on the manufacturer's specifications, accepted industry procedures, and safety concerns. They have the expert knowledge to make these important decisions without favoritism toward the insurance company, auto body shop, or car owner.

Auto Damage Appraisers often work outside the office, inspecting damaged automobiles, and new technology (such as laptop computers and cell phones) makes communication easier.

Salaries

Auto Damage Appraisers working for insurance companies tend to earn slightly higher average earnings than independent appraisers because they have a steady income. Average annual earnings of Auto Damage Appraisers are $42,630; ranging from a low of less than $27,410 to a high of more than $60,470.

Employment Prospects

Employment of Auto Damage Appraisers is expected to grow about as fast as the average for all occupations through 2012, according to the U.S. Bureau of Labor Statistics. Many job openings also will result from the need to replace workers who transfer to other occupations or leave the labor force.

Insurance companies and agents are selling more auto insurance policies, which eventually will lead to more claims being filed that will require the attention of an Auto Damage Appraiser. This occupation is not easily automated, because most appraisal jobs require an on-site inspection, but employment growth will be limited by industry downsizing and the implementation of new technology that is making the job of Auto Damage Appraiser more efficient.

Insurance companies hire most of the appraisers, although insurance sales agents and brokers and independent adjusting and claims processing firms employ them as well. Two percent of appraisers are self-employed.

Advancement Prospects

Auto Damage Appraisers typically begin as auto body repair workers, and then move on and get jobs with insurance companies or independent adjusting firms. Like automotive body and related repairers and automotive service technicians, Auto Damage Appraisers must be familiar with the structure and functions of different automobiles and parts.

Beginning appraisers work on small claims under the supervision of an experienced worker; they are promoted as they demonstrate competence in handling assignments and progress in their coursework. Trainees are promoted as they demonstrate competence in handling assignments; eventually, they may be promoted to claims approver or claims manager.

Once they achieve a certain level of expertise, some Auto Damage Appraisers choose to start their own independent auto damage appraising firms.

Education and Training

Training and entry requirements vary widely for Auto Damage Appraisers, but a bachelor's degree or equivalent experience and industry coursework is preferred. No specific college major is recommended, but knowledge of computer applications also is extremely important. Appraisers usually need several years of work-related experience, on-the-job training, and/or vocational training. Some colleges offer an undergraduate program associated with Auto Damage Appraisers. Further education may also be required to pursue this career.

Continuing education is very important because of the introduction of new car models and repair techniques. The Independent Automotive Damage Appraisers Association provides seminars and training sessions in different aspects of auto damage appraising.

Some companies require applicants to pass a series of written aptitude tests designed to measure communication, analytical, and general mathematical skills. Appraisers should have an estimate system, a digital camera, and the ability to transmit the completed appraisal assignment by e-mail.

Special Requirements

Some states require Auto Damage Appraisers to be licensed. Appraisers may become Automotive Service Excellence (ASE) certified by passing the ASE Damage Analysis and Estimating Certification exam. This test identifies those appraisers who possess the skills required to properly analyze and estimate automotive collision damage. The ASE Damage Analysis and Estimating test is intended for those professionals who may not actually repair cars but have the special knowledge needed to assess collision damage, estimate repair costs, and work with vehicle owners. The scored test consists of 50 questions that address damage analysis, estimating, legal and environmental practices, vehicle construction, vehicle systems knowledge, parts identification and source, and customer relations and sales skills. The ASE Damage Analysis and Estimating Test is offered every May and November at more than 700 test centers nationwide.

To become ASE certified, an appraiser must pass the exam and present proof of two years of relevant work experience related to damage analysis and estimating (not hands-on collision repair). Appraisers may substitute two years of relevant formal training for up to one year of the work experience requirement. To remain certified, appraisers must be retested every five years. This requirement ensures ASE-certified estimators are keeping up with changing technology.

Experience, Skills, and Personality Traits

Employers usually look for Auto Damage Appraisers who have a minimum of three years experience in claim-related physical damage appraisals and experience with collision damage estimating. Appraisers also should have experience with estimating software. Auto Damage Appraisers must have a good grasp of mathematics, clerical tasks, and accounting. They should also have a sound mechanical understanding of machines and tools, including repair and maintenance. They must also understand local laws, court procedures, government regulations, and agency rules.

Appraisers must be honest, reliable, and able to follow guidelines and client instructions. In addition, appraisers must be able to complete damage appraisal and total loss assignments in a fast, efficient, and professional manner. Appraisers may need to help adjusters obtain police reports and help with scene investigations and canvass an area for witnesses.

Like automotive body repairers and automotive service technicians and mechanics, Auto Damage Appraisers must be familiar with the structure and functions of different automobiles and parts. An appraiser must have a strong customer service orientation, attention to detail, and the ability to work independently. Strong oral and written communication skills and computer competency are a must.

Unions and Associations

Auto Damage Appraisers may belong to the Independent Automotive Damage Appraisers Association (www.iada.org).

Tips for Entry

1. Try to obtain skills by working on your own cars and by taking every relevant course available during high school or vocational school.
2. An internship or summer job at an insurance company can provide invaluable experience.
3. Check your college job placement service and work with them to land a position as an appraiser.
4. Visit the Web site of the Independent Automotive Damage Appraisers Association, which maintains a job placement service online, at www.iada.org/jobs.cfm.
5. Jobs may be advertised in the classified section of newspapers under headings such as "Professional" or "General."
6. Send your résumé and a cover letter to the personnel department of insurance companies in the locations where you would like to work.
7. Continue your education and try to get any certifications that you can, such as ASE certification.

AUTO DAMAGE CLAIMS ADJUSTER

CAREER PROFILE

Duties: Investigate claims, negotiate settlements, and authorize payments

Alternative Title(s): None

Salary Range: $26,680 to $71,350+

Employment Prospects: Good

Advancement Prospects: Good

Best Geographical Location(s): All parts of the country have good opportunities for Auto Damage Claims Adjusters

Prerequisites:

Education or Training—Four-year college degree

Experience—A business or an accounting background helpful

Special Skills and Personality Traits—Good communication and computer skills; ability to get along well with others; attention to detail

CAREER LADDER

```
┌─────────────────────────────────┐
│   Auto Damage Claims Manager    │
│    or owner of Independent       │
│        Adjusting Firm            │
└─────────────────────────────────┘

┌─────────────────────────────────┐
│   Auto Damage Claims Adjuster    │
└─────────────────────────────────┘

┌─────────────────────────────────┐
│          Entry Level             │
└─────────────────────────────────┘
```

Position Description

Auto Damage Claims Adjusters perform a wide range of functions, but their most important role is to act as intermediary with the public. Insurance adjusters must determine the validity of a claim, determine how much to reimburse the client, and negotiate a settlement. Insurance companies and independent adjusting firms hire adjusters to handle claims, interpret and explain policies or regulations, and resolve billing disputes. Auto Damage Claims Adjusters handle minor claims filed by automobile policyholders, contacting claimants by telephone or mail to obtain information on repair costs.

Many companies centralize this operation through a claims center, where the cost of repair is determined and a check is issued immediately. More complex cases are referred to senior adjusters.

Some clients may choose to hire a public Auto Damage Claims Adjuster who performs the same services as adjusters who work directly for companies. Public adjusters help their clients prepare and present claims to insurance companies and try to negotiate a fair settlement. They work in the best interests of the client, rather than the insurance company.

Claims adjusters primarily plan and schedule the work required to process a claim, investigating claims by interviewing the claimant and witnesses, consulting police and hospital records, and inspecting property damage to determine the extent of the company's liability. Many adjusters have digital cameras so they can take photographs of the damage to be sent to the company. Claims adjusters also may consult with other professionals (accountants, architects, engineers, or lawyers) who can offer a more expert evaluation of a claim. Then the information (including photographs and statements) is included in a report used to evaluate a claim. When the policyholder's claim is legitimate, the Auto Damage Claims Adjuster negotiates with the claimant and settles the claim. When claims are contested, adjusters may testify in court and refer claims to an investigator. If adjusters suspect a case might involve fraud, they refer the claim to an investigator.

Many insurance companies are emphasizing better customer service. One way they are achieving this is by offering access to claims services at any time. New software programs can give estimates of damage based on the information input directly into the computer, which allows claims to be processed faster and more efficiently. Claims Adjusters working for small insurance companies may still answer phones and take claims information, and then handle the claims themselves.

In general, Auto Damage Claims Adjusters are able to arrange their work schedule to accommodate evening and weekend appointments with clients; typically, they work 50 or 60 hours a week. Claims adjusters often work outside the office, inspecting damaged automobiles, but others report to the office every morning to get their assignments. Laptop computers and cell phones make work easier for claims adjusters. Many adjusters work inside their office only a few hours a week. Some adjusters' business is done entirely out of their home.

Salaries

Average earnings for Auto Damage Claims Adjusters are $43,020 a year; the lowest 10 percent earn less than $26,680, and the highest 10 percent earn more than $71,350, according to the U.S. Bureau of Labor Statistics.

Claims adjusters working for insurance companies tend to earn slightly higher average earnings than independent adjusters because they have a steady income. Many claims adjusters receive additional bonuses or benefits as part of their job. Adjusters often are furnished a laptop computer, a cellular telephone, and a company car or are reimbursed for use of their own vehicle for business purposes.

Employment Prospects

Insurance companies hire the vast majority of Auto Damage Claims Adjusters. Insurance sales agents and brokers and independent adjusting and claims processing firms employ them as well; 2 percent of adjusters are self-employed.

Employment of claims adjusters is expected to grow about as fast as the average for all occupations over the 2000–2012 period, according to the U.S. Bureau of Labor Statistics. Many job openings will occur to replace workers who transfer to other occupations or leave the labor force.

Larger companies are relying more on customer service representatives in call centers to handle the recording of the necessary details of the claim, allowing adjusters to spend more of their time investigating claims. New technology also cuts down on the time it takes for an adjuster to complete a claim, which increases the number of claims one adjuster can handle. Despite recent productivity increases as the result of modern technology, adjuster jobs are not easily automated; adjusters still are needed to contact policyholders, inspect damaged cars, and consult with experts. An increase in the number of auto policies sold eventually will result in more claims.

Advancement Prospects

Beginning Auto Damage Claims Adjusters work on small claims under the supervision of an experienced worker. As they learn more about claims investigation and settlement, they are assigned larger, more complex claims. Trainees are promoted as they demonstrate competence in handling assignments and progress in their coursework.

Employees who demonstrate competence in claims adjuster work may be promoted to claims approver or claims manager. Once claims adjusters achieve a certain level of expertise, some choose to start their own independent adjusting firms.

Education and Training

Training and entry requirements vary widely for Auto Damage Claims Adjusters. However, most companies prefer to hire college graduates. No specific college major is recommended. A claims adjuster with a business or an accounting background might specialize in claims of financial loss due to auto damage.

Special Requirements

Some companies require applicants to pass a series of written aptitude tests designed to measure communication, analytical, and general mathematical skills. About one-third of the states require independent public adjusters to be licensed; check with your state insurance department to see if your state requires a license. Applicants in these states usually must comply with one or more of the following:

- Pass a licensing examination covering the fundamentals of adjusting
- complete an approved course in insurance or loss adjusting
- furnish character references
- be at least 20 or 21 years of age and a resident of the state
- file a surety bond.

Claims adjusters who aren't self-employed can usually work under the company license and do not need to become licensed themselves.

It is very important for Auto Damage Claims Adjusters to receive continuing education in claims, since new federal and state laws and court decisions are often passed that affect how claims are handled or who is covered by insurance policies.

Some states that require adjusters be licensed also require a certain number of continuing education credits per year in order to renew the license. Many companies offer training sessions to inform their employees of industry changes, and many schools and adjuster associations offer courses and seminars in various claims topics. Correspondence courses via the Internet are making long-distance learning possible. Adjusters also can earn credits by writing articles for claims publications or giving lectures and presentations.

Many adjusters choose to pursue certain certifications and designations to distinguish themselves. The Insurance Institute of America offers an Associate in Claims (AIC) designation upon successful completion of four essay examinations. Adjusters can prepare for the examination through independent home study or company and public classes. The institute also offers a certificate upon successful completion of the Introduction to Claims program and an examination.

Registered Professional Adjusters, Inc., offers the Registered Professional Adjuster (RPA) designation. For public adjusters, the National Association of Public Insurance Adjusters offers both the Certified Professional Public Adjuster (CPPA) and Senior Professional Public Adjuster (SPPA) designations. Most designations require at least 5 to 10 years' experience in the claims field, passing examinations, and earning a certain number of CE credits a year. For information about the Associate in Claims (AIC) designation, or the Introduction to Claims program, contact the Insurance Institute of America, 720 Providence Rd., P.O. Box 3016, Malvern, PA 19355, or on the Internet at www.aicpu.org. For information on the Registered Professional Adjuster (RPA) designation, contact Registered Professional Adjusters, Inc., P.O. Box 3239, Napa, CA 94558.

Experience, Skills, and Personality Traits
Because they often work closely with claimants, witnesses, and insurance professionals, Auto Damage Claims Adjusters must be able to communicate effectively with others. Knowledge of computer applications also is extremely important.

Unions and Associations
Auto Damage Claims Adjusters can belong to several different professional organizations, such as the Insurance Institute of America, the International Claim Association, or the National Association of Public Insurance Adjusters.

Tips for Entry
1. For information on public adjuster jobs, contact the National Association of Public Insurance Adjusters, 112-J Elden St., Herndon, VA 20170.
2. Jobs may be advertised in the classified section of newspapers under headings such as "Professional" or "General."
3. Send your résumé and a cover letter to the personnel department of claims adjusting firms in the locations where you would like to work.
4. Continue your education and try to get any certifications that you can.
5. Check out the job bank on the website of the International Claim Association (www.claim.org).

AUTO SERVICE STATION MANAGER

CAREER PROFILE

Duties: Supervises the overall operation of auto service stations

Alternate Title(s): Gas Station Manager

Salary Range: $19,580 to $60,000+

Employment Prospects: Good

Advancement Prospects: Fair

Best Geographical Location(s): All parts of the country can provide good locations for service stations

Prerequisites:

Education or Training—High school diploma with courses in automobile mechanics, marketing education, mathematics, business education, and computer applications

Experience—Experience working on cars an asset; some employers require a driver's license

Special Skills and Personality Traits—Ability to manage and motivate employees; good sales skills; ability to deal well with the public

Licensure/Certification—Hydrocarbon training and certification required for jobs involving light maintenance duties or filling of propane cylinders

CAREER LADDER

```
Auto Service Station Manager
of a larger service station
or Service Station Owner
```

```
Auto Service Station Manager
```

```
Auto Service Station Attendant
```

Position Description

Auto Service Station Managers supervise the overall operation of service stations, both traditional gas stations and gas station–convenience stores. They are responsible for planning and carrying out policies for managing service stations, including hiring and training workers; preparing work schedules; setting prices for products and services; collecting payment from customers for services rendered; ordering gasoline, oil, supplies, and auto parts; and reconciling sales with gasoline pump meter readings. Service station managers oversee attendants who sell fuel, diesel, propane, automotive products, and convenience store items at full-service stations, and may handle cash and credit card transactions. Additional duties may include balancing cash at the end of a shift, stocking products on shelves, and cleaning up inside and outside the booth or convenience store.

Today, many service stations are run as commission leases, in which a large national petroleum company hires a manager to operate the company-owned station. The manager in this case is responsible for hiring and paying other employees. Fuel prices are set by the petroleum company, and the manager is paid a typical commission of between 2 and 10 cents per gallon of gas sold.

Salaries

Salaries range from a low of $19,580 to a high of more than $60,000, depending on the location of the service station and whether it is affiliated with a national company or chain.

Employment Prospects

Employment prospects are only fair for Auto Service Stations Managers, since government statistics project there will be a decrease of 5 percent in this occupation through the year 2010, as service stations become more and more automated and many stations sell out to larger petroleum companies.

Advancement Prospects

Auto Service Station Managers can advance by buying the station where they work, or by moving on and getting a job at a larger service station, with more responsibilities and higher salary.

Education and Training

Graduation from high school is preferred for entry into this occupation. High school students may prepare by taking courses in automobile mechanics, marketing, mathematics, business, and computer applications.

Some knowledge of motor vehicles is an asset. In addition, training is usually provided on the job in order to familiarize the employee with safety and security practices. This on-the-job training may also be supplemented with company training programs on safety and customer service. Some oil/gasoline distributors offer special training programs for managers of company-owned stations.

Special Requirements

Some employers may require a driver's license if moving vehicles is part of the job. Hydrocarbon training and certification is required to perform light maintenance on or to fill up propane cylinders.

Experience, Skills, and Personality Traits

Auto Service Station Managers generally work eight-hour shifts that often include evenings, weekends, and holidays. Many service stations are open 24 hours a day. The work is physically demanding and stressful, and requires that the manager be a business whiz, a computer expert, a personnel director, and a customer service specialist. Service station owners typically look for people who are honest, sociable, energetic, responsible, and reliable.

Unions and Associations

Auto Service Station Managers may belong to a variety of auto-related groups, such as the Automotive Service Association, the International Automotive Technicians' Network, or the National Institute for Automotive Service Excellence.

Tips for Entry

1. Positions for Auto Service Station Manager are advertised in the newspaper classified ad section.
2. Send your résumé and a cover letter to all the service stations in your area. You may get called for an interview even if the job has not been advertised in the paper.
3. If you graduated from vocational or postsecondary school, find out if the school has a job placement service and work with them to land a position.

AUTO SERVICE STATION ATTENDANT

CAREER PROFILE

Duties: Perform duties at gas stations as requested by customers and diagnose and repair cars; perform state inspections and vehicle emissions tests; maintain and perform preventive care

Alternate Title(s): Gas Station Attendant

Salary Range: $6.26 to $12.06 per hour

Employment Prospects: Good

Advancement Prospects: Good

Best Geographical Location(s): All locations throughout the country have job possibilities for Auto Service Station Attendants

Prerequisites:

Education or Training—High school or postsecondary vocational school automotive service technician training program

Experience—Experience in car repairs

Special Skills and Personality Traits—Good diagnostic skills; attention to detail; mechanical ability

Licensure/Certification—Driver's license required

CAREER LADDER

Auto Service Station Manager

Auto Service Station Attendant

Entry Level

Position Description

Auto Service Station Attendants, also known as gas station attendants, pump gas, clean windshields, check batteries and water levels in radiators, check the oil level in engines and the fluid level in automatic transmissions, check tires for correct air pressure, and handle cash payments or prepare slips for credit card customers. They also sell and install parts and accessories such as tires, batteries, fan belts, and windshield wiper blades, and may sell groceries and related items.

Auto Service Station Attendants also may perform minor maintenance and repair work such as changing oil, rotating and repairing tires, and replacing mufflers. In performing maintenance and repair work, Auto Service Station Attendants may use screwdrivers, pliers and wrenches, motor analyzers, and wheel alignment machines.

The Auto Service Station Attendant also may be responsible for keeping the service areas, building, and restrooms clean. In some stations, attendants help the manager take inventory of automobile parts in stock, set up displays, and keep business records. If a gasoline service station provides emergency road service, the attendant occasionally may drive a tow truck to help motorists with mechanical problems or tow their cars back to the station.

Attendants work indoors and outdoors in all kinds of weather; while the office may be heated, service areas are not. Attendants do considerable lifting and stooping and spend much time on their feet. Possible injuries include cuts from sharp tools and burns from hot engines, but safety precautions help protect against more serious injuries. Because of the nature of the work, attendants frequently get dirty as they pump gasoline and work around oil and grease.

Salaries

Hourly earnings of Auto Service Station Attendants start at the minimum wage to $6.26 an hour, although experienced workers earn up to $12.06 an hour; Average hourly wage ranges from $8.11 to $8.71. In addition, attendants may earn commissions on the accessories they sell and the services they provide, such as adding oil, lubricating cars, or assisting mechanics. In some stations, employers provide fringe benefits such as accident and health insurance and paid vacations. Employers generally furnish uniforms and pay for their cleaning.

Full-time attendants work 40 hours a week or more. Because many stations are open at least 12 hours a day, six days a week, work schedules may include evenings, weekends and holidays. Top-paying states are Alaska (average $10.24/hour), Colorado ($9.96), and California ($9.91).

Employment Prospects

Part-time work is almost always available, but full-time employment will continue to decline as the trend toward self-service stations means little need for attendants. Moreover, better gas mileage has reduced fuel consumption and lessened the need for a large supply of Auto Service Station Attendants. However, some job openings are expected to occur as attendants transfer to other occupations or retire.

Attendants with mechanical skills will have the best chance of landing a job. Employers report some trouble in finding experienced applicants to fill vacancies, although there are plenty of inexperienced applicants. This means workers new to the field may have a difficult time finding the first job.

Advancement Prospects

There are several ways for Auto Service Station Attendants to advance. Auto Service Station Attendants gradually acquire and practice their skills by working with more experienced attendants or mechanics. With a few months' experience, beginners can perform many routine service tasks and make simple repairs.

Additional training qualifies attendants to become mechanics. Those with business management capabilities may be promoted to station manager. Many experienced station managers and automobile mechanics go into business for themselves.

Education and Training

Most employers prefer high school graduates, and on-the-job training is generally provided.

Special Requirements

A driver's license is required so that attendants can move vehicles being serviced at the station.

Experience, Skills, and Personality Traits

Auto Service Station Attendants need mechanical ability, knowledge of basic arithmetic, and the ability to speak well and clearly. They should be polite, neat, and able to work independently.

Auto Service Station Attendants sometimes work indoors in clean, well-ventilated well-lit lift areas, but some shops are drafty and noisy, so a high tolerance to noisy, dirty environments is important. They also may be required to work in outdoor conditions.

Unions and Associations

Auto Service Station Attendants do not usually belong to unions or associations.

Tips for Entry

1. Try to obtain skills by working on your own cars, and by taking every relevant course available during high school or vocational school.
2. An internship or summer job at a service station can provide invaluable experience.
3. Check jobs in the newspaper classified ad section under "Trades: mechanical" or "Auto" or "General Help Wanted."
4. Contact local service stations in your area.

AUTOMOTIVE WRITER

Duties: Write automotive-related articles for newspapers or magazines, work in automotive-related public relations, or write automotive-related books

Alternate Title(s): Motorsports Writer

Salary Range: $17,620 to $80,000+ a year

Employment Prospects: Good

Advancement Prospects: Excellent

Best Geographical Location(s): Detroit, California, and the southern states are among the best areas where a concentration of automotive industries and racetracks are located

Prerequisites:

Education or Training—College journalism degree with a minor in engineering, or an engineering degree with a minor in journalism

Experience—Experience working on cars or racing helpful

Special Skills and Personality Traits—Ability to work well under pressure; good concentration skills; good computer skills; good writing skills

```
┌─────────────────────────────┐
│     Automotive Editor       │
└─────────────────────────────┘

┌─────────────────────────────┐
│     Automotive Writer       │
└─────────────────────────────┘

┌─────────────────────────────┐
│  Automotive Writing Intern  │
└─────────────────────────────┘
```

Position Description

Automotive Writers may work for a newspaper, a racing or car magazine, or as a freelancer writing car-related articles or books for a wide variety of publishers. Some Automotive Writers work for public relations departments of organizations such as NASCAR or for the auto industry. Others are automotive correspondents for TV networks or shows, such as Speed Channel or ESPN. Many Automotive Writers are experienced race car drivers or former mechanics; others have college degrees in writing, communications, or public relations before branching out into automotive writing.

All major newspapers hire Automotive Writers, including the Associated Press, the *Washington Post, New York Times, Detroit Free Press, Detroit News,* and *Orlando Sentinal.* Car-related publications are natural choices, including *AutoSport, Car and Driver, AutoWeek, American Woman Road and Travel, Motor Trend Magazine,* and others.

Auto Writers research and write articles or books. Auto Writers may conduct interviews; those who work in public

relations also may prepare press releases, arrange media opportunities and other publicity events, and provide help to media to publicize their client.

Salaries

Automotive Writers may work either on a freelance basis, selling articles to various magazines or writing motorsports-related books. Writers who produce freelance articles may expect to earn between $3,000 and $6,000 per article; those who write books may earn an advance of $10,000 to $20,000 per book. Staff Automotive Writers average between $22,350 and $47,170 a year, depending on experience, talent, and size or location of the publication. The lowest 10 percent earn less than $17,620; the highest 10 percent earn $69,450.

Employment Prospects

As with any other job, making a career in motorsports writing requires many hours of preparation, hard work, and networking. With hard work and perseverance, there should be a good chance of finding work in this field, as employment will grow about as fast as the average for all occupations through 2012. Some Automotive Writers break into the business by selling individual articles to a newspaper or automotive magazine (freelance). Other Automotive Writers get a staff job upon college graduation.

Advancement Prospects

With experience, Automotive Writers can move into writing articles for larger, more prestigious newspapers or magazines, or obtain staff jobs at larger publications. After many years, some Automotive Writers leave staff jobs to become freelance writers and run their own writing businesses. Other Automotive Writers move into public relations with a motor speedway, racing organization, or automotive corporation. Eventually, some Automotive Writers may move into editor positions, managing staffs of other writers and running publications.

Education and Training

A four-year college degree in journalism with a minor in engineering is an ideal background for an Automotive Writer (alternatively, an engineering degree with a minor in journalism is also a good idea). Choose a university with a strong journalism department and a daily student newspaper, so that you can work at the paper and build up a number of published articles. Writers who think they might like to cover motorsports for television might also consider taking some broadcast journalism courses as well.

Since it is easier to get a writing job in the automotive field if you have some automotive experience, you should develop your skills as either a mechanic or your driving and mechanical skills by getting involved in auto racing. Investigate a mechanics training program at a racing school or enroll in an auto mechanics course at the local community college.

Experience, Skills, and Personality Traits

Excellent English and writing ability is important, as is the ability to work well under deadline pressure and an interest in cars and/or motorsports. Attention to detail, inquisitiveness, creativity, and motorsports or automotive experience are all important.

Unions and Associations

Automotive Writers may belong to the American Auto Racing Writers & Broadcasters Association, the American Society for Journalists and Authors, or the National Motorsports Press Association.

Tips for Entry

1. Develop multiple skills: become proficient in writing, photography, high performance driving, and video production, and obtain auto-related technical knowledge.
2. Check with your journalism school's career guidance center for job leads.
3. Experience is key. Start writing for anybody who will accept your work. Cover high school sports for your local newspaper, and then sell articles and photographs to smaller automotive publications.
4. Develop your photography skills. Most small magazines require Automotive writers to be able to take good photos to accompany their articles.
5. You cannot write about it well unless you really understand it, so develop your driving and mechanical skills by getting involved in racing. Attend a racing school (check out www.racingschools.com for information on more than 100 schools throughout America and Europe).
6. Branch out—many magazines besides strictly motor sports publications accept car-related articles. Consult magazines such as *The Robb Report,* and even *Good Housekeeping.*

AUTOMOTIVE MUSEUM DIRECTOR

CAREER PROFILE

Duties: Formulate policies, plan budgets, and raise funds for the automotive museum

Alternate Title(s): None

Salary Range: $50,000 to $83,750+

Employment Prospects: Fair

Advancement Prospects: Fair

Best Geographical Location(s): All locations throughout the country have job possibilities for experienced Automotive Museum Directors

Prerequisites:

Education or Training—B.A. or B.S. with emphasis on museum studies, or master's degree in museum studies or related field from a recognized four-year college or university; several years of professional automotive museum experience

Experience—Experience or knowledge of automobile history, auto mechanics, motor racing, and/or related subjects

Special Skills and Personality Traits—Creativity; attention to detail; good people skills; good management and computer skills

CAREER LADDER

```
┌─────────────────────────────┐
│   Automotive Museum Director │
│      of Larger Museum        │
└─────────────────────────────┘

┌─────────────────────────────┐
│   Automotive Museum Director │
└─────────────────────────────┘

┌─────────────────────────────┐
│  Automotive Museum Technician│
└─────────────────────────────┘
```

Position Description

Automotive Museum Directors formulate policies, plan budgets, and raise funds for their museums. They coordinate the activities of their staff to establish and maintain collections. Automotive Museum Directors search for, buy, appraise, analyze, describe, arrange, catalog, restore, preserve, exhibit, maintain, and store valuable automobiles that can be used by researchers or for exhibitions, publications, broadcasting, and other educational programs. They plan and oversee the arrangement, cataloging, and exhibition of the car collections and, along with technicians, maintain the collections.

Automotive Museum Directors may coordinate educational and public outreach programs, such as tours, workshops, lectures, and classes, and may work with the boards of institutions to administer plans and policies. They also may research topics or items relevant to their automotive collections.

The director works closely with others to develop the annual budget and long-range financial, educational, and philosophical goals, including identifying, soliciting, and securing funding from individuals, corporations, foundations, public sector, and develop fund-raising programs.

Salaries

Average annual earnings of Automotive Museum Directors is about $63,580, ranging from a low of less than $50,000 to a high of more than $83,750. Earnings of Automotive Museum Directors vary considerably by type and size of museum.

Employment Prospects

Competition for jobs as Automotive Museum Directors is expected to be keen as qualified applicants far outnumber job openings, since there are relatively few car museums in the United States. College graduates with highly specialized training or experience in the automotive world, along with extensive computer skills and perhaps an advanced degree, should have the best opportunities for jobs.

Automotive Museum Directors need to have substantial work experience in automotive collection management, exhibit design, restoration, and database management skills to obtain a position.

Although an Automotive Museum Director's job is attractive to many who have the necessary training and subject knowledge, there are only a few openings at any one time. Consequently, candidates may have to work part time, or even as a volunteer director at an automotive museum after completing their formal education.

Advancement Prospects

Automotive Museum Directors in smaller museums may move into positions in larger museums. Individual research and publication are important if you are interested in working at larger museums.

Education and Training

As their role has evolved, Automotive Museum Directors increasingly need business backgrounds in addition to an understanding of the automobiles in their collections and a master's degree in an appropriate field. Since Automotive Museum Directors may have administrative and managerial responsibilities, courses in business administration, public relations, marketing, and fund-raising also are recommended. Substantial work experience in collection management, exhibit design, or restoration, as well as database management skills, is necessary for permanent status.

In smaller automotive museums, museum director positions may be available to individuals with a bachelor's degree. For some positions, an internship at an automotive museum supplemented by courses in museum practices is necessary.

Directors also need good computer skills and the ability to work with electronic databases, and they should also be familiar with digital imaging and scanning technology.

Experience, Skills, and Personality Traits

Automotive Museum Directors usually need experience in the automotive field and previous museum work experience, particularly in exhibit design. Being personable and able to work well with others is a plus, and computer experience is absolutely required. Directors also must be flexible because of the wide variety of their duties; they should have good manual dexterity so they can build exhibits or restore cars. Leadership ability and business skills are also important for Automotive Museum Directors, while marketing skills are valuable for increasing museum attendance and fund-raising.

Unions and Associations

Automotive Museum Directors may belong to a number of museum-related organizations, such as the American Association of Museums.

Tips for Entry

1. Visit the Web site of the American Association of Museums to check for job ads (http://www.aam-us.org/aviso/index.cfm).
2. Unpaid voluntary work or student internships in automotive museums can provide experience, which may lead to paid work. Approach the individual automotive museum with a detailed résumé.
3. Send your résumé to every automotive museum in the country to get into position for an opening.

DRIVING INSTRUCTOR

CAREER PROFILE

Duties: Teaches practical and theoretical driving skills to clients

Alternate Title(s): Driver Trainer, Driver Education Teacher

Salary Range: $9 to $15 an hour

Employment Prospects: Good

Advancement Prospects: Fair

Best Geographical Location(s): All locations have opportunities for Driving Instructors

Prerequisites:

  Education or Training—High school education; some states require college degree

  Experience—Driving and teaching experience helpful

  Special Skills and Personality Traits—Patience; calm attitude; good communication skills and good people skills

  Licensure/Certification—Driver's license; instructor licensing and certification requirements vary by state

CAREER LADDER

```
┌─────────────────────────────────────┐
│   Owner of Driver Training School    │
└─────────────────────────────────────┘


┌─────────────────────────────────────┐
│         Driving Instructor           │
└─────────────────────────────────────┘


┌─────────────────────────────────────┐
│            Entry Level               │
└─────────────────────────────────────┘
```

Position Description

Driving Instructors explain the basic mechanical workings of the car to the client, demonstrate and explain how to operate a car, coach clients while they are driving, teach clients the road rules and about road safety, and prepare clients for their driver's license tests. Some Driving Instructors may teach advanced qualifications or defensive driving courses.

Driving Instructors may instruct students to drive a car by teaching them how to steer, change gears (if manual), interpret and understand traffic conditions, reverse, park, and understand mechanical components and functions. They teach road traffic regulations and advise students when they are ready for the test, teach road craft and defensive driving skills, and advise and teach advanced driving techniques when required for emergency situations and/or to further driving knowledge.

Driving Instructors with special licenses may teach people to drive buses and trucks.

Some Driving Instructors use their own cars converted to dual control, while others use company vehicles. The work can be stressful, the hours long and irregular. Most clients are teenagers, but Driving Instructors also work with adults who want private lessons and are hoping to pass the road test. The Driving Instructor helps clients prepare for their driver's test with review lessons and private lessons, doing a lot of parallel parking and other basic skills and procedures needed to pass the driver's test.

Most Driving Instructors' working day takes place in their cars. They also work from home and travel to schools, homes, or workplaces to pick up or drop off clients, and teach mainly in their cars; occasionally they teach in classrooms.

Driving Instructors usually teach by appointment and work irregular hours, often working evenings and weekends. Their work is often challenging, since they have to train learner drivers on public roads.

Driving Instructors spend a lot of time with people from a wide range of backgrounds. They may also have contact with professionals such as occupational therapists when teaching people with disabilities to drive.

Salaries

Most Driving Instructors are self-employed. Some instructors also contract their services to driving schools. Beginning instructors may earn between $9 to $15 per hour, depending on performance and experience.

Employment Prospects

The demand for Driving Instructors is growing, in part because of fluctuating student population numbers and attitude changes among the public. Favorable auto insurance rates for students who have taken driving instruction, along with many high schools no longer automatically offering driver training, has increased the number of potential jobs.

Most clients taught by Driving Instructors are school-age, since many parents are now realizing that their children would benefit more from being taught by a qualified instructor. The nationwide trend for both parents to work full time has also meant an increase in demand for Driving Instructors, as parents do not have the time needed to teach their children to drive.

Advancement Prospects

The primary way for a Driving Instructor to advance would be for the person to open his or her own driving school.

Education and Training

In most states, there are no specific educational requirements to become a Driving Instructor; however, some states require teacher certification, which presupposes a college degree.

Driving Instructors should have a thorough knowledge of the driving techniques and motor vehicle laws in the state in which they teach. They should know about the mechanical and practical operation of vehicles, as well as defensive driving techniques. Those who are self-employed should also know how to run a small business.

Special Requirements

Driving Instructors need to have held a full driver's license for the class they want to teach. In addition, commercial driving schools and Driving Instructors are usually licensed and regulated by the individual state's Department of Motor Vehicles (DMV).

To become a Driving Instructor or to operate a driver training school, certain requirements must be met, often including filing of certificate of insurance, no DWI (driving while intoxicated) record, completion of courses in driver training and instructional techniques, completion of tests administered by DMV, approval of facilities and vehicles, approval of instructional curriculum and training methods, and verification of previous teaching experience.

Licensing processes, facilities, requirements and qualifications of Driving Instructors, and curriculum differ somewhat depending upon the state and the type of training offered.

Experience, Skills, and Personality Traits

Driving Instructors need advanced driving skills and excellent communication skills in order to teach clients. They must be able to organize their own time and set priorities, and they should have good decision-making ability. Driving Instructors should be friendly and patient, and must remain calm in emergencies. They should be punctual, mature and responsible, able to inspire confidence in their clients, and alert and able to make good judgments. Driving Instructors need to have good reflexes, good eye-hand coordination and good hearing (with or without hearing aids). They should also be reasonably fit and healthy and have a neat appearance. Because Driving Instructors teach all ages, they must be able to communicate with all types of students.

Unions and Associations

Driving instructors may belong to a teachers' union, such as the American Federation of Teachers (www.aft.org).

Tips for Entry

1. Contact local school districts to see if any offer driver training and need instructors.
2. Check the "help wanted" section of your local newspaper under "professional" for driver training instructor ads.
3. Send your résumé or visit local driver instructor schools and network with the school employees about possible employment.

VOCATIONAL-TECHNICAL SCHOOL INSTRUCTOR

CAREER PROFILE

Duties: Provide instruction to secondary and postsecondary students for all types of automotive-related jobs, such as auto mechanic, auto upholsterer, welder, auto body repairer, or customizer

Alternate Title(s): Vocational-Technical Teacher

Salary Range: $24,960 to $68,530+

Employment Prospects: Excellent

Advancement Prospects: Excellent

Best Geographical Location(s): All parts of the country should have openings for good Vocational-Technical School Instructors, but fast-growing states of California, Texas, Florida, New York, and Arizona should be especially good

Prerequisites:

Education or Training—High school diploma (associate's degree helpful but not required)

Experience—At least three years of professional experience as an auto technician

Special Skills and Personality Traits—Good communication skills; ability to motivate and relate well to students; patience; independence

CAREER LADDER

> **Vocational-Technical School Director**

> **Vocational-Technical School Instructor**

> **Vocational-Technical School Assistant**

Position Description

Postsecondary Vocational-Technical School Instructors provide instruction for all types of automotive-related jobs, such as auto mechanic, auto upholsterer, welder, auto body repairer or customizer, and so on. Classes are often taught in an industrial setting where students are given hands-on experience. For example, welding instructors show students various welding techniques, watch them use tools and equipment, and have them repeat procedures until they meet specific standards.

Increasingly, postsecondary Vocational-Technical School Instructors are integrating academic and vocational curriculums so students obtain a variety of skills that can be applied to the real world. Postsecondary Vocational-Technical School Instructors must prepare lessons, grade papers, attend faculty meetings, and keep abreast of technical developments in the automotive field. Vocational-technical schools also are playing a greater role in students' transition from school to work by helping establish internships and by providing information about prospective employers.

Postsecondary Vocational-Technical School Instructors are employed by schools and automotive institutes that specialize in training people in a specific field, such as welding or auto repair. They also work for state and local governments and job training facilities.

Postsecondary Vocational-Technical School Instructors usually have flexible schedules, although they must be present for classes (usually 12 to 16 hours a week) and for faculty and committee meetings. Otherwise, instructors are free to decide when and where they will work, and how much time to devote to course preparation, grading, and other activities. Some vocational instructors teach night and weekend classes. Most vocational institutions require instructors to work nine months of the year.

Vocational auto repair teachers who work at the secondary school level help students evaluate their abilities, talents, and interests so that the student can develop realistic academic and automotive career options. Vocational high school teachers also can advise on trade, technical school, and apprenticeship programs.

Salaries

Earnings for Vocational-Technical School Instructors vary widely by subject, academic credentials, experience, and region of the country. Part-time instructors usually receive few benefits.

Average annual earnings of Vocational-Technical School Instructors are about $44,367, ranging from a low of less than $24,960 to a high of more than $68,530. Earnings vary according to rank and type of institution and geographic area. Most faculty members also earn money in addition to their base salary, from consulting, teaching other courses, or fixing cars on the side. Part-time faculty usually have fewer benefits than do full-time faculty.

Employment Prospects

Job prospects will continue to improve in the automotive training field, which offers attractive nonacademic job opportunities and attracts fewer applicants for academic positions, according to the U.S. Department of Labor. The job outlook for postsecondary teachers should be much brighter than it has been in recent years. Employment is expected to grow much faster than the average for all occupations through 2012.

Projected growth in vocational school enrollment over the next decade stems largely from the expected increase in the population of 18- to 24-year-olds. Adults returning to college and an increase in foreign-born students also will add to the number of students, particularly in the fastest-growing states of California, Texas, Florida, New York, and Arizona. Because many of the students will be from minority groups, demand for minority teachers will be high.

Welfare-to-work policies and the growing need to regularly update skills will continue to create new opportunities for vocational-technical teachers, particularly at community colleges and vo-tech schools. There also is expected to be a large number of openings due to the retirements of faculty who were hired in the late '60s and '70s to teach the baby boomers.

Vocational-Technical School Instructors are in short supply, and distance learning, particularly over the Internet, is expected to create a number of new jobs. Those in rural areas and with family responsibilities are embracing distance education as a way to get the education they want, while minimizing the commute to a campus. In addition, employers are expected to use distance learning as a way to update their employees' skills. The U.S. Army has recently announced plans to offer distance learning to its troops. Increasing demand for distance education will result in the need for more teachers of online classes.

Advancement Prospects

For most types of Vocational-Technical School Instructors, advancement involves a move into administrative and managerial positions, such as departmental chair or director of the vocational institute.

Education and Training

Requirements for postsecondary Vocational-Technical School Instructors include work experience and formal education ranging from a license or certificate to a college degree. Training requirements for postsecondary Vocational-Technical School Instructors vary by state and by automotive subject. In general, teachers need a bachelor's degree or higher, plus work or other experience in their field. In some fields, a license or certificate (such as ASE master mechanic status) that demonstrates solid qualifications may be all that is required. Teachers update their skills through continuing education to maintain certification. They must also maintain ongoing dialogue with businesses to determine the most current skills needed in the workplace.

Vocational instructors in secondary schools normally need work or other experience in their field and a license or certificate for full professional status. Most states require secondary school vocational instructors to have a bachelor's degree, and some states also require teacher certification.

Experience, Skills, and Personality Traits

Vocational-Technical School Instructors should be able to communicate ideas well, motivate, and relate well to students. They should have inquiring and analytical minds and a strong desire to pursue and disseminate knowledge, while being motivated and able to work in an environment where they receive little direct supervision.

Unions and Associations

Vocational-Technical School Instructors may belong to a teachers' union, such as the American Federation of Teachers (www.aft.org).

Tips for Entry

1. For information on postsecondary vocational-technical school teaching positions, contact the department of vocational-technical education in your state.
2. General information on adult and vocational education is available from the Association for Career and

Technical Education, 1410 King Street, Alexandria, Virginia 22314 or online at www.acteonline.org.

3. Check the ERIC Clearinghouse on Adult, Career, and Vocational Education, 1900 Kenny Road, Columbus, Ohio 43210 or visit the Web site at www.ericacve.org.

4. Contact local school districts and vocational schools in the areas where you would like to work to check for open positions. Send your résumé for the school district to keep on file in case openings occur mid-year.

5. Check the classified ads for "help wanted: professional."

AUTO RECYCLER

CAREER PROFILE

Duties: Recycle quality auto parts and provide expert dismantling to ensure complete customer satisfaction

Alternate Title(s): Auto Salvage Expert

Salary Range: $20,800 to $41,600+

Employment Prospects: Good

Advancement Prospects: Good

Best Geographical Location(s): All parts of the country can provide opportunities for auto recycling positions

Prerequisites:

Education or Training—High school diploma, with courses in automobile mechanics, marketing education, mathematics, business education, and computer applications

Experience—Experience working on cars an asset

Special Skills and Personality Traits—Attention to detail; good research skills; good people skills

CAREER LADDER

Auto Recycle Shop Owner

Auto Recycler

Apprentice Auto Recycler

Position Description

Cars that reach the end of the road are still far from being thrown onto the junk heap, regardless of their condition. Due to the high cost of replacement parts and the vast number of cars on the road, auto recycling has become a highly organized, efficient means of getting the most out of available parts. In fact, recycling car parts and materials has become big business—the kind that helps keep the automotive service and repair industry moving.

As cars became more complex, with onboard computers responsible for monitoring everything and special tools and equipment required for even small jobs—auto recycling in recent years has changed. Once dealing primarily in junkyard sales, Auto Recyclers now focus on inventory management for the resale of quality, reusable parts. Nothing is wasted. Auto Recyclers work in independent recycling businesses.

Because of the high resale value of many components, many Auto Recyclers now manage indoor warehousing systems so parts are not damaged by the weather. This inventory is then available for "instant" sale.

This process has also helped to increase quality control, since the condition of the part is assessed before it is added to inventory.

Hundreds of salvage companies list their available inventories on shared computer files. When a customer calls looking for a specific part, the Auto Recycler can access the inventories of many locations until the right part is found at an acceptable price. The part can be ordered and shipped via computer.

The Auto Recycler spends time helping employees dismantle and inventory cars. Some days the Auto Recycler may spend time buying cars for salvage through auctions, insurance companies, or private vendors. Since some cars the Auto Recycler buys are relatively new, they may be rebuilt with parts from another similar car and resold by the Auto Recycler as a reliable used car or truck. Customers for these used cars include auto body shops, general repair garages, and materials recycling plants.

Salaries

The starting wage for an Auto Recycler is about $10 an hour, for an annual starting salary of about $20,800. After five years, the Auto Recycler may earn more than $20 an hour, for a yearly salary of about $41,600. Owners of recycling businesses can earn much more.

Employment Prospects

The outlook is good for this growing business, and many more employees are expected to enter the auto recycling business. This is driven in part by the high price of car parts today, which creates an ongoing demand for high-quality used parts.

Advancement Prospects

Auto Recyclers may advance by getting a job with a larger recycling shop and may eventually buy a shop and go into business. Some Auto Recyclers go on to become auto/body repair shop managers, used car dealership managers, or materials recycling experts.

Education and Training

A high school education is required for most auto recycling jobs, and courses in math, English, computer science, business, and mechanics may be helpful. Additional experience in auto repair is very helpful, and related business experience is valuable for Auto Recyclers who eventually want to open their own shops. Most Auto Recyclers participate in on-the-job training or begin as an apprentice to a more experienced Auto Recycler.

Experience, Skills, and Personality Traits

An Auto Recycler should have good business management and computer skills, and be excellent at handling customers. Auto Recyclers also must be able to handle a busy pace with multiple responsibilities. An Auto Recycler must rely on a detailed knowledge of cars to ensure the recycler buys cars that can be salvaged for high-quality parts in excellent condition. He or she must know how to price the purchases and parts for sale to ensure good business profits. Being able to work well with people—customers, suppliers, and employees—is an important part of keeping a business thriving. Important skills include good planning and organizing skills, mechanical knowledge, and bookkeeping and customer service skills.

Unions and Associations

Auto Recyclers may belong to associations, such as the National Institute for Automotive Service Excellence and the Automotive Service Association.

Tips for Entry

1. Hands-on experience is important; try to improve your skills by working on your own cars, and by taking every relevant course available during high school or vocational school.
2. An internship or summer job at an auto recycling shop, car dealer, service station, or car repair shop can provide invaluable experience.
3. Check Web sites of local auto recycling shops to spot job openings.
4. Positions should be advertised in the newspaper classified ad section under "trades: mechanical" or "auto."

APPENDIXES

APPENDIX I
AUTOMOTIVE-RELATED ASSOCIATIONS

Alliance of Automobile Manufacturers
1401 H Street, NW, Suite 900
Washington, DC 20005
Phone: (202) 326-5500
http://www.autoalliance.org

**American Association of Franchisees
and Dealers**
P.O. Box 81887
San Diego, CA 92138-1887
Phone: (800) 733-9858
http://www.aafd.org

**American Auto Racing Writers
and Broadcasters Association**
922 North Pass Avenue
Burbank, CA 91505
Phone: (818) 842-7005
http://www.motorsportsforum.com/ris01/
aarwba.htm

American Bus Association
1100 New York Avenue, NW, Suite 1050
Washington, DC 20005
http://www.buses.org

American Hot Rod Association (AHRA)
Spokane Raceway Park/AHRA
North 101 Hayford Road
Spokane, WA 99224
Phone: (509) 244-3663
http://www.spokaneracewaypark.com/
Drags/index.html

**American International Automobile
Dealers Association**
211 North Union Street, Suite 300
Alexandria, VA 22314
Phone: (703) 519-7800
http://www.aiada.org

**American Public Transportation
Association**
1666 K Street, NW, Suite 1100
Washington, DC 20006
http://www.apta.org

**The American Society of Mechanical
Engineers**
Three Park Avenue
New York, NY 10016
http://www.asme.org

American Trucking Association
2200 Mill Road
Alexandria, VA 22314
Phone: (703) 838-1700
http://www.trucking.org

American Welding Society
550 N.W. Lejeune Road
Miami, FL 33126-5699
http://www.aws.org

ARCA
P.O. Box 5217
Toledo OH, 43611-0217
Phone: (734) 847-6726
Fax: (734) 847-3137
http://www.arcaracing.com

**Association for Career
and Technical Education**
1410 King Street
Alexandria, VA 22314
Phone: (703) 683-3111
http://www.acteonline.org

**The Association for Manufacturing
Technology**
7901 Westpark Drive
McLean, VA 22102
Phone: (703) 893-2900
    or (800) 524-0475
http://www.mfgtech.org

**Association of International
Automobile Manufacturers, Inc.**
1001 19th Street, North
Suite 1200
Arlington, VA 22209
Phone: (703) 525-7788
http://www.aiam.org

Autoclassroom.com
http://autoclassroom.com

**Automatic Transmission Rebuilders
Association**
2400 Latigo Avenue
Oxnard, CA 93030
Phone: (805) 604-2000
http://www.atra.net

**Automotive Aftermarket Industry
Association (AAIA)**
4600 East-West Highway, Suite 300
Bethesda, MD 20814-3415
Phone: (301) 654-6664
http://www.aftermarket.org

**Automotive Engine Rebuilders
Association**
330 Lexington Drive
Buffalo Grove, IL 60089-6998
Phone: (847) 541-6550
http://www.aera.org

Automotive Industry Action Group
26200 Lahser Road, Suite 200
Southfield, MI 48034
Phone: (248) 358-3570
http://www.aiag.org

Automotive Industry Planning Council
http://www.autoipc.org

Automotive Recyclers Association
3975 Fair Ridge Drive, Suite 20-North
Fairfax, VA 22033
Phone: (703) 385-1001
http://www.autorecyc.org

Automotive Service Association
P.O. Box 929
Bedford, TX 76095
Phone: (817) 283-6205
    or (800) 272-7467
http://www.asashop.org

**Automotive Training Managers
Council**
101 Blue Seal Drive, S.E., Suite 101
Leesburg, VA 20175
Phone: (703) 669-6670
http://www.atmc.org

**Automotive Warehouse Distributors
Association**
4050 Pennsylvania, Suite 225
Kansas City, MO 64111
Phone: (816) 523-8693
http://www.awda.org

Automotive Youth Education System (AYES)
50 W. Big Beaver, Suite 145
Troy, MI 48084
Phone: (248) 526-1750 or (888) 664-0044
http://www.ayes.org

Canadian Vehicle Manufacturers' Association
170 Attwell Drive, Suite 400
Toronto, Ontario
M9W 5Z5
Phone: (416) 364-9333 or (800) 758-7122
http://www.cvma.ca

ERIC Clearinghouse on Adult, Career, and Vocational Education
1900 Kenny Road
Columbus, OH 43210
http://www.ericacve.org

Independent Automotive Damage Appraisers Association
P.O. Box 1166
Nixa, MO 65714
http://www.iada.org

Indy Racing League (IRL)
http://www.indyracing.com

Institute of Electrical and Electronics Engineers
445 Hoes Lane
Piscataway, NJ 08855-1331
http://www.ieee.org

Institute of Industrial Engineers, Inc.
25 Technology Park/Atlanta
Norcross, GA 30092
http://www.iienet.org

International Association of Business Communicators
One Hallidie Plaza, Suite 600
San Francisco, CA 94102
Phone: (415) 544-4700 or (800) 776-4222
http://www.iabc.com

International Automotive Technicians' Network
411 West Lambert Road, Suite 409
Brea, CA 92821
Phone: (714) 257-1335
http://www.iatn.net

International Franchise Association
1350 New York Avenue, NW, Suite 900
Washington, DC 20005-4709
Phone: (202) 628-8000
http://www.franchise.org

International Motor Sports Association (IMSA)
1394 Broadway Avenue
Braselton, GA 30517
Phone: (706) 658-2120
http://www.imsaracing.net

Mobile Air Conditioning Society Worldwide
P.O. Box 88
225 South Broad Street
Lansdale, PA 19446
Phone: (215) 631-7020
http://www.macsw.org

National Automobile Dealers Association
8400 Westpark Drive
McLean, VA 22102
http://www.nada.org

National Automotive Technicians Education Foundation
101 Blue Seal Drive S.E., Suite 101
Leesburg, VA 20175
http://www.natef.org

National Hot Rod Association
2035 Financial Way
Glendora, CA 91741
Phone: (626) 914-4761
Fax: (626) 963-5360
http://www.nhra.com

National Institute for Automotive Service Excellence
101 Blue Seal Drive, S.E., Suite 101
Leesburg, VA 20175
Phone: (877) ASE-TECH
http://www.asecert.org

National Institute for Metalworking Skills
3251 Old Lee Highway, Suite 205
Fairfax, VA 22030
Phone: (703) 352-4971
http://www.nims-skills.org

National Limousine Association
2365 Harrodsburg Road, Suite A325
Lexington, KY 40504
Phone: (800) 652-7007
http://www.limo.org

National School Transportation Association
625 Slaters Lane, Suite 205
Alexandria, VA 22314

National Tooling and Metalworking Association
9300 Livingston Road
Fort Washington, MD 20744
http://www.ntma.org

North American Council of Automotive Teachers (NACAT)
11956 Bernardo Plaza Drive, Dept. 436
San Diego, CA 92128
Phone: (858) 487-8126
http://www.nacat.com

Precision Machine Products Association
6700 West Snowville Road
Brecksville, OH 44141-3292
http://www.pmpa.org

Professional Truck Driving Institute of America, Inc.
8788 Elk Grove Boulevard, Suite 20
Elk Grove, CA 95624
Phone: (916) 686-5146

School Bus Fleet
3520 Challenger Street
Torrance, CA 90503
http://www.schoolbusfleet.com

Service Technicians Society
400 Commonwealth Drive
Warrendale, PA 15096-0001
Phone: (800) 787-9596
http://www.sts.sae.org/jsp/jsps/stsindex.jsp

Society of Automotive Engineers
400 Commonwealth Drive
Warrendale, PA 15096
Phone: (724) 776-4841
http://www.sae.org

Society of Manufacturing Engineers
One SME Drive
P.O. Box 930
Dearborn, MI 48121
Phone: (800) 733-4763
http://www.sme.org

Sports Car Club of America (SCCA)
P.O. Box 19400
Topeka, KS 66619-0400
Phone: (785) 357-7222
or (800) 770-2055
http://www.scca.org

Taxicab Limousine, and Paratransit Association
3849 Farragut Avenue
Kensington, MD 20895
Phone: (301) 946-5701
Fax: (301) 946-4641
http://www.tlpa.org

Truck Driver Institute of America
2200 Mill Road
Alexandria, VA 22314
Phone: (703) 838-8842
http://www.ptdi.org

United Motorcoach Association
113 South West Street, 4th Floor
Alexandria, VA 22314
Phone: (800) 424-8262
http://www.uma.org

United States Auto Club (USAC)
4910 West 16th Street
Speedway, IN 46224
Phone: (317) 247-5151
http://www.usacracing.com

APPENDIX II
INFORMATION ON AUTOMOTIVE TRAINING

AUTO DAMAGE APPRAISING

Independent Automotive Damage Appraisers Association
P.O. Box 1166
Nixa, MO 65714
http://www.iada.org
The association provides information on careers in auto damage appraising.

AUTOMOTIVE TECHNICIAN TRAINING

Accrediting Commission of Career Schools and Colleges of Technology
2101 Wilson Boulevard, Suite 302
Arlington, VA 22201
http://www.accsct.org
Offers a directory of accredited private trade and technical schools that offer programs in automotive technician training.

Automotive Youth Educational Systems (AYES)
2701 Troy Center Drive, Suite 450
Troy, MI 48084
http://www.ayes.org
Offers information on automobile manufacturer-sponsored programs in automotive service technology.

National Automotive Technicians Education Foundation
101 Blue Seal Drive, S.E., Suite 101
Leesburg, VA 20175
http://www.natef.org
Offers a list of certified automotive technician training programs.

National Institute for Automotive Service Excellence (ASE)
101 Blue Seal Drive, S.E., Suite 101
Leesburg, VA 20175
http://www.asecert.org
Offers information on how to become a certified automotive service technician.

SkillsUSA-VICA
P.O. Box 3000
1401 James Monroe Highway
Leesburg, VA 22075

http://www.skillsusa.org
Offers a list of public automotive technician training programs.

AUTOMOTIVE BODY REPAIRING TRAINING

Accrediting Commission of Career Schools and Colleges of Technology
2101 Wilson Boulevard, Suite 302
Arlington, VA 22201
http://www.accsct.org
Offers a directory of accredited private trade and technical schools that offer training programs in automotive body repair.

Automotive Service Association, Inc.
1901 Airport Freeway
Bedford, TX 76021-5732
http://www.asashop.org
Provides general information about automotive body repairer careers.

Inter-Industry Conference On Auto Collision Repair Education Foundation (I-CAR)
3701 Algonquin Road, Suite 400
Rolling Meadow, IL 60008
Phone: (888) 722-3787
http://www.i-car.com
Offers general information on auto body repair careers.

National Automotive Technician Education Foundation
101 Blue Seal Drive, S.E., Suite 101
Leesburg, VA 20175
http://www.natef.org
Provides a directory of certified automotive body repairer programs.

National Institute for Automotive Service Excellence (ASE)
101 Blue Seal Drive, S.E., Suite 101
Leesburg, VA 20175
http://www.asecert.org
Provides information on how to become a certified automotive body repairer.

SkillsUSA-VICA
P.O. Box 3000
1401 James Monroe Highway
Leesburg, VA 22075

http://www.skillsusa.org
Provides a list of public automotive body repair training programs.

CHAUFFEURING

Executive Chauffeuring School
1198 Pacific Coast Highway, Suite D-232
Seal Beach, CA 90740

AUTOMOTIVE ENGINEERING

Accreditation Board for Engineering and Technology, Inc.
111 Market Place, Suite 1050
Baltimore, MD 21202-4012
http://www.abet.org
Organization can provide information for high school students interested in obtaining information on ABET-accredited engineering programs.

American Society for Engineering Education
1818 N Street, NW, Suite 600
Washington, DC 20036-2479
http://www.asee.org
Organization provides information on general engineering education and career resources.

Institute of Industrial Engineers, Inc.
25 Technology Park/Atlanta
Norcross, GA 30092
http://www.iienet.org
Organization provides further information about industrial engineers.

National Council of Examiners for Engineers and Surveying
P.O. Box 1686
Clemson, SC 29633-1686
http://www.ncees.org
Provides information for nonlicensed engineers and college students interested in obtaining information on Professional Engineer licensure.

National Society of Professional Engineers
1420 King Street

Alexandria, VA 22314-2794
http://www.nspe.org
Provides information for nonlicensed engineers and college students interested in obtaining information on Professional Engineer licensure.

UNC Charlotte Motorsports and Automotive Engineering Program
University of North Carolina
9201 University City Boulevard
Charlotte, NC 28223
Phone: (704) 687-3335
http://www.coe.uncc.edu/motorsports/index.html

ENGINEERING TECHNOLOGY

Accreditation Board for Engineering and Technology, Inc.
111 Market Place, Suite 1050
Baltimore, MD 21202
http://www.abet.org
Provides information on ABET-accredited engineering technology programs.

Junior Engineering Technical Society (JETS)
1420 King Street, Suite 405
Alexandria, VA 22314-2794
http://www.jets.org
For $3.50, JETS will provide a package of guidance materials and information (product number SP-01) on a variety of engineering technician and technology careers; free information is available on the JETS Web site.

National Institute for Certification in Engineering Technologies (NICET)
1420 King Street
Alexandria, VA 22314-2794
http://www.nicet.org
Information on certification of engineering technicians.

MACHINIST TRAINING

National Tooling and Metalworking Association
9300 Livingston Road
Fort Washington, MD 20744
http://www.ntma.org
Organization provides a list of training centers and apprenticeship programs.

PMA Educational Foundation
6363 Oak Tree Boulevard
Independence, OH 44131-2500
http://www.pmaef.org
Organization provides general occupational information and a list of training programs.

MOTORSPORTS MANAGEMENT

Rowan-Cabarrus Community College Motorsports Management Technology
Associate in Applied Science Degree/Certificate Program
North Campus (Rowan County)
P.O. Box 1595
Salisbury, NC 28145

South Campus (Cabarrus County)
1531 Trinity Church Road
Concord, NC 28027
Phone: (704) 637-0760
    or (704) 788-3197, ext. 221
http://www.rccc.cc.nc.us/programs/msm.html
The Motorsports Management Technology curriculum is designed to provide students with the knowledge and skills necessary to perform mid-management level functions in motorsports-related companies.

MOTORSPORTS MECHANICS

Bobby Isaac Motorsports Program
Catawba Valley Community College, East Campus
Hickory, NC
Phone: (828) 327-7000, ext. 4284
http://www.cce.cvcc.edu/?a=race

VO-TECH EDUCATION

ERIC Clearinghouse on Adult, Career, and Vocational Education
1900 Kenny Road
Columbus, OH 43210
http://www.ericacve.org

APPENDIX III
AUTO RACING SCHOOLS

Aintree Racing Drivers' School Ltd.
1 Fairoak Court
Whitehouse
Runcorn
Cheshire WA7 3DX
United Kingdom
Phone: +44 (0) 1942 270230
http://www.racing-school.co.uk

Ambassador Racing School
14840 Speedway Drive
Wimauma, FL 33598
Phone: (813) 634-1076
http://www.racingkarts.com

Apex Racing Schools
727 Silver Spur Road
Rolling Hills Estates, CA 90274
http://www.apexracing.com

Bertil Roos Indystyle Racing School
P.O. Box 221
Blakeslee, PA 18610
Phone: (800) 722-3669
http://www.racenow.com

Bill Sisley Kart Racing School
Buckmore Park Kart Circuit
Maidstone Road
Chatham
Kent ME5 9QG
United Kingdom
Phone: 01634 201562
http://www.buckmore.co.uk

Billy Pauch Driving School
611 Highway 519
Frenchtown, NJ 08825
Phone: (908) 996-7278

**Bob Bondurant School of High
    Performance Driving**
P.O. Box 51980
Phoenix, AZ 85076-1980
http://www.bondurant.com

**Bob Cornish Graduate School Of Auto
    Racing**
P.O. Box 1188
Willows, CA 95988
Phone: (530) 520-3414
http://www.performancecoach.com

**Bobby Isaac Motorsports Technology
    Program**
2550 Highway 70 SE
Hickory, NC 28602
Phone: (828) 327-7000 ext. 4284
http://www.teamconcept2000.com

**Bragg-Smith Advanced Driving
    School Inc.**
3601 South Highway 160
Pahrump, NV 89048
Phone: (775) 727-6363
http://www.bragg-smith.com

Bridgestone Racing Academy
P.O. Box 373
Pontypool, ON L0A 1K0
Canada
Phone: (905) 983-1114
http://www.race2000.com

Bridgestone Winter Driving School
1850 Ski Time Square
P.O. Box 774167
Steamboat Springs, CO 80477
Phone: (800) WHY-SKID
E-mail: mail@winterdrive.com
http://www.winterdrive.com

BSR Inc. Driving School
P.O. Box 190
Summit Point, WV 25446
Phone: (304) 725-6512
http://www.bsr-inc.com

Buck Baker Racing
1613 Runnymede Lane
Charlotte, NC 28211
Phone: (704) 366-6224
    or (800) 529-BUCK
http://www.buckbaker.com

Car Guys Driving School
Car Guys, Inc.
P.O. Box 1310
Rockville, MD 20849-1310
Phone: (800) 800-4897 or (301) 984-8300
http://www.carguys.com

Competitive Edge Racing School
14919 Northeast 147th Court
Woodinville, WA 98072

Phone: (800) 699-7080
http://www.racingschool.com

Complete Auto Racing School
15332 Antioch Street #515
Pacific Palisades, CA 90272
Phone: (888) 98-U-RACE
http://www.carsracing.com

Danny Collins Racing School
1626 Albion Street
Denver, CO 80220
Phone: (303) 388-3875

**David Loring/Motion Dynamics
    Drivers School**
P.O. Box 2245, Route 16
Conway, NH 03818
Phone: (603) 447-3543
http://www.mdracing.com

Derek Daly Speedcentre
7055 Speedway Boulevard, Suite E-102
Las Vegas, NV 89115
Phone: (888) 463-3735
http://www.derekdaly.com

Dirt Track Racing Workshops
4830 Industrial Parkway
Indianapolis IN 46226
Phone: (317) 357-3643

Donniebrooke Motorsport
4444 Shoreline Drive
Spring Park, MN 55384
Phone: (800) 825-2502

**Donnie Moran Racing Driving
    School**
4325 Fawn Drive
Dresden, OH 43821
Phone: (740) 754-2299
E-mail: Donnie@donniemoran.com
http://www.donniemoran.com/
    driving_school.htm

Drive Tech Racing School
14611 Rancho Vista Drive
Fontana, CA 92335
Phone: (800) 678-8864
http://www.drivetech.com

Driving 101
6915 Speedway Boulevard
Las Vegas, NV 89115
Phone: (702) 651-6300
http://www.driving101.com/?raceindustry

Driving Dynamics
54 Birch Avenue
Little Silver, NJ 07739
Phone: (732) 219-0404
http://www.drivingdynamics.com

Duvall Driving School
614 South Green River Road
Cowpens, SC 29330
Phone: (864) 489-3863

**Fast Track High Performance Driving
    School**
5540 Morehead Road
P.O. Box 160
Harrisburg, NC 28075-0160
Phone: (704) 455-1700
http://www.fasttrackracing.com

FinishLine Racing School
3113 South Ridgewood Avenue
Edgewater, FL 32141
Phone: (904) 427-8522
http://www.finishlineracing.com

Frank Hawley's Drag Racing School

EAST:
11223 C.R. 225
Gainesville, FL 32609
Phone: (352) 336-8111
http://www.frankhawley.com

WEST:
P.O. Box 484
LaVerne, CA 91750-0484
Phone: (909) 622-2466
http://www.frankhawley.com

**Go4it High Performance
    Driving/Racing Schools**
374 North 96th Street
Louisville, CO 80027
Phone: (303) 666-4113
http://www.go4itservices.com

Grand Prix Promotions
P.O. Box 507
4133 Weld County Road 34
Mead, CO 80542
Phone: (970) 535-4255

Hawaii International Racing School
91-201 Malakole Street
Kapolei, HI 96707

Phone: (808) 673-1601
http://www.hawaiiracewaypark.com

High Performance Course Ltd.
Phone: 01858 545 946
E-mail: info@high-performance-
    course.co.uk
http://www.high-performance-
    course.co.uk

Jim Hall Karting School
1555-G Morse Avenue
Ventura, CA 93003
Phone: (805) 654-1329
E-mail: jhrkart@west.net
http://www.jhrkartracing.com

**Jimmy Sills School of Open Wheel
    Racing**
2435 Morrene Drive
Placerville, CA 95667
Phone: (800) 508-8448
http://www.sprintcar.com

**Jim Russell Racing Drivers School
    (Infineon Raceway)**
29305 Arnold Drive
Sonoma, CA 95476
Phone: (707) 939-7600 or (800) 733-0345
http://www.jimrussellusa.com

**Jim Russell Racing Drivers School at
    Mont Tremblant**
http://www.jimrussell.com

**Jim Russell Racing Drivers School at
    Donington Park**
http://www.jimrussel.com

Knockhill Race School
Knockhill Racing Circuit
Dunfermline
Fife KY12 9TF
Scotland
United Kingdom
Phone: 01383-723337
http://www.knockhill.com

Legends Motorsports
1953 9th Avenue NW
Calgary, Alberta T2N 4N3 Canada
Phone: (403) 203-1977
http://www.racingadventures.com

Legends Racing School
P.O. Box 600
Concord, NC 28026
Phone: (704) 455-3240
http://www.600racing.com

Mid-Ohio School
545 Metro Place South, Suite 400
Dublin, OH 43017-1100
Phone: (614) 793-4615
http://www.midohioschool.com

NASA Performance Driving School
P.O. Box 21555
Richmond, CA 94820
Phone: (530) 232-6272
http://www.nasaproracing.com

Outlaw Driving School
P.O. Box 210739
Dallas, TX 75211
Phone: (214) 331-4664
http://www.outlawdrivingschool.com

**Panoz Racing School At Road
    Atlanta**
5300 Winder Highway
Braselton, GA 30517
Phone: (770) 967-6143
    or (800) 849-RACE
http://www.panozracingschool.com

**Paul Smith's Top Fuel/Funny Car Drag
    Racing School**
1080 Linton Boulevard B-5, Suite 12
Delray Beach, FL 33444
Phone: (561) 738-0864

**Performance Drivers Association
    School**
1372 Main Avenue
Clifton, NJ 07011
Phone: (973) 253-3900
http://www.imp-auto.com

Phil Price Rally School
Coed Harbour
Llangunllo LD7 1TD
Knighton Powys
Wales, United Kingdom
Phone: 01547 550300
http://www.philprice.co.uk

Pitarresi Pro Drive Racing School
1940 North Victory Boulevard
Portland, OR 97217
Phone: (503) 285-4449
http://www.prodrive.net

PM Kart Racing School
11414 Deerfield Road
Cincinnatti, OH 45242
Phone: (513) 294-5020
    or (800) 407-0252
http://www.pmracing.com

**Powell Motorsport Advanced Driving
    School**
3140 Highway 7A
Blackstock, Ontario LOB 1B0
Canada
Phone: (905) 986-2277
    or (905) 985-1600
http://www.powellmotorsport.com

ProFormance Race Drivers School
2244 Lefeuvre Road
Abbotsford, British Columbia V4X 1C6
Canada
Phone: (800) 567-RACE
    or (604) 820-2270
http://www.proformanceracing.com

ProFormance Racing School
P.O. Box 791
Bellevue, WA 98009
Phone: (425) 271-7098
http://www.proformanceraceschool.com

Putnam Race Cars
13500 Woodedge Drive
Bowie, MD 20720
Phone: (301) 262-4100
http://www.jrdragster.net

Race On Driving Experience
Phone: (866) 4RACE-ON (472-2366)
    or (901) 527-6174
http://www.4raceon.com

Race Training Center
P.O. Box 484
LaVerne, CA 91750
Phone: (877) 901-RACE [7223]
http://www.racetrainingcenter.com

Raceworks Racing Academy
17001 Midway Road
Tracy, CA 95376
Phone: (877) 923-RACE [7223]
http://www.racekid.com

Racing Adventures
8776 East Shea #B3A-117
Scottsdale, AZ 85260-6629
Phone: (602) 618-RACE [7223]
E-mail: racingadventures@nucleus.com
http://www.racingadventures.com

Richard Petty Driving Experience
6022 Victory Lane
Concord, NC 28027
Phone: (704) 455-9443

http://www.1800bepetty.com

Road Atlanta Driver Training Center
5300 Winder Highway
Braselton, GA 30517
Phone: (800) 849-RACE [7223]
    or (770) 967-6143
E-mail: info@roadatlanta.com
http://www.roadatlanta.com

**Rod Hall Advanced Off-Road Racing
    School**
1360 Kleppe Lane
Sparks, NV 89431
Phone: (775) 331-5032
http://www.rodhall.com

Roy Hill's Drag Racing School
4926 Walker Mill Road
Sophia, NC 27350
Phone: (336) 498-7964
http://www.royhill.com

Russell Racing School
Phone: (800) 733-0345
http://www.russellracing.com

Silverstone Racing School
Silverstone Circuit
Northamptonshire NN12 8TN
United Kingdom
Phone: 01327 320412
E-mail: race@silverstonemotorsport.co.uk
http://www.silverstone-circuit.co.uk

Skip Barber Racing School
P.O. Box 1629
29 Brook Street
Lakeville, CT 06039
Phone: (800) 221-1131 or (860) 435-1300
E-mail: speed@skipbarber.com
http://www.skipbarber.com

Southard's Racing School
P.O. Box 1810
New Smyrna Beach, FL 32170
Phone: (904) 428-3307
http://www.racingschool.net

**Southern Thunder American Truck
    Racing**
7320 47th Street North
Pinellas Park, FL 33781
Phone: (727) 321-3715
http://www.southernthunder.com

Speedtech Auto Racing School
4333 Motorsports Drive
Concord, NC 28027

Phone: (877) 807-7333
E-mail: speedtech500@speedtech500.com
http://www.speedtech500.com

Speed Zone Racing School
P.O. Box 3912
Riverside, CA 92519
Phone: (909) 686-3826
http://www.adamskart.com

Start!! Racing
P.O. Box 396
Millerton, NY 12546
Phone: (800) 243-1310
http://www.startracing.com

**Stephens Brother's School Of High
    Performance Driving**
2232 S. Nogales Avenue
Tulsa, OK 74107-2826
Phone: (918) 583-1136
http://www.mavier.com/
    stephens_bros_racing

Stock Car Racing Experience
P.O. Box 500
Blakeslee, PA 18610
Phone: (877) 786-2522
    or (570) 643-6921
http://www.877stockcar.com

Team Texas Racing School
15468 Highway 156
Justin, TX 76247
Phone: (940) 648-1043
http://www.teamtexas.com

**Track Time Performance Driving
    Schools, Inc.**
1104 North Meridian
Youngstown, OH 44509
Phone: (330) 793-9451
http://www.tracktime.com

**Western Adventures 4x4 Driving
    School**
P.O. Box 2451
Ramona, CA 92065
Phone: (760) 789-1563
    or (619) 573-0607
E-mail: frenchie@tmisnet.com
http://www.4×4now.com/4wstrwa.htm

Winter Driving School
P.O. Box 774167
Steamboat Springs, CO 80477
Phone: (970) 879-6104
http://www.winterdrive.com

APPENDIX IV
AUTOMOTIVE MUSEUMS

ALABAMA

Barber Vintage Motorsports Museum
2721 5th Avenue South
Birmingham, AL 35233
Phone: (205) 252-8377
http://www.barbermuseum.org

International Motorsports Hall of Fame
P.O. Box 10183198
Talladega, AL 35160
Phone: (205) 362-5002
http://www.motorsportshalloffame.com

Mercedes-Benz USA Visitor Center
1 Mercedes Drive
Tuscaloosa, AL 35490
Phone: (888) 286-8762
http://www.mbusi.com

ALASKA

**Alaska Historical and Transportation
    Museum**
P.O. Box 920
Palmer, AK 99645
Phone: (907) 745-4493
http://www.alaska.net/~~rmorris/mati1.htm

**Museum of Alaska Transportation and
    Industry**
P.O. Box 870646
Wasilla, AK 99687
Phone: (907) 376-1211
http://www.museumofalaska.org

ARIZONA

Hall of Flame Museum of Firefighting
6101 East Van Buren
Phoenix, AZ 85008
Phone: (602) 275-3473
http://www.hallofflame.org

ARKANSAS

Museum of Automobiles
Petit Jean Mountain
Morrilton, AR 72110
Phone: (501) 727-5427
http://www.museumofautos.com

CALIFORNIA

All Cadillacs of the Forties
12811 Foothill Boulevard
Sylmar, CA 91342
Phone: (818) 361-1147 or (800) 808-1147

Blackhawk Automotive Museum
3700 Blackhawk Plaza Circle
Danville, CA 94506
Phone: (925) 736-2280
http://www.blackhawkauto.org

**Blaker Antique Auto and Clock
    Collection**
1301 Fulkerth Road
Turlock, CA 95380
Phone: (209) 634-4931

Concours Motorcars
619 East Fourth Street
Santa Ana, CA 92703
Phone: (714) 953-5303

Dan Rouit Flat Track Museum
309 West Rialto Street
Clovis, CA
Phone: (559) 291-2242
http://www.vft.org/rouit.htm

Deer Park Car Museum
29013 Champagne Boulevard
Escondido, CA 92026
Phone: (619) 749-1666

Firehouse Museum
1972 Columbia Street
San Diego, CA 92117
Phone: (619) 232-FIRE

Hays Old Truck Town
2000 East Main Street
P.O. Box 2317
Woodland, CA 95776
Phone: (916) 666-1044; (916) 661-1167
http://www.truckmuseum.org

Heidrick Ag History Center
1962 Hays Lane
Woodland, CA 95776
Phone: (530) 666-9700
http://www.aghistory.org

J. Paul Getty Museum
17985 West Pacific Coast Highway
Malibu, CA 90265
http://www.getty.edu/museum

Justice Brothers Racing Museum
2734 East Huntington Drive
Duarte, CA 91010
Phone: (626) 359-9174
http://www.justicebrothers.com/jb6.html

Metropolitan Historical Collection
5330 Laurel Canyon Boulevard
North Hollywood, CA 91607
Phone: (213) 769-1515

Millers Horse and Buggy Ranch
9425 Yosemite Boulevard
Modesto, CA 95351
Phone: (209) 522-1781

Movieland Cars of the Stars Museum
P.O. Box 5130
7711 Beach Boulevard or 6920
    Orangethorpe Avenue
Buena Park, CA 90602
Phone: (714) 522-1154
    or (213) 583-8025

Petersen Automotive Museum
6060 Wilshire at Fairfax
Los Angeles, CA 90036
Phone: (213) 930-CARS
http://www.petersen.org

**Route 66 Territory Visitors Center
    and Museum**
Thomas Winery Plaza
7965 Vineyard Avenue, Suite F5
Rancho Cucamonga, CA 91730
Phone: (800) JOG-RT66
http://www.classicar.com/museums/
    ranchovc/ranchovc.htm

San Diego Automotive Museum
2080 Pan American Plaza #12
San Diego, CA 92101
Phone: (619) 231-AUTO
E-mail: sdauto@cts.com
http://www.sdautomuseum.org

Toyota Museum
1901 South Western Avenue
Torrance, CA 90509
Phone: (213) 618-4000

Towe Auto Museum
2200 Front Street
Sacramento, CA 95818
Phone: (916) 442-6802
http://www.toweautomuseum.org and
http://www.classicar.com/museums/
    toweford/toweford.htm

Vintage Museum of Transportation
    and Wildlife
1421 Emerson Avenue
Oxnard , CA 93033
Phone: (805) 486-0666 or (805) 486-
    2586

Wagons to Wings Museum
15060 Foothills Road
Morgan Hill, CA 95037
Phone: (408) 779-4136

COLORADO

Dougherty Museum Collection
8382 1075th Street
Longmont, CO 80501
Phone: (303) 766-2520

Forney Transportation Museum
4303 Brighton Boulevard
Denver, CO 80216
Phone: (303) 297-1113
http://www.forneymuseum.com

Front-Wheel Drive Auto Museum
250 North Main Street
Brighton, CO 80601
Phone: (303) 659-5295; (303) 659-6536

House of Cars Car Museum
1102 South 21st Street
Colorado Springs, CO 80907
Phone: (303) 473-7776

Pikes Peak Auto Hill Climb Visitors
    Center and Race Car Museum
135 Manitou Avenue
Manitou Springs, CO 80829
Phone: (719) 685-4400

CONNECTICUT

Antique Auto Museum
P.O. Box 430
Manchester, CT 06040

Hartford Automobile Club
815 Farmington Avenue
West Hartford, CT 06119
Phone: (203) 233-8511

Museum of Connecticut History
231 Capitol Avenue
Hartford, CT 06115
Phone: (203) 566-3056

DELAWARE

Delaware Agricultural Museum
866 North Dupont Highway
Dover, DE 19901
Phone: (302) 734-1618

Magic Age of Steam
P.O. Box 127
Route 82
Yorklyn, DE 19726

WASHINGTON, DC

Smithsonian Institution
14th and Constitution
Washington, DC 20560
Phone: (202) 357-2700

FLORIDA

Birthplace of Speed Museum
160 East Granada Boulevard
Ormond Beach, FL 32074
Phone: (904) 672-5657

Elliott Museum
Hutchinson Island
Stuart, FL 33494
Phone: (407) 225-1961

Don Garlits Museum of Drag Racing
13700 Southwest 16th Avenue
Ocala, FL 34473
Phone: (352) 245-8661
http://www.garlits.com/Museum/
    museum.html

Fort Lauderdale Antique Car Museum
1527 Southwest 1st. Avenue
Fort Lauderdale, FL 33315
Phone: (954) 779-7300

Historical Society of Martin County-
    Elliott Museum
825 Northeast Ocean Boulevard
Stuart, FL 34996
Phone: (407) 225-1961
http://www.classicar.com/MUSEUMS/HI
    STMART/HISTMART.HTM

Sarasota Classic Car Museum
5500 North Tamiami Trail
Sarasota, FL 34239
Phone: (941) 355-6228
http://www.sarasotacarmuseum.org

Silver Springs Antique Car
    Collection
State Road 40
Ocala, FL 32670
Phone: (904) 236-2121

Tallahassee Antique Car Museum
3550A Mahan Drive
Tallahassee, FL 32308
Phone: (850) 942-0137
http://www.tacm.com

GEORGIA

Museo Abarth
111 Via Bayless
Marietta, GA 30066-2770
Phone: (678) 928-1446
http://www.classicar.com/MUSEUMS/
    ABARTH/ABARTH.HTM

Stone Mountain Antique Car
    and Treasure Museum
Stone Mountain Memorial Park
2542 Young Road
Stone Mountain, GA 30088
Phone: (404) 981-0194
http://www.protsman-antiques.com

IDAHO

Grant's Antique Cars and Museum
5603 Franklin Road
Boise, ID 83705
Phone: (208) 342-8800
    or (208) 343-3113

Idaho State Historical Society
    Transportation Museum
Boise, ID 83705
Phone: (208) 334-2844

Vintage Wheel Museum
218 Cedar Street
Sandpoint, ID 83864
Phone: (208) 263-7173
http://www.ohwy.com/id/v/vintwhmu.htm

ILLINOIS

Dale's Classic Cars
12th and West Lake Street
Glenview, IL 60025
Phone: (618) 244-4116

**Fagan's Antique and Classic
Automobile Museum**
162nd Street and Clairmont Avenue
Markham, IL 60426
Phone: (312) 331-3380

Gasoline Alley
1765 North Milwaukee
Libertyville, IL 60048
Phone: (312) 362-8700

Grant Hills Antique Auto Museum
U.S. Highway 20
Galena, IL 61036
Phone: (815) 777-2115

**Hartung's License Plate Automotive
Museum**
3623 West Lake Street
Glenview, IL 60025
Phone: (847) 724-4354
http://www.classicar.com/MUSEUMS/
HARTUNG/HARTUNG.HTM

Lazarus Motor Museum
P.O. Box 368
211 Walnut Street
Forreston, IL 61020
Phone: (815) 938-2250

**Museum of Science and Industry-
Collections**
57th Street and Lake Shore Drive
Chicago, IL 60637
Phone: (312) 684-1414

**Quinsippi Island Antique Auto
Museum**
2215 Spruce
Quincy, IL 62301

Volo Antique Auto Museum
27582 West Highway 120
Volo, IL 60073
Phone: (815) 385-3644
http://www.volocars.com

INDIANA

Antique Auto and Racecar Museum
Stone City Mall
3348 16th Street
Bedford, IN 47421
Phone: (812) 275-0556
http://www.autoracemuseum.com

Antique and Classic Auto Museum
2130 Middlebury Street
Elkhart, IN 46516

Phone: (219) 522-0539
http://www.classicar.com/museums/
srmiller/srmiller.htm

Auburn-Cord Duesenberg Museum
P.O. Box 271
1600 South Wayne Street
Auburn, IN 46706
Phone: (260) 925-1444
http://www.acdmuseum.org

Door Prairie Auto Museum
2405 Indiana Avenue
P.O. Box 1771
LaPorte, IN 46350
Phone: (219) 326-1337
http://www.dpautomuseum.com/index.htm

**Indianapolis Motor Speedway and Hall
of Fame Museum**
4790 West 16th Street
Speedway, IN 46224
Phone: (317) 248-6747

**National Automotive and Truck
Museum of the United States**
1000 Gordon M. Buehrig Place
P.O. Box 686
Auburn, IN 46706-0686
Phone: (219) 925-4560
http://www.clearlake.com/natmus/nat.htm

Plew's Indy 500 Museum, Inc.
9648 West Morris Street
Indianapolis, IN 46231

Studebaker National Museum
525 South Main Street
South Bend, IN 46600
Phone: (219) 235-9714; (219) 284-9479
http://www.classicar.com/museums/stude/
stude.htm

IOWA

Auto Museum
P.O. Box 188
Highway 75
Sioux Center, IA 51250
Phone: (712) 722-1611

National Sprint Car Hall of Fame
One Sprint Capital Place
P.O. Box 542
Knoxville, IA 50138-0542
Phone: (800) 874-4488
http://www.classicar.com/museums/
sprint/sprint.htm
http://www.sprintcarhof.com

Van Horn's Truck Museum
Highway 65
Mason City, IA 50401
Phone: (515) 423-0655

Wheels O' Time Museum
11923 North Knoxville (Route #40)
P.O. Box 9636
Peoria, IL 61612-9636
Phone: (309) 243-9020
or (309) 691-3470

KANSAS

Smokey's Car Museum
1909 Miller's Lane
McPherson, KS 67460
Phone: (316) 241-5160

Van Arnsdale Motor and Antique Cars
323 West Broadway
Highway 50
Macksville, KS 67557
Phone: (316) 348-3105

**Wheels and Spokes Classic Auto
Display**
P.O. Box 360
Hays, KS 67601
Phone: (913) 628-6477

KENTUCKY

Calvert Auto Museum
P.O. Box 245
Highway 95
Calvert City, KY 42029

National Corvette Museum
350 Corvette Drive
Bowling Green, KY 42101-9134
Phone: (502) 781-7973
or (800) 53-VETTE
http://www.corvettemuseum.com

**Rineyville Sandblasting Model A Ford
Museum**
179 Arvel Wise Lane
Elizabethtown, KY 42701
Phone: (502) 862-4671

LOUISIANA

**Ark-La-Tex Antique and Classic
Vehicle Museum**
601 Spring Street
Shreveport, LA 71101
Phone: (318) 222-0227
http://www.softdisk.com/comp/classic

Cars of Yesteryear Museum
P.O. Box 15080
12137 Airline Highway
Baton Rouge, LA 70801
Phone: (504) 293-8070
      or (504) 293-0581

Crump's Cars of Yesteryear Museum
P.O. Box 15080
12137 Airline Highway
Baton Rouge, LA 70801
Phone: (504) 293-8070

Firefighters Museum
427 Laurel Street
Baton Rouge, LA 70801

MAINE

Boothbay Auto Museum
P.O. Box 123
Route 27
Boothbay, ME 04537
Phone: (207) 633-4727
http://www.lincoln.midcoast.com/
      ~railvill

Cole Land Transportation Museum
405 Perry Road
Bangor, ME 04401
Phone: (207) 990-3600
http://www.classicar.com/museums/
      coleland/cole.htm

Jay Hill Antique Auto Museum
State Route 4
Jay, ME 04239
Phone: (207) 645-4330

Seal Cove Auto Museum
P.O. Box 128
Seal Cove, ME 04674
Phone: (207) 244-9242

Wells Auto Museum
Route 1
P.O. Box 496
Wells, ME 04090
Phone: (207) 646-9064
http://www.classicar.com/museums/wells/
      wells.htm

MARYLAND

Fire Museum of Maryland, Inc.
1301 York Road
Lutherville, MD 21093
Phone: (410) 521-7500

MASSACHUSETTS

Heritage Plantation of Sandwich
Grove Street
P.O. Box 566
Sandwich, MA 02563
Phone: (508) 888-3300

Museum of Transportation
15 Newton Street
Brookline, MA 02146
Phone: (617) 522-6547
http://www.mot.org

MICHIGAN

Alfred P. Sloan Museum
1221 E. Kearsley Street
Flint, MI 48503
Phone: (810) 760-1169
http://www.classicar.com/museums/sloan/
      sloan.htm

Automotive Hall of Fame Inc.
The People Place
21400 Oakwood Boulevard
Dearborn, MI 48121
Phone: (313) 240-4000
http://www.automotivehalloffame.org

Walter P. Chrysler Museum
DaimlerChrysler
1 Chrysler Drive
Auburn Hills, MI 48326-2778
http://www.daimlerchrysler.com/museum

Detroit Historical Museum
5401 Woodward Avenue
Detroit, MI 48202
Phone: (313) 399-0886
      or (313) 647-1957

Gilmore Car Museum
6865 Hickory Road
Hickory Corners, MI 49060
Phone: (269) 671-5089
http://www.gilmorecarmuseum.org

Henry Ford Museum
20900 Oakwood Boulevard
Dearborn, MI 48121
Phone: (313) 271-1620
http://www.hfmgv.org

**Novi Motorsports Hall of Fame
   and Museum**
26200 Town Center Drive
Novi, MI 48050
Phone: (313) 349-7223
http://www.mshf.com

Oldsmobile/GM Heritage Center
414 East Michigan Avenue
Lansing, MI 48933
Phone: (517) 482-0717
http://www.oldsmobileheritage.com

Poll Museum of Transportation
353 East Sixth Street
Holland, MI 49423
Phone: (616) 399-1955

Spirit of Ford
1151 Village Road
Dearborn, MI 48124
http://www.spiritofford.com

MINNESOTA

Ellingson Car Museum
20950 Rogers Drive
Rogers, MN 55374
Phone: (763) 428-7337
http://www.ellingsoncarmuseum.com

MISSISSIPPI

Mississippi Classique Cars Unlimited
5 Turkey Bayou Road
P.O. Box 249
Lakeshore, MS 39558
Phone: (601) 467-9633

MISSOURI

Autos of Yesteryear
Route 63 North
Rolla, MO 65401
Phone: (314) 364-1810

Auto World Museum
54 North
Fulton, MO
Phone: (573) 642-2080

Kelsey's Antique Cars Museum
P.O. Box 564
Camdenton, MO 65020
Phone: (314) 346-2506

National Museum of Transport
8015 Barrett Station Road
St. Louis, MO 63122
Phone: (314) 965-7998

Ozark Auto Show and Museum
West Highway 76
Branson, MO 65616
Phone: (417) 334-4191

St. Louis Car Museum and Sales
1575 Woodson
St. Louis, MO 63114
Phone: (314) 993-1330
http://www.stlouiscarmuseum.com

Turpen Enterprises Classic
and Antique Cars
1206 West Highway 76
Branson, MO 65616
Phone: (417) 334-5700

NEBRASKA

Chevyland U.S.A.
Route 2
Elm Creek, NE 68836
Phone: (308) 856-4208
http://www.classicar.com/museums/
    chevylan/chevylan.htm

NEVADA

Don Laughlin's Classic Car Collection
1650 Casino Drive
Laughlin, NV 89029
Phone: (702) 298-2535

Imperial Palace Auto Collection
3535 Las Vegas Boulevard
South Las Vegas, NV 89109
Phone: (702) 794-3174
http://www.autocollections.com

National Automobile Museum
10 Lake Street
South Reno, NV 89501
Phone: (702) 333-9300
http://www.automuseum.org

NEW HAMPSHIRE

Westminster MG Car Museum
P.O. Box 37
South Street
Walpole, NH 03608
Phone: (603) 756-4121

NEW JERSEY

National Auto Racing Hall of Fame
and Museum
Flemington Speedway
Route 31
Flemington, NJ 08822
Phone: (908) 782-5053

Roaring 20s Autos
Road 1
P.O. Box 178-G
Wall, NJ 07719

NEW MEXICO

Antique Auto Barn
National Parks Highway 16-180
Carlsbad, NM 88220
Phone: (505) 885-2437

YesterDave's Auto Museum
10601 Montgomery Boulevard NE
Albuquerque, NM
Phone: (505) 293-0033

NEW YORK

Automobile Museum of Rome and
    Restoration Shop
Route 46-49
West New London Road
Rome, NY 13440
Phone: (315) 336-7032

Buffalo Transportation Pierce-Arrow
    Museum
263 Michigan Avenue
Buffalo, NY 14203
Phone: (716) 855-1931
http://www.pierce-arrow.com

Bridgewater Auto Museum
P.O. Box 152
U.S. Route 20
Bridgewater, NY 13313

Collector Cars Inc.
56 West Merrick Road
Freeport, NY 11520
Phone: (516) 378-6666

Corvette Americana Museum
P.O. Box 167
Cooperstown, NY 13326
Phone: (607) 547-4135

Hall of Fame and Classic Car Museum
P.O. Box 240
1 Speedway Drive
Weedsport, NY 13166
Phone: (315) 834-6606

Himes Museum of Motor Racing
    Nostalgia
15 O'Neil Avenue
Bayshore, NY 11706
Phone: (516) 666-4912

Northeast Classic Car Museum
24 Rexford Street (NYS Route 23)
Norwich, NY 13815
Phone: (607) 334-2886
http://www.classiccarmuseum.org

Old Rhinebeck Aerodrome
42 Stone Church Road
Rhinebeck, NY 12572
Phone: (845) 758-8610
http://www.oldrhinebeck.org

Watkins Glen Racing Museum and
    National Motor Racing Hall of Fame
110 North Franklin Street
Watkins Glen, NY 14891
Phone: (607) 535-2779

NORTH CAROLINA

Charlotte's Motor Car Museum
4545 Highway 29
Harrisburg, NC 28075
Phone: (888) 736-2519
http://www.backingupclassics.com

C. Grier Beam Truck Museum
117 North Mountain Street
Cherryville, NC 28021
Phone: (704) 435-1346
    or (704) 253-7651

Estes-Winn Antique Car Museum
111 Grovewood Road
Asheville, NC 28804
Phone: (704) 253-7651

North Carolina Transportation
    Museum
P.O. Box 165
411 South Salisbury Avenue
Spencer, NC 28159
Phone: (704) 636-2889
http://www.classicar.com/museums/nctra
    nsp/nctransp.htm

Rear View Mirror Museum
300 East Baltic Avenue
Nags Head, NC 27959
Phone: (919) 441-1132; 441-4493
    or (800) 368-8085

Richard Childress Racing Museum
180 Industrial Drive
P.O. Box 360
Welcome, NC 27374
Phone: (333) 731-3389
    or (800) 476-3389
http://www.rcracing.com

Richard Petty Museum
Route 4, Box 86
Branson Mill Road
Randleman, NC 27317
Phone: (919) 495-1143

OHIO

Canton Classic Car Museum
Market Avenue at 6th Street SW
Canton, OH 44703
http://www.cantonclassiccar.org

Charlie Sens Antique Auto Museum
2074 Mount Gilead Road
Marion, OH 43302-8991
Phone: (614) 389-4686
http://www.classicar.com/museums/
sens/sens.htm

Crawford Auto-Aviation
10825 East Boulevard
Cleveland, OH 44106
Phone: (216) 721-5722

Goodyear World of Rubber
1144 East Market Street
Akron, OH 44316

National Packard Museum
1899 Mahoning Avenue NW
Warren, OH 44482
Phone: (330) 394-8484
http://www.packardmuseum.org

Welsh Jaguar Classic Car Museum
5th and Washington Streets
P.O. Box 4130
Steubenville, OH 43952
Phone: (614) 282-1010
http://www.classicar.com/museums/
welshjag/welshjag.htm

OKLAHOMA

Mac's Antique Car Museum
1319 East 4th Street
Tulsa, OK 74120
Phone: (918) 583-7400

Oklahoma Firefighters Museum
2716 Northeast 50th Street
Oklahoma City, OK 73105
Phone: (405) 424-3440

OREGON

Tillamook County Pioneer Museum
2106 2nd Street
Tillamook, OR 97141
Phone: (503) 842-4553

77 Grand Prix Museum
16355 Southeast Yamhill
Portland, OR 97233
Phone: (503) 252-5863

PENNSYLVANIA

Alan Dent Antique Car Museum
P.O. Box 254
Lightstreet, PA 17839

America on Wheels Museum
Allentown, PA
http://www.americaonwheels.org

**Antique Automobile Club of America
Museum**
P.O. Box 234
161 Museum Drive
Hershey, PA 17033
Phone: (717) 566-7100
http://www.aaca.org/museum

Boyertown Museum of Historic Vehicles
28 Warwick Street
Boyertown, PA 19512
Phone: (215) 367-2090
http://www.boyertown.net/museum.html

Eastern Museum of Motor Racing
100 Baltimore Road
York Spring, PA 17372
Phone: (717) 528-8279
http://www.emmr.org/index.html

Grice Clearfield Community Museum
119 North 4th Street
Clearfield, PA 16830
Phone: (814) 765-6185; (814) 765-2601

JEM Classic Car Museum
Route 443 RD1
Andreas, PA 18211
Phone: (717) 386-3554

Kelley's Auto Museum and Gift Shop
P.O. Box 137
Lehigh Road
Gouldsboro, PA 18424
Phone: (717) 842-2797

Pollock Auto Showcase
70 South Franklin Street
Pottstown, PA 19464
Phone: (215) 323-7108

Reilly Classic Motorcars
175 Market Street
Kingston, PA 18704
Phone: (717) 288-7767

**Rolls-Royce Foundation Library
and Museum**
505 Fishing Creek Road
Lewisberry, PA 17339

SOUTH CAROLINA

**National Motorsports Press Association
(NMPA) Stock Car Hall of Fame**
P.O. Box 500
Highway 151-34
Darlington, SC 29532
Phone: (803) 393-2103

Wings and Wheels
P.O. Box 93
Santee, SC 29142

SOUTH DAKOTA

Ledbetter's Auto Museum
U.S. 16
West Custer, SD 57730

Performance Car Museum
3505 South Phillips Avenue
Sioux Falls, SD 57105
Phone: (605) 338-4884

Pioneer Car Museum
Interstate 90
Murdo, SD
Phone: (605) 669-2691
http://www.classicar.com/museums/
pioneer/pioneer.htm

**Telstar Mustang-Shelby-Cobra
Museum**
1300 South Kimball Street
Mitchell, SD 57031
Phone: (605) 996-6550
http://www.telstarmuseum.com

TENNESSEE

Car Collector Hall of Fame
1534 Demon Breun Street
Nashville, TN 37203
Phone: (615) 255-6804

Cox's Car Museum
P.O. Box 253
Gatlinburg, TN 37738

Dixie Guns Old Car Museum
P.O. Box 130
Highway 51S
Union City, TN 38261
Phone: (901) 885-0700

Reed's 1950 Antique Car Museum
Route 2, Lost Sea Pike
Sweetwater, TN 37874
Phone: (615) 887-7718

Smokey Mountain Car Museum
2970 Parkway
P.O. Box 1385
Pigeon Forge, TN 37861

TEXAS

Alamo Classic Car Showcase and Museum
P.O. Box 546
6401 South Interstate 35
New Braunfels, TX 78132
Phone: (210) 606-4311

Central Texas Museum of Automotive History
Highway 304
Rosanky, TX 78953
Phone: (512) 237-2635

Classic Car Showcase & Wax Museum
P.O. Box 543
Star Route
Kerrville, TX 78028

GAF Auto Museum
118 Kodak Boulevard
P.O. Box 7189
Longview, TX 75607
Phone: (903) 758-0002; (800) 234-0124

Moore's Classic Auto Museum
505 North Loop West Yale Exit
Houston, TX 77008
Phone: (713) 868-2243

Pate Museum of Transportation
1227 West Magnolia, Suite 420
Fort Worth, TX 76104
Phone: (817) 332-1161

UTAH

Antique-Classic Special Interest Auto Museum
355 West 700 South
Salt Lake City, Utah 84101
Phone: (801) 322-5509
    or (801) 322-5186

Bonneville Speedway Museum
1000 Wendover Boulevard
Wendover, UT 84083
Phone: (801) 665-7721

Kimball-Browning Car Museum
2501 Wall Avenue
Ogden, UT 84401
Phone: (801) 629-8535

VERMONT

Westminster MG Car Museum
Route 5
Westminster, VT 05158
Phone: (603) 756-4121

VIRGINIA

Historic Car & Carriage Caravan at Luray Caverns
P.O. Box 748
Luray, VA 22835
Phone: (703) 743-6551

Pettit's Museum of Motoring Memories
P.O. Box 445
Luisa, VA 23093

Roaring Twenties Antique Car Museum
Route 1, Box 576
Hood, VA 22723
Phone: (703) 948-6290

Virginia Museum of Transportation, Inc.
303 Norfolk Avenue
Roanoke, VA 24016
http://www.vmt.org

WISCONSIN

Dells Auto Museum
591 Wisconsin Dells Parkway
Wisconsin Dells, WI 53965
Phone: (414) 648-2151
    or (608) 254-2008

J & J Muscle Car Collection
U.S. Highway 10
Medina, WI 54944
Phone: (414) 779-6259

Midway Auto Museum
P.O. Box 183, Route 2
Birnamwood, WI 54414
Phone: (715) 449-2901

Rhine Center Garage Historic Museum
Route 1
Elkhart Lake, WI 53020
Phone: (414) 876-3030

Uihlein Antique Racing Car Museum
236 Hamilton Road
Cedarsburg, WI 53102

Wisconsin Alfa Heaven, Inc.
2698 Nolan Rd
Aniwa, WI 54408-9667
Phone: (715) 449-2141

Wisconsin Automotive Museum
147 North Rural
Hartford, WI 53027
Phone: (414) 673-7999
http://www.wisconsinautomuseum.com

Zunker's Antique Car Museum
3722 MacArthur Drive
Manitowac, WI 54220
Phone: (414) 684-4005

BIBLIOGRAPHY

ACT Auto Staffing (America's Auto Career Super Market), http://www.actautostaffing.com

Alternative Fuels Vehicle Tech, http://www.natef.org/career/afv.cfm

American Trucking Association: Careers in Trucking, http://www.truckline.com/safetynet/drivers/careers.html

Auto Body Repair Career Guide, http://www.khake.com/page11.html

Auto Careers, http://www.autocareers.com.au/entry.htm

Auto Glass Installers, http://www.iseek.org/sv/13000.jsp?pg=13000&id=100249

Auto Industry Careers: Job Profiles, http://www.auto industry.co.uk/education/careers/index

Auto Mechanics/Technicians career info, http://www.schoolfinder.com/careers/Profile.asp?CareerCode=7321 aut&URL=careerindex

Automobile Parts Counter Worker, http://www.calmis.cahwnet.gov/file/occguide/Autopart.htm

Automotive Trade Association, http://www.autoconsulting.com/autotrade.htm

Auto Service Technology Career Guide, http://www.khake.com/page12.html

Autosport International Careers in Motorsport, http://www.autosport-international.com/Default_PUBLIC.asp?SetID=1&TextID=23

Boraas, Tracey. *Automotive Master Mechanic (Career Exploration).* Mankato, Minn.: Capstone Press, 2000.

Bureau of Labor Statistics, U.S. Department of Labor, Occupational Outlook Handbook, 2004-05 Edition, http://www.bls.gov

Bus and Truck Mechanics career information, http://www.iscck.org/sv/13000.jsp?pg=13000&id–100026

Career Infonet, http://www.acinet.org/acinet/occ_rep.asp?soccode=493023&from=&Level=&keyword=AUTOMOTIVE&stfips=42&x=41&y=11

Career Resource Libary, Transportation and Material Moving Occupations, http://www.acinet.org/acinet/library.asp?category=1.4.22#1.4.22.2

Careers in Car Design, http://co2.technologyeducator.com/links/links2.htm

Career Zone, Job Profile, Insurance Appraisers, Auto Damage, http://nycareerzone.org/graphic/profile.jsp?onetsoc=13-1032.00

Farm Equipment Mechanics, http://www.iseek.org/sv/13000.jsp?pg=13000&id=100076

Farr, Michael and LaVerne L. Ludden, *200 Best Jobs for College Graduates.* 2d ed. Indianapolis, Ind.: JIST Publishing, 2003.

Formula One Careers, http://www.f1mech.co.uk/careers.htm

Fuel Cell industry careers, http://www.fuelcells.org/career/baxter.htm

Garner, Geraldine. *Great Jobs for Engineering Majors.* 2d ed. New York: McGraw-Hill, 2002.

Hollembeak, Barry. *Today's Technician: Automotive Electricity and Electronics* 2d ed. Clifton Park, N.Y.: Delmar Publishers, 1997.

How to Become an Auto Mechanic, http://www.ehow.com/ehow/ehowDetails.jsp?index=1105&id=5134

Indy Racing League, http://www.suite101.com/welcome.cfm/irl

Lee, Richard and Mary Price Lee. *Careers for Car Buffs & Other Freewheeling Types.* New York: McGraw-Hill, 2003.

Metcalf, Robert. *The Successful Race Car Driver: A Career Development Handbook.* Troy, Mich.: Society of Automotive Engineers, 2000.

Mission: Careers, http://www.carsyouth.ca/carsyouth/reference/career_info/opportunities.cfm

Mission: Careers, Repair and Maintenance, http://www.carsyouth.ca/carsyouth/reference/career_info/repair.cfm

Motorsport Careers, http://motorstats.eddsport.co.uk/careers.asp

Motorsport, Cranfield University, http://www.motorsport.cranfield.ac.uk/interest.htm

McKinney, Anne (ed). *Real-Resumes for Auto Industry Jobs.* Fayetteville, N.C.: Prep Publishing, 2003.

Myfuture: Automotive electrician, http://www.myfuture.edu.au/services/default.asp?FunctionID=5050&ASCO=421211A

Myfuture: Exhaust fitter careers, http://www.myfuture.edu.au/services/default.asp?FunctionID=5050&ASCO=799111D

National Auto Dealers Association, Auto Career Links, http://www.nada.org/Content/NavigationMenu/Member Services/EducationandTraining/AutomotiveCareers/WheretoBegin.htm

National Automotive Technicians Education Foundation: automotive technician, http://www.natef.org/career.cfm

Radosevich, MIke. *What you Need to Succeed: Making Car Sales a Career Rather Than a Job.* Minneapolis, Minn.: Kirk House Publishers, 2003.

Scharnberg, Ken. *Opportunities in Trucking Careers.* New York: McGraw-Hill, 1999.

Schmidt, Peggy and M. Krebs. *Cars: Careers Without College.* Lawrenceville, N.J.: Petersons Guides, 1999.

Smith, Carroll. Drive To Win: *The Essential Guide to Race Car Driving, Motorbooks International.* Osceola, Wis.: 1996.

Street Performance racing schools, http://www.street performance.com/search.php?display=DRVSC

Tire Repairers and Changers, http://www.iseek.org/sv/13000.jsp?pg=13000&id=100212

Weber, Robert M. *Opportunities in Automotive Service Careers.* New York: McGraw-Hill, 2001.

INDEX

ABOUT THE AUTHOR

G. Michael Kennedy, the author of *Take Care of Your Car the Lazy Way* (Macmillan), is a former race car driver and former chief mechanic for the Jim Russell International Race Driver School in Canada. An ASE-certified master auto technician and registered VW master technician, Kennedy trained at Hewland Engineering in Maidenhead, Berks (England) and has more than 30 years of experience as a master technician with VW, Porsche, Audi, Saab, and Suburu, in addition to experience in rebuilding and repairing classic vintage collector cars.